THE

# KINGDOM OF CHRIST ON EARTH:

## TWELVE LECTURES

DELIVERED BEFORE THE

STUDENTS OF THE THEOLOGICAL SEMINARY,

ANDOVER.

BY

SAMUEL HARRIS,

DWIGHT PROFESSOR OF SYSTEMATIC THEOLOGY IN YALE COLLEGE.

PUBLISHED BY REQUEST OF THE STUDENTS.

Andover:
PUBLISHED BY WARREN F. DRAPER,
MAIN STREET.
1874.

ANDOVER: PRINTED BY WARREN F. DRAPER.

PRESS, RAND, AVERY & CO.

# NOTE.

---

THESE Lectures were delivered to the Students of Andover Theological Seminary in December, 1870. All except one of them have since appeared in the Bibliotheca Sacra. They are now published in a volume in accordance with the desire expressed to the Author by persons in whose judgment he has confidence, and in the form in which they were originally delivered.

S. H.

YALE THEOLOGICAL SEMINARY,
October, 24, 1874.

# CONTENTS.

## LECTURE I.

### THE IDEA OF CHRIST'S KINGDOM ON EARTH, IN ITSELF AND IN ITS HISTORY, PROOF THAT IT IS FROM GOD.



## LECTURE II.

### THE ANTAGONISM OF CHRIST'S KINGDOM TO THE WORLD OR THE KINGDOM OF SATAN.



## LECTURE III.

### THE PECULIARITY OF CHRISTIAN VIRTUE INVOLVED IN THE FACT THAT IT IS THE RESULT OF REDEMPTION.

## LECTURE IV.

### THE DIVINE AGENCY IN THE ESTABLISHMENT, ADMINISTRATION, AND TRIUMPH OF CHRIST'S KINGDOM.



## LECTURE V.

### THE CHURCH THE ORGANIC OUTGROWTH OF THE LIFE-GIVING AND REDEEMING GRACE OF CHRIST PENETRATING HUMAN HISTORY IN THE HOLY SPIRIT.



## LECTURE VI.

### THE NECESSITY AND CHARACTERISTICS OF THE HUMAN AGENCY IN ADVANCING CHRIST'S KINGDOM.



## LECTURE VII.

### THE SACRIFICIAL LOVE OF CHRIST THE TYPE AND MEASURE OF CHRISTIAN LOVE.

## LECTURE VIII.

### THE CHRISTIAN LAW OF SERVICE.



## LECTURE IX.

### CHARACTERISTICS OF THE GROWTH OF CHRIST'S KINGDOM.



## LECTURE X.

### THE PROGRESS OF CHRIST'S KINGDOM IN ITS RELATION TO CIVILIZATION.



## LECTURE XI.

### THE SCRIPTURAL DOCTRINE OF THE TRIUMPH OF CHRIST'S KINGDOM DISTINGUISHED FROM MILLENARIANISM.

## LECTURE XII.

### THE PROGRESS OF CHRIST'S KINGDOM IN ITS RELATION TO THE SPIRIT OF THE PRESENT AGE.

THE

# KINGDOM OF CHRIST ON EARTH.

## LECTURE I.

### THE IDEA OF CHRIST'S KINGDOM ON EARTH, IN ITSELF AND IN ITS HISTORY, PROOF THAT IT IS FROM GOD.

THE theme of the present lecture is this: "The idea of Christ's kingdom, in itself and in its historical origin, development, and prevalence, is proof that it is from God and that it will be realized on earth." In unfolding this proof the following points are to be considered:

I. The Idea of Christ's Kingdom is an Existing Power in Human Thought and Action.

The thinking of Christendom is now earnestly directed upon the person and work of Jesus, the Messianic King. The number of treatises recently published on the significance of his life and work, the extent to which they are circulated, and the interest with which they are discussed, are remarkable. More than one of them have been translated into different languages of Christendom and have had a sale that is extraordinary in the history of bookselling.

This power over the thinking of our day of one who lived in an age and country so remote, is a pregnant fact. If, as careless observers say, this is a superficial age given to novel-reading, it is significant that such an age is interested in a personage of antiquity who addresses himself only to that which is most profoundly spiritual in man. If, as is more correctly said, the age is unsurpassed in earnestness, this power of Jesus is equally significant in view of the direction of that earnestness—the political and social questions urgent in every Christian nation, involving in some instances the constitution and even the existence of the nation; the industrial interests absorbing human enterprise; the philosophy and science apparently leading away from religion.

In the generation preceding this, other questions pertaining to the life and work of Jesus were the subjects of excited controversy. This is another fact of similar significance. So in every age of intellectual or moral earnestness since Christ came, his person and kingdom have been powerful in human thought and action.

No other personage of antiquity has power over the age sufficient to awaken general interest in any discussion or controversy respecting him. Homer is one of the greatest of the ancients. His authorship of the Iliad and Odyssey, and even his existence, are denied. Yet the public is utterly indifferent to the question, and it would be impossible to awaken any general interest in its discussion.

This interest in Jesus is not speculative, but practical, pertaining to him as the world's Redeemer and King. The idea of his kingdom on earth, and the expectation of its progress and triumph in fulfilment of the prophecy and promise of the gospel, have become familiar elements of human thought and determinant forces in human action. The sublime idea of the conversion of the world to Christ has become so common as to cease to awaken wonder. Its realization is the object throughout Christendom of systematic, persistent, and energetic action, and elicits every year heroic consecration and self-sacrifice. The prayer, "Thy kingdom come," is perpetually offered.

Besides this direct interest in the conversion of the world, modern civilization is characterized by ideas derived from the gospel of the kingdom; the brotherhood of man and the fatherhood of God; philanthropy; the promise of human progress; the rights of man; the removal of oppression; the reign of justice and love displacing the reign of force.

These facts must be accounted for. This idea and expectation of Christ's reign over men in righteousness, an idea and expectation never associated with any other personage, have so penetrated human history that they demand explanation. The only rational explanation is, that the idea and the promise are from God, and will be realized on earth.

II. The Idea of the Kingdom is in itself a Proof of its Divine Origin.

The consummation which it proposes to realize on earth is the universal reign of justice and love.

This consummation is not the reign of abstract truth and right, but the reign of Christ, the Messianic King, who is the truth and the life impersonated.

It is to be realized not by the spontaneous fermentation of human thought, nor by a natural law of progress, nor by the propagation of philosophical or ethical truth, or scientific discovery and inventions, but by the divine grace in Christ coming down upon humanity from above, and establishing itself in humanity as a power of redemption. The doctrine of the kingdom presupposes the knowledge of God, of sin, of condemnation, and of all that pertains to natural religion. Its distinctive and essential characteristic is redemption as an historical action of God in humanity. It emphasizes the person and the propitiatory work, as well as the reign and administration of the King. God in Christ, the divine in the human, enters human history as Redeemer, and makes propitiation for the sins of the world. The love, which God is, and which became incarnate in Christ, comes in the Holy Spirit and establishes itself in humanity as an energy of saving grace, and abides through all human history, working redemption for man. Through him the redeeming love of God in Christ is perpetually penetrating humanity and becoming the life of the world. Thus Christ reigns and administers his government on earth. Christ, the King anointed on the holy hill of Zion, seated at the right hand of Majesty on high, all power given to him in heaven and on earth, reigns over his kingdom on earth, administering his government through the Holy Spirit, through whom the life that is in Christ is perpetually penetrating and vitalizing humanity, evolving from the kingdom of darkness his kingdom of righteousness and peace and joy in the Holy Ghost.

In this the doctrine of the kingdom is distinguished from philosophy, ethics, politics, and sociology. These emphasize speculative truth, law, and institutions. Christianity, on the contrary, is not dogmatic, but historical; not speculation, but action; not command and condemnation, but invitation and promise; not organization, but spiritual life. Accordingly, the abstract word Christianity is not in the Bible; but Jesus, the Christ, the Redeemer who ever liveth, the incarnate energy of God's love always active in redemption, is on every page of the New Testament, and his Messianic reign is the theme of the whole Bible.

The citizens of the kingdom are all who, renewed by the Holy Spirit, are converted from the life of selfishness to the life of faith and love, "delivered from the power of darkness, and translated into the kingdom of God's dear Son." These become a brotherhood, united in fellowship by their common faith in Christ, and are workers together with God to extend his kingdom through the world. The kingdom, growing from generation to generation on earth, extends also to heaven, where Christ reigns in person, and where the redeemed at death become a brotherhood of glorified and immortal saints, still honoring the same King, of whom the whole family in heaven and on earth is named, and serving him in the interest of his kingdom.

The law of the kingdom is the law of love. The life of every citizen is a life of service. Every one acknowledges his obligation or debt to all men everywhere, as much as in him lies, to bring them into the kingdom. The service and the love are sacrificial, like Christ's. His sacrificial love is the type and measure of all Christian love.

The prophecy and promise of growth and ultimate triumph are inherent in the idea of the kingdom. The idea and expectation of the conversion of the world, of human progress to the universal reign of justice and love, are essential to

Christianity and inseparable from it. They are a gift to mankind from Christ.

The promise, in its extent, reaches to all mankind. Society over all the world is to be transfigured into the kingdom of God. As to its depth, it reaches the greatest sinner. In its indirect, but necessary results, it promises the purification of society, the Christianizing of civilization and of all institutions, the carrying out into the details of social life of the principles of Christian love.

For the realization of the promise the kingdom depends not on force, but on the moral power of Christ's life and love, on the preaching of the truth as it is in Christ, and on the power of love in the hearts and lives of Christians, made effectual by God's redeeming grace, always active in the Holy Spirit.

Such is the biblical doctrine of the kingdom of Christ. It presents a complete philosophy of human history. It leaves still incomprehensible the mysteries which transcend the limits of a finite mind; it even thrusts them on our notice in startling antinomies, as if to emphasize the infinitude of God, and awe us into reverence. But within the sphere of human intelligence it meets and answers the great questions which have occupied the human mind concerning the relations of man to God, the significance of his history, the law, end, and blessedness of his being. If it were fully realized, the perfection and blessedness both of the individual and of society would be attained. As such, it is a conception complete, satisfactory, and sublime. Were it only a creation of a poet's genius, it would, as a conception, surpass every creation of genius. What epic, what drama, can be compared with the drama — if it is a drama — of man's fall and his redemption? Were it only a theory which some philosopher had elaborated in his study, it would surpass all the products of the profoundest human thought — as a philosophy of human history so perfect that no mind can add to it or detract from it or alter it, without impairing its completeness

The existence of this conception is to be accounted for. Its completeness as a conception, its grandeur as it presents itself to the imagination, its profoundness, comprehensiveness, and satisfactoriness, as it is taken up by thought, and applied to the complicated problem of man's life and destiny, indicate that it is from God.

We proceed to seek the historical origin of this wonderful idea. We trace it to the teaching of Jesus, by whom, if it was not originated, it was introduced as a power into the thinking and civilization of the world. This brings us to the third step in the argument.

III. Christ's Preaching of the Kingdom, and of Himself as the Messianic King, demands for its consistent Explanation the Admission that the Kingdom is from God, and that Jesus is its divinely anointed King.

Jesus preached the kingdom of God as coming on earth, and himself as its Messiah or divinely anointed King, and all the germinant truths involved therein, which have been the seeds of Christian civilization. This doctrine was essential and determinant in his idea of his own mission, and was the central topic of his preaching. This remains true, if we accept only what the severest historical criticism is obliged to acknowledge.

John the Baptist had preached that the kingdom of heaven was at hand, and had warned the people to repent in preparation for its coming. To the people repeatedly, and once, at least, to an official deputation from the Sanhedrim, he had declared that the prophesied Messianic King had come. Jesus began his own ministry by preaching: "The kingdom of heaven is at hand." Throughout his public ministry his preaching consisted in presenting himself to the people as the divinely anointed and predicted King, in explaining the nature of the kingdom, his own redemptive work in setting it up, and the conditions of entering it, and in insisting on its spiritual character and growth, in refutation of the persistent error that it was to be a political kingdom, established and advanced by force. At his baptism he was proclaimed "the Son of God," which was a well-known prophetic title of the Messiah. The temptation in the wilderness turned on the question what sort of a kingdom he should set up, and by what sort of agency; and he rejects every satanic proposal to establish an outward kingdom by force, even by his own miraculous power. When, at the first passover after his baptism, he presented himself at Jerusalem and purified the temple, it was a formal and official presentation of himself as the Messianic King to the nation as such, in the person of their rulers, in the seat of the government, and the temple of the religion. The Sermon on the Mount is an elaborate exposition of the spiritual nature of the kingdom, declaring in what it makes man's supreme blessedness to consist; what is the character of its citizens, and their relation to the world as bringing to it light and salvation; what the relation of the kingdom to the law of God, and the positive and spiritual significance of its requirements; what the simplicity and godly sincerity of its members, the nature of worship, the law of beneficence, the necessity of entire consecration, the beauty and safety of faith in God, and the completeness of the new life, beginning in faith, and vitalizing and rectifying the conduct to the remotest and minutest action. In his parables and his conversations with his disciples he is continually explaining what the kingdom is, and correcting current mistakes respecting it. At last, it is for this persistent preaching of himself as the divinely anointed King that he is arrested, condemned, and crucified. At his trial he declares before Pilate that he is the King, but explains: "My kingdom is not of this world." Over his cross was written the reason of his condemnation: "Jesus of Nazareth, the king of the Jews."

This doctrine of the kingdom is the key to our Saviour's ministry, without which it is impossible rightly to understand it. This doctrine gives the point, significance, and consistency of his particular discourses and conversations. It gives, also, the point, significance, and consistency of his ministry as a whole, as consisting not so much in what he teaches as in what he personally is and does as the Redeemer of men, anointed to set up and administer God's kingdom of grace. If Jesus had been simply a teacher and an example, and so is to be studied as on the same plane with philosophers, lawgivers, and reformers, it would be impossible to explain why his public ministry was so short; why his teaching, considered as a system either of sociology, ethics, philosophy, or theology, was so fragmentary and incomplete; why his teaching centred on himself, presenting himself as the way, the truth, and the life, and urging regard to himself personally, "for my sake," as the motive to draw men from sin to the heroism of love; and, finally, why he suffered an ignominious death, and why that death, both in his own teaching and in that of the apostles, was exalted to supreme significance. But all this becomes significant and consistent when we know that he is not merely our teacher and example, but our Redeemer, expressing in the incarnation and under human limitations God's justice and mercy; being, in his humiliation, suffering, and death, the propitiation for the sins of the world; rising from the grave the Conqueror of sin and death; ever living to infuse his own life into humanity, and quickening in the world the kingdom of righteousness over which he reigns. Then his own preaching, while on earth, must culminate not in philosophy, nor ethics, nor sociology, nor even in theology, but in the gospel of Christ: "Come unto *me*, all ye that labor and are heavy-laden, and I will give you rest." Then the leading motive to the life of love must be regard to and trust in him personally; the love must spring from faith in Christ. Then his name must be above every name. And the gospel is necessarily exclusive, and declares: "Neither is there salvation in any other; for there is none other name under heaven given among men whereby we must be saved."

Observe, also, that Jesus taught this doctrine not as an interesting speculation, but as a gospel, a prophecy and a promise certain to be realized. His own confidence in its realization, serene amid the opposition which stormed about him, is sublime. Suppose that you had been one of his hearers. You see a young man, with the coarse garb, the hard hands, the limited education, the habits and demeanor of a laboring man. Listening, from time to time, to his teachings, his conception of his kingdom gradually forms itself in its grandeur before your mind. You become intensely interested; you admire the grand conception; but you think it a vision too beautiful to be realized, and that it would be fanatical and visionary to attempt or expect it. Especially you wonder that one so uninfluential should offer himself as the king to realize this beautiful conception, and to make his name potent to rule all hearts. But Jesus preaches the prophecy and promise of the kingdom with unwavering assurance that the kingdom is about to come, and will extend till it fills the world. It becomes evident, however, that the people of his day cannot receive his doctrine. Whenever he goes to Jerusalem he is contemptuously rejected by those in authority, who early begin to plot against his life. He is obliged for safety to retire to Galilee, and prosecute his ministry in country places. Even there few receive him, and those from the humbler walks of life. Even his own family think he is quite gone crazy, and come to take him and confine him. At last it becomes evident that he must either abandon his pretensions or suffer an ignominious death. Yet his confidence in his kingdom remains unshaken.

On one occasion, near the close of his life, Jesus asked his disciples: "Who do men say that I am?" They replied that some acknowledged him to be a prophet, some acknowledged him as Elijah, the expected harbinger of the Christ; but, even at that late period in his ministry, they could make no favorable report of any increasing readiness to receive him as the Christ. He then asked: "Who say ye that I am?" Peter said: "Thou art the Christ." Jesus pronounced a blessing on him for recognizing him as the Christ, and immediately uttered that sublime prophecy of the irresistible prevalence of his kingdom: "Upon this rock I will build my church, and the gates of hell shall not prevail against it." On another occasion, foreseeing that the malignity of the rulers would soon bring him to the cross, he declares that the cross itself shall be the means of his triumph: "I, if I be lifted up from the earth, will draw all men unto me." Afterwards, in Bethany, just before his arrest, a woman anointed him with a costly perfume. Jesus, while saying that she had anointed him for his burial, yet declares the certain triumph of his kingdom: "Wheresoever this gospel of the kingdom shall be preached in the whole world, there shall also this that this woman hath done be told for a memorial of her." This faith in his great idea, declared more confidently when all outward circumstances seemed to demonstrate its futility, and worldly wisdom could only pronounce it proof that he was visionary or insane, is sublime.

It appears, therefore, that the doctrine of his kingdom and the claim for himself to be the Messianic King were central, essential, and persistent in Christ's own conception and preaching of himself and his mission. If this doctrine and claim were not true, then he was either an impostor or a visionary. But in the light of historical criticism, it is conceded that he was not an impostor. Then the only theory which remains possible is that of Renan, that he was a visionary, and his claims for himself the result of illusion. We have, now, a complete alternative. Either Jesus was the Messiah, as he claimed to be, or else he was a visionary, and in all his public life the victim of his own illusions. But the hypothesis that he was a visionary is impossible, for two reasons. First, it is an hypothesis on which a consistent, rational, and satisfactory explanation of the teaching, work, and life of Jesus as an historical personage is impossible. Secondly, because the world owes to him the doctrine of the kingdom of God on earth, with all the truths germinant in it, which from his day till now have been vital forces of human progress; and it is impossible that this grandest, mightiest, and most beneficent idea which ever was a power in human thought and life, originated in the illusions of a visionary. If this is visionary illusion, then visionary illusion is the grandest, mightiest, and most beneficent reality in human history.

Our position, therefore, is established. The teaching, work, and life of Jesus admit no rational and consistent explanation, except on the supposition that he is the divinely anointed Redeemer of the world, and that his kingdom is from God, and is destined to prevail.

IV. Consider Christ's Doctrine of the Kingdom in Contrast with the History of Human Thought in Heathen Nations before his Coming.

This is necessary to the full force of the preceding arguments. The truths of Christianity have so become the common property of the human mind, the elements of all thinking, the law of all action, the maxims of human rights, the principles of progress, the germinant forces of civilization, that we fail to appreciate the indebtedness of the world to Jesus as their author. We must go back into the darkness, and witness the rising of that Sun. I sometimes think if we did not know Jesus so well, we should know him better.

This, however, is only what is true of all luminaries; the greater the luminary, the more it is lost in the light which it creates. When a candle is lighted, we notice the candle, rather than its light. We admire the brilliancy of the stars; they have light enough to reveal themselves, not to dispel the darkness. When the moon, "sweet regent of the sky," comes up and throws "her silver mantle" over the dark; when the still concave of the firmament seems full of solid effulgence; when every object, silvered on one side, seems to start out of the darkness, and, as you move, shifting the light and shade, to take on fantastic forms, the moon itself is seen, if at all, only as one bright object in the brilliant scene. But when the sun rises, and brings the day, we use the light, but do not look at the sun. So Jesus, the Sun of Righteousness, is lost in the light which he creates. Modern rationalism uses the very light which Christ has given as an argument against Christianity. It asks: "What need of a supernatural revelation in the midst of all this light?" As if one should ask: "What need of the sun in the daytime, when it is so light?" Heathen philosophers attract admiration to themselves. Like the stars, they have light enough to reveal themselves, not enough to dispel the night.

The point here to be made is that before Christ heathen literature and civilization were destitute of the idea and promise of a kingdom of God on earth, and of the germinant and life-giving thoughts involved in it.

The heathen had not the idea of God as being essentially love; nor of that love as a divine energy in human history, redeeming men from sin; nor of a kingdom of those redeemed from selfishness to faith and love, growing in power and extent, and destined to fill the world; nor of the obligation of men to consecrate themselves in self-devoting love to the service of mankind in seeking first the establishment of this kingdom; nor of the sacredness and worth of the individual man — a soul worth more than the world — a man so priceless that Christ "tasted death for every man"; nor of the consequent doctrines of the equality of men before God, the sacredness of human rights, and the foundation of society and government on justice and right, instead of force.

They had not the idea of a universal religion. Polytheism is essentially divisive. National gods are embittered with the national enmities. The gods of the hills fight against the gods of the valleys. The religion gives no common ground of unity, no common and supreme god, no common divine law, no common standard of appeal, no fellowship of common faith or hope. The cleavage between the nations cuts through the deepest foundations of thought, feeling, and interest, and leaves them more hopelessly dissevered than ships driven asunder on the ocean; for it cleaves the ocean itself, and leaves them no common element in which to separate.

They had not the idea of the brotherhood of man, nor of universal philanthropy, definitely proposing the blessedness of mankind as an end. Even Plato teaches that foreigners are natural enemies, and may be conquered and spoiled, if the state has power to do it. Everywhere is the law of might, not the law of love.

Finally, the heathen had not the prophecy nor the promise of a better future for man in the establishment of a universal reign of justice and love. The idea of human progress was not a power in their civilization. Their golden age was in the past.

When we search the history and literature of the heathen world, listening for some word of hope for man, we seem to stand on the shore of the ocean in a stormy night. We hear the sound of a vast activity, but only an activity that is baleful — the roar and tumult of the storm, the moaning and hissing of the waves as they break in vain on the relentless rocks, the groaning of an everlasting unrest beneath the impenetrable night.

How, then, is it to be explained that Jesus, this young man who has never learned, comes from his carpenter's shop, and announces at once this grand doctrine of the kingdom of God on earth — a conception which answers the questions that had tasked the profoundest minds of the race without result, which comprises a consistent philosophy of human history and destiny — a conception missed by the greatest geniuses of heathen civilization, yet grasped by Jesus at the outset in its simplicity and grandeur, and proclaimed, without emendation or change, without doubt or vacillation, through his entire ministry? The only rational explanation is that he was what he claimed to be — the Messianic King.

V. The Force of the Argument is further enhanced by the Relation of Christ's Teachings to the Previous Literature of the Jews.

Here it is objected, by those who put Jesus on the same

plane with the philosophers, that his idea of the kingdom was not original — that he derived it from the Hebrew literature. But this only leads to a new line of argument.

In the first place, this literature itself cannot well be accounted for without admitting its supernatural origin.

The Book of Genesis, one of the oldest of writings, declares, in its first sentence, the doctrine of one God, the Creator of all things, and therein solves the great problem of God's relation to his works, on which human thought for centuries afterwards, where that writing was not known, expended its most powerful efforts in vain. This of itself is evidence that it is from God to every one who is familiar with these fruitless efforts, and who has noted how in the Oriental nations these efforts issued in pantheism, confounding God with his works; and in the Western nations in the deification of human heroes, retaining God's personality at the expense of his unity and his deity.

Then, on the same page, another great truth which the wisdom of the heathen has missed — the unity and brotherhood of man.

Immediately, as we turn the page, we strike the great facts of sin and redemption — man a sinner and condemned, God's promise of redemption. Here this ancient writing strikes the key-note of that wonderful series of documents, the Jewish scriptures — the great idea which, through all these varied writings, in every style of composition, by authors of the most different conditions, writing without concert and at long intervals, through more than a thousand years, is never lost; is by each new writer taken up and further developed — this promise of redemption, no glimpse of which is found in the literature of Greece and Rome — the key-note, not of the Old Testament only, but also of that divine harmony in many parts which sweeps through all human history, and swells triumphant in the music of heaven. At first, we have only the promise of redemption to come from God in some way through the human race itself — the seed of the woman. To Abraham the promise is renewed, with the more explicit definition that blessedness is to come to all mankind through his seed. Afterwards it is successively defined still further in the line of Isaac, of Jacob, of David. In the time of Moses we first have explicit intimation that the deliverer shall be an individual person. In the time of Samuel, and more clearly in the time of David, we find the idea of a kingdom and a king. In the Psalms and prophecies the kingdom and its king are delineated with ever-increasing clearness. We wonder, as we read, at the characteristics ascribed to them: "He shall judge the poor with righteousness; protection for the widow, the fatherless, and the weak; he shall break every yoke, and let the oppressed go free; he shall bind up the broken-hearted; in his days shall the righteous flourish, and abundance of peace so long as the moon endureth." Such a conception of a kingdom of universal justice, peace, and love, presented not as a poetic fancy, but as a prophecy and a promise, reiterated century after century in those old days of national exclusiveness, hate, oppression, and violence; pervading the literature of a people pre-eminently bigoted and intolerant, whose literature is in exact contrariety to the national character, and therefore cannot have been the natural outgrowth and expression of the national life; pervading that literature while totally wanting in the literature of every contemporary people — such a conception cannot be explained, except as that literature itself explains it, that that people had been chosen by God to receive and perpetuate his promise of the Christ.

In the next place, we have the fact that Jesus came at the appointed time, claiming to be the predicted king. The expectation of the prophesied Messiah had saturated the thinking of the Jewish people. The critics who insist that there are no clear predictions of Christ in the Old Testament must reconcile their criticism with this fact. This expectation the Jews carried with them through all the Eastern nations in their dispersion. When the luminary is broken, all the scattered fragments shine. How came it to pass that just at the time when the Christ was generally expected Jesus should appear and fulfil the prophecy? It can be explained only on the supposition that he was the long-predicted king.

It is often urged that history is the necessary development of the primordial forces in human nature; that each age is the necessary outgrowth from its predecessors, and literature and great men are the necessary product of the spirit of their age. But Jesus could not have been the product of his age. Before his coming the Jewish expectation of the Messiah had hardened into the expectation of a temporal king, conquering and ruling by force. The age in which he appeared was of all ages the most barren of spiritual life. Polytheism had given place to philosophical scepticism. Judaism had decayed into the formalism of the Pharisee and the unbelief of the Sadducee. Jesus was in all respects the opposite of his age, and could not have been its natural product. That the life of such a people culminated in such a personage is proof that he was from God. If the Hebrew literature of the Old Testament demands a divine intervention to account for it, the argument is strengthened and made unanswerable by the fact that the literature of that same people culminated in that later and more wonderful series of documents, the New Testament.

Thus, whether we study pagan literature and civilization, or Jewish, the courses of human history antecedent to Christ's coming converge on him. In him is revealed the truth which the thinking of the heathen world had been groping to discover: in him are met the wants which the sin-conscious heart of the heathen world had been yearning to satisfy; in him are fulfilled the promise and the prophecy revealed by God through the Jewish prophets. In this sense he is the Desire of all nations. Not Ethiopa alone, but all the nations of antiquity, stretched forth their hands unto him.

VI. It remains to consider Christ's Doctrine of the Kingdom in its Relation to the History of the World after his Coming.

If you had been one of his hearers when he was on earth,

you might have said: "This man's conception of his kingdom surpasses all human conceptions in sublimity. In depth, compass, and completeness of thought, in grandeur of imagination and loftiness of genius, in purity of heart and power of love, he is in advance of all the great minds of antiquity — so in advance that comparison ceases, and contrast alone is possible. But if he expects this conception to be realized, he must be a visionary. Has he forgotten how infinitesimal in the rush of the world's affairs is the influence of one man; and does he expect to transform the world? Has he forgotten how powerless the greatest are after they die, how shadowy the great names and systems of the past; and does he expect to lift his crumbling arm out from the grave, and sway with it the living world? Especially, has he forgotten how feeble is the greatest man to command the love of men; and does this provincial, this poor man, this man without office or honorable position or influence with the great, this unlettered man, this outcast among his own people — does this man expect to rule the world by men's love to him? Does he expect to set up his power, where power is hardest to win, in the hearts of men, so that faith in and love to him will in all generations turn the energies of human hearts into a mighty enthusiasm to deliver mankind from sin? And does he expect that this power of his personal influence, this motive which he continually urges, 'for my sake,' will at last touch all hearts, and transform society everywhere into his kingdom?"

Still more would you think him a visionary, could you then know that his public ministry is to continue less than four years; that he is to suffer the most ignominious of deaths as a leader of sedition; that he is anticipating that death as the consummation of his work, into which the motive power of his name is to be concentrated; that, making but few converts himself, he is depending for the establishment of his kingdom after his death on the preaching of those few converts, with the story of his short life and ignominious death as the subject of their preaching, and thus sending them out, a few sheep among many wolves, he is expecting the sheep to conquer the wolves.

And your belief that he is a visionary would be still more strengthened could you then look forward through the ages and foresee the coming changes. The Roman empire, then co-extensive with Occidental civilization, will be destroyed. The imperial throne of the Caesars, at whose base then rippled the peaceful and sunlit waves of a world-wide obedience, will sink when the fountains of that great deep shall be broken up. Barbarians, whose very existence was then unknown, will overwhelm the abodes of civilization. From the consequent confusion, desolation, and darkness the kingdoms of modern Europe will slowly and painfully emerge; new discoveries and inventions will change the courses of human thought and action; a new civilization will arise, so different from the ancient as to make that difficult of comprehension to the moderns; a new continent will be discovered; new philosophy and science, new arts and agencies, new institutions and laws will possess the earth. And this man expects his personal influence to live through all these changes; and not to live only, but to vitalize, energize, and guide them; to establish itself in the seats of the ancient and decaying civilization; to meet the barbarians and to make them Christians; in the ages of darkness attending and following the overthrow of the Roman empire to cause all men to bow in outward homage to the name of Jesus, and to quicken faithful ones truly to love him, and to seek for his sake to save men from sin; to kindle revival and reformation from age to age; to follow the star of empire in its westward way; to preside over the birth and growth of nations; to live in the latest progress of art, science, philosophy, and civil polity; in advance of all spiritual thought, the law of all human action, the ideal of human perfection, the source of the hope of pardon, of purification from sin, and of peace with God; at once the source, the motive, the strength, and the goal of all moral and spiritual progress.

And if Jesus was only a man, and on the same plane with

philosophers, then he was a visionary, the greatest of all history. But, from the day when he began to preach "The kingdom of heaven is at hand," until now, his name has been a power in human thought and life; the kingdom has been in the world gathering individuals into itself, and vitalizing civilization with its divine ideas, a central force in the history of all enlightened and progressive nations. Therefore he was not a visionary.

But if Jesus was not a visionary, then he is man's Redeemer and Lord. Then, with more than the wonder of those who cried: "What manner of man is this, that even the winds and the sea obey him?" we exclaim: "What manner of man is this, who rules amid the tumult of the ages, and the courses of human thought obey him, and the farthest progress of man is confessedly towards the realization of his idea?" He is man's Redeemer and Lord; his idea of his kingdom, by its existence on the earth, and by its perpetuation and power through the ages, is proof that it is from God and is destined to prevail.

The argument is now complete. The idea of a kingdom of God on earth and the prophecy of its realization are present in modern thought and among the forces that determine modern progress and civilization. The idea is so complete as a solution of the problem of man's history and destiny, so sufficient, if realized, to constitute the perfection and blessedness of society, and as a conception of the ways of God with man so comprehensive and sublime, that in itself it demonstrates that it is from God. We then trace this grand conception back to the teaching of Jesus; we consider his preaching of it in its relation to the age in which he lived, in its relation to the antecedent history of human thought, both among the heathen and the Jews, and in its power in all subsequent human history. The conclusion is irresistible that the idea and prophecy of the kingdom of God existing as a power in the world's progress and civilization can be rationally accounted for only on the ground that it is from God and is destined to prevail.

In the nineteenth Psalm the law of God is compared to the sun and the stars. As these by shining declare their divine origin and the glory of God, so does God's law by its own perfection declare its divine origin and God's glory. Similar is the argument which has now been unfolded. God's kingdom, like the sun, must reveal itself and its divine glory by its own shining, by enlightening and vivifying the world. No one doubts that the modern astronomy will prevail through the world. Its principles and laws do but express the actual realities of the starry and solar systems. The more thoroughly the heavens are explored, the more complete must be the evidence that astronomy is true. So the doctrine of Christ's kingdom expresses the divine idea of redemption, which God in his administration of human affairs is constantly carrying out to its realization.

Human history, then, must contain and express the idea, and the study of human history must give proof of God's redeeming love, working in it to establish his kingdom of grace. His kingdom is progressive, like the growth of a mustard-seed. Therefore the argument is as yet incomplete. But every new generation, and especially every epoch in human progress, adds to its force. Already it is possible from the study of human history to construct an argument that history itself demands for its rational explanation the presence and power of God in it as a Redeemer establishing his kingdom. When in the future the kingdom shall possess the earth, then history itself will have proved the truth of Christ's claims, and God's redeeming grace and his kingdom will be as demonstrable from the facts of human history as the laws of astronomy are from the facts of the starry heavens.

We, then, on this new continent and in this distant age, acknowledge Jesus as the Christ, our Redeemer and Lord. With the thousand times ten thousand and thousands of thousands who in the ages past have loved him, and now praise him in heaven, with all the living of every kindred and people and tongue who now trust and serve him, we bow before him, and join the great confession: "Thou art the Christ, the Son of the living God."

Him we behold a sorrowful man in the dimness of a far-off age and land, burdened and smitten by the power of sin, suffering for us, the just for the unjust, to bring us to God. Him, we behold above the convulsions of the ages, the halo about his majestic head shining as the sun down all the tract of time, his voice speaking promise and peace amid the confusion of human affairs. Him, we behold seated on the right hand of majesty on high, all power given unto him in heaven and on earth, and on his head are many crowns. Him, we joyfully confess "King of kings and Lord of lords"; we offer the prayer which he has taught us: "Thy kingdom come"; we accept the command and the promise which he has given us: "Seek ye first the kingdom of God and his righteousness, and all these things shall be added unto you"; and, in the expectation that his kingdom shall fill the earth, we consecrate our lives to his service. And, entering into the joy of all the redeemed, with all who have tasted and seen that the Lord is gracious, we offer him our homage: "Worthy is the Lamb that was slain to receive power and wisdom and strength and honor and glory and blessing; for thou hast redeemed us to God out of every kindred and tongue and people and nation. Unto him that loved us, and washed us from our sins in his own blood, and hath made us kings and priests unto God and his Father, unto him be glory and dominion forever and ever. Amen."

# LECTURE II.

## THE ANTAGONISM OF CHRIST'S KINGDOM TO THE WORLD OR THE KINGDOM OF SATAN.

CHRIST'S kingdom is created out of the world by God's action redeeming men from sin. It exists and grows by God's redeeming grace delivering sinful men from the power of darkness and translating them into the kingdom of his Son. It implies a perpetual process of transforming the world into itself.

The first thought which flows from this fundamental conception, and is now to be our subject, is this: Christ's kingdom is in antagonism to the world or the kingdom of Satan. God's redeeming grace and the kingdom which it calls into being are in perpetual conflict with the power and kingdom of evil for the deliverance of man.

This kingdom of evil is called in the Bible the power of darkness, as opposed to the kingdom of God's dear Son; the kingdom of Satan, as opposed to the kingdom of Christ; the world, as opposed to the kingdom of heaven. The last is the most frequent designation, not because the world is conterminous with the reign of evil, but because it is subject to it, and the part of it immediately in contact with the kingdom of righteousness. It is only as we understand this use of "the world," as representing the kingdom and power of darkness in its direct antagonism to Christ's kingdom, that we get the full significance of many of the sayings of Christ and his apostles. We miss their power if we suppose "the world," as they often use it, means only earthly goods.[1]

[1] "If ye were of the world, the world would love his own; but because ye are not of the world but I have chosen you out of the world, therefore the world

This antagonism appears in the opening of Genesis. Man sinless in Eden is encircled and protected by the law which prohibits him from evil. When by transgression he has overleaped the law, which encircled and protected him, into the midst of circumjacent evil, the law becomes a sword of fire shutting him out from good, himself a victim of the power of evil, and henceforth a part of it. Nor was the antagonism that of the law only, but deliverance from the curse of the law is itself to come through conflict and suffering: "it shall bruise thy head, and thou shalt bruise his heel." Men are not represented here as each in an isolated individuality, but as related to powers of good and of evil which existed before man existed, and the scope of whose action outreaches the sphere of human life. This is in analogy with nature. A man's health does not depend altogether on his personal care of it. There are cosmic agencies under which the earth itself sickens and belches out pestilential miasmata; and the black death, the cholera, and plagues of whatever name move around the globe. And there are always invigorating cosmic influences from the sun, the air, the ocean, and the land, without which no human forethought could sustain life. So the Bible, from its very opening, represents the spiritual relations of man. The writer of Genesis knew not the earth's relation to other worlds and systems; but he knew that man's relations extended beyond the earth. The power of darkness has put its blight on man. God is seeking the lost man to bring him back to righteousness and peace. The earth is a battle-field for the soul of man between the powers of heaven and of hell.

hateth you." "The prince of this world cometh, and hath nothing in me." "Wherein in time past ye walked according to the course of this world, according to the prince of the power of the air, the spirit that now worketh in the children of disobedience." "For we wrestle not against flesh and blood, but against ..... the rulers of the darkness of this world." "Love not the world, neither the things which are in the world. If any man love the world, the love of the Father is not in him." "Whosoever is born of God overcometh the world; and this is the victory that overcometh the world, even our faith." John xv. 19; xiv. 30; Eph. ii. 2; vi. 12; 1 John i. 15; v. 4.

This conflict appears throughout the Old Testament. The history of the Jews brings it vividly before the mind, and, as it were, incorporates it into human consciousness. In their history this conflict appears, first, in the separation of this people by a divine call, the promise of blessedness to all mankind through the Messiah to spring from them, and the conditioning of the continuance of God's favor to them on their fidelity to him, involving throughout their history the recognition of Paul's principle, "He is not a Jew who is one outwardly, but only he who exercises faith like Abraham's." It appears, secondly, within the chosen people in the continual preaching of the prophets against dependence on birth and outward service, and their testimony to the spirituality of God's requirements and the universality of his promise; and in the faithfulness of the few, like the seven thousand in Elijah's day, and like Simeon and Anna, who stood with the prophets in every generation in antagonism to the national Pharisaism and corruption. It appears, thirdly, in the outlook of the prophecies into the future, revealing the kingdom of the Messiah in its conquest of the world.

When Christ came he not only declared this conflict, but his own life set it forth.. From the temptation in the wilderness until his death he was assailed by the powers of darkness; but before he died he saw Satan as lightning fall from heaven, — the token of victory.

It is remarkable that at the beginning of each dispensation we have this conflict set forth between chosen champions, and open to the gaze of all generations. In the beginning, Adam, type of unaided man, meets the adversary and falls. In the opening of the gospel dispensation, Jesus, the Redeemer, type of man quickened by God's grace, meets the adversary and conquers.

The conflict of Christ's kingdom against the kingdom of Satan is constantly insisted on by the apostles, and in the Apocalypse is pictured, as in a panorama, until its final triumph.

Thus the scriptures, from beginning to end, set forth this conflict in didactic expositions, in prophecy, and in history. The history of redemption is the history of this conflict. The history of this conflict is essentially the history of man.

It remains to consider some of the truths involved in this scriptural conception.

I. It assumes the Existence of Sin as the Essential Evil.

The theory, which is gaining currency, that sin is a necessary process in the development of a finite spirit, annihilates the significance of both sin and evil. A process necessary to the development of the being cannot be sin, because it is constitutionally necessary for the perfection of the being; it cannot be essentially evil, since it is the necessary means of the highest good. According to this theory the soul is invigorated by sin as the body is said to be sometimes by a fever. Children are born with a constitutional liability to certain diseases, which can be removed only by having them; and the parent rejoices when his child has taken one of these diseases and is well through it. So the Infinite Father rejoices as his children take and go through the disease of sin. Some have it more lightly than others, but all come out at last freed from the liability to have it again; all alike, even by way of the brothel or the gallows, are passing on through the necessary stages of growth to their full perfection. On this theory, there is neither sin nor evil in the universe, and there can be no antagonism to them. Rather God and man will desire every one to pass through the necessary amount of sin as rapidly as possible. This theory, in annihilating the significance of sin and evil, annihilates the significance of Christianity, which is redemption from sin. Nor is the theory tenable on any consistent doctrine of rationalism. It belongs to sheer naturalism, and is tenable only on the supposition that man is merely a germ or force of nature necessarily developed under the action of cosmic agencies.

II. Love, whether in God or Man, must be in irreconcilable Antagonism and Warfare against Sin, and cannot consent that any Being should be Blessed in it.

1. This is evident *from the nature of sin as transgression of law.*

Law is not the fiat of will, not even of God's will; but is the truth of reason. Reason necessarily knows itself as authoritative and law-giving; and every rational being knows himself under obligation to obey reason, that is, to act in harmony with rationality. Will, as the power of choice and volition, will as the basis of character, is subject to law, and incapable of creating law. Even when enforcing law in government, it is only as authorized and required so to do by the superior law of reason to which it is subject. Any other enforcement by will of its own behests is not the reign of law, but of caprice. It is subjugation by force to a despotic will. It is the reign of force: "might makes right." God's will originates no law, but obeys the eternal principles of the divine reason, and in obedience to them enforces them as law throughout the universe. That which is highest in the universe is not power nor will; it is reason.

When Positivism argues that the order of nature proves the absence of will, the argument is irrelevant; for law is not of will, but of reason. Every conception of the universe as a cosmos, an orderly and beautiful whole, implies that reason is supreme in it, that it is pervaded by rationality, is expressive of rational principles, and subject to them as laws. This is implied in the arrangement of all individuals in scientific classes and systems, and the reduction of all forces under scientific laws. It is the basis of induction; it is the fundamental postulate, inadequately expressed in the principle of the uniformity of nature, on which all induction rests. Without it induction reaches no conclusion, observation only accumulates facts signifying nothing, the difference between the rational and the absurd is annihilated, rationality is extruded from the universe, and science itself becomes impossible.

As the thoughts or principles of the supreme reason, the law of nature and the moral law are alike. When in the action both of molecules and of masses we discover mathematical laws, when we discover that natural objects are all arranged in scientific classes and systems, we do but discover the principles of the divine reason expressed in the works of God, and may adopt as literal truth the exclamation of the rapt Kepler, "O God, I think thy thoughts after thee." In like manner moral law is the eternal thoughts of God, the principles of reason, the constituent elements of rationality respecting the conduct and character of rational beings, which every such being by virtue of his rationality must recognize as a law to himself.

The laws of nature, so far as now known, are many. The law of rational agents is one; its real principle is expressed in the one word — LOVE. Love, then must present itself first as law. This law must be absolute, supreme, unchangeable. If law were the fiat of will, a beginning, a change, an abrogation would be conceivable. But law, as the truth of reason, is necessarily eternal and unchangeable; for to change it would be to change rationality itself, to annihilate the difference between the rational and the absurd, to make reason itself irrational.

It follows that sin is an attempt on the part of a rational being to realize an absurdity. It is a fight against reason. And in this, the transgression of the law of love is analagous to the trangression of the laws of nature. The will may refuse submission to the reason, and work in antagonism to it, but it cannot exalt itself so as to nullify or abrogate the law. Thus in the sphere of nature a man may spend his life in trying to produce in mechanism perpetual motion; but in spending his life thus, he expends, wastes, loses it; the effort to realize an absurdity must be in vain. So a sinner spends, wastes, loses himself in a vain effort to realize an absurdity. The divine law is: "Love God and man." The principle which sin aims to realize is that self is supreme, and God and all creatures should serve it; more monstrous than the old astronomy, that the earth is the centre around which all planets and suns revolve daily. The result must be the waste and perdition of the soul. In the Bible, therefore, the sinner is called indiscriminately a sinner or a fool. It is impossible for any man to miss losing himself or being a castaway when he consumes his energies in antagonism to eternal reason, and to all the laws which rule the universe, and to the cosmic agencies which act in harmony therewith, and thus takes the essential evil into his own character and constitutes of it his own life.

Observe, here, that the selfish character is itself the essential evil. When you put your finger in the fire, the evil is not the pain suffered, but the destruction of the finger. The pain is a good; it evinces the continuance of life in the finger resisting the fire that destroys it and warning you to withdraw it. The evil is complete when the calcined bone lies insensible, consuming in the fire. So the evil of sin is not the suffering which it causes, but the bosom pleasure which it gives. The suffering is a good, evincing the continuance of moral sensibility and warning of the evil. The evil is the heart's joy in sin, when the soul is happy in sin, insensible in the fire that consumes it; when the soul chooses the evil, prefers it to the good, accepts it with joy as the good. The full significance of this preference is given in the words of Milton's Satan:

"All good to me is lost;
Evil, be thou my good."

Sin, as the transgression of law, being essential evil, love cannot consent that any rational being be blessed in it; love itself must visit it with penalty. Therefore reason, as supreme law, demands love on pain of perdition. Thus is declared the absolute antagonism of love, as supreme, inexorable, eternal law, to sin as the essential evil. The eternal perdition of the ungodly signifies that, under the law of supreme and universal reason, which is the law of love, sin has no tolerance now or hereafter, here or in any place; that in all places in his boundless domain, in all ages of his reign forever, God meets sin only with antagonism. If this is not so, sin is not essential, but only incidental evil; no conceivable doctrine of immutable right is possible; reason ceases to be contrary to the irrational, and rationality itself ceases to have significance; the powers of the universe, no longer expressing the perfect law of love, are in truce with absurdity and wrong; and evil extinguishes itself by an apotheosis into good.

> "If this fail,
> The pillared firmament is rottenness,
> And earth's base built on stubble."

2. The same is evident *from the nature of love, as the real principle of law.*

As we have seen, the law which reason imposes on rational beings is the law of love. Love, in itself considered, is the choice of universal being as the supreme end in preference to self. In other words, it is universal good-will. But because universal goodwill is required of every rational being by reason, it is the real principle of a law. Thus the exercise of love is also obedience to law, and involves the harmony of the will with the reason, and its consent and allegiance to the law which reason imposes. Therefore there is necessarily a duality in love; it contains two elements; or rather presents itself in two aspects. Considered in itself, as universal good-will, we call it good-will or benevolence. Considered as the harmony of the will with the reason, the consent or allegiance of the will to law, we call it righteousness. If we had corresponding words of Latin derivation, we should call the former *bene-volence*, the latter *recte-volence;* the former having regard to universal well-being, the latter to universal right, or to the supremacy and universal reign of law.

The duality of reason and will is inherent in the conception of a rational being. The duality of love, as the abiding preference of the will choosing universal well-being as the supreme end, and its harmony therein with reason and obedience to its law, is a necessary consequent. We are thus able to supply a defect in Edwards's doctrine of virtue, finding for righteousness not merely a place by tolerance, but a necessity for it in the philosophical exposition of the facts.

But, as the duality of reason and will is in unity, they being names of the mind itself in different aspects, the duality of love is also in unity. Since universal good-will is what reason commands as law, the exercise of it is in itself the harmony of the will with the reason, the consent or allegiance of the will to law. It is thus the harmony of the mind with itself in its two inseparable aspects of rationality and freedom. In God is the same duality in unity—a will that is almighty in eternal harmony with a reason that is absolute; so that the word which is the life-giving gospel, "God is love," is also the true and deepest philosophy of his being. In the love which the gospel requires, the human mind not only comes into harmony with itself, but also with God and with the laws of the entire universe. Ethical philosophers continually omit from their systems one or the other of these two aspects of love; they make virtue to consist either in universal good-will with no recognition of law, or else in obedience to law with no recognition of its real principle of universal love. In the former case, the universe is resolved into a joint-stock company, in which each person has weight according to his number of shares; God himself is of more account than man only because he is greater in quantity; and the idea of a supreme law is lost. Then the appropriate prayer would be that which the Maid of Orleans is said to have extorted from Lahyre: "O Jehovah, I pray thee do as much for Lahyre in this time of his distress, as he would do for thee, if he were Jehovah and thou wert Lahyre"; or that attributed to Richard Coeur de Lion, in the chronicles of his crusade: "How unwilling should I be to forsake thee in so forlorn and dreadful a condition if I were thy Lord and Advocate as thou art mine." This is the appropriate liturgy of the Benthamites. In the latter case, the theory of virtue comes round into itself in a circle; virtue is choosing the right for its own sake; it is obedience to duty; it is a regard to worthiness, without defining what is worthy. Thus the law has no real principle, but consists only of the empty requirement of obedience to itself.

Love is thus duplex and yet one; like the sun's ray of light and of heat; like electricity acting at opposite poles with seemingly antagonistic phenomena, yet one force; like all the bipolar forces of nature, two and yet one — two in order to be one.

As such, love must react in antagonism to sin; and the intensity of the reaction must be proportioned to the intensity of the love. The love, which in its essential nature is consent and allegiance to the law, must be as essentially antagonism to transgression. It is as impossible to conceive of love without reaction against sin, as to conceive of light which casts no shadow when obstructed, or of mechanical action without reaction. That comfortable tolerance of wrong, which is mistaken for Christian charity, is proof of the sluggishness of the moral life — sluggishness such that the vitals of virtue may be stabbed and the soul not wince, as the jelly-fish may be torn in pieces and give no sign of pain or offence.

3. The same is evident *from the nature of love considered as to the object loved.*

We are to love God and our neighbor; that is, all beings, or "universal being." But all rational beings are subjects both of character and happiness. No chemistry of thought can identify these two. Love, therefore, must have respect both to the character and the happiness of the being that is loved. Here appears again the duality in unity of love. As love insists on a right character it is righteousness; as it seeks the blessedness of its object in a right character, it is benevolence.

We may present the same thought in another light. Love seeks universal well-being. But the universal well-being or *summum bonum*, which love seeks, is not happiness or enjoyment. It is primarily right character, the perfection and harmony of the being, and secondarily, the happiness or joy incidental to it. This is blessedness. The only blessedness is the blessedness of the righteous. Happiness or joy is an incident of ill-being as really as of well-being. A drunken man is very happy, but we pity and despise him for his maudlin joy. The very wretchedness of the sinner is his joy in his sin; joy that is unworthy of him; joy in that in which a right-hearted man is capable only of shame and sorrow; joy which makes the subject of it incapable of the blessedness of the righteous; joy which is the heat of the fire that is consuming him. Reason rejects as absurd the doctrine of Bentham, that virtue is the art of maximising happiness — all happiness the same in kind to be measured only by quantity — the happiness of Paul glorying in tribulation and heroic sacrifice and toil for the salvation of men the same in kind with the joy of the sensualist, to be measured by the pailful, like the swill which satisfies a swinish appetite. The joys incident to gratified desires are inseparable from sensitivity, and therefore remain to the sinner. But these joys intensify the eagerness and increase the swiftness with which he rushes to ruin. By them his steps take hold on hell; in them he reaches out his eager hands to perdition, stooping downwards as he runs. And while with progress in sin the desires and passions grow more powerful to stimulate, the attendant joys become less satisfying, and are transformed into ghastliness; like the greed which rusts and consumes the miser's soul, and the reeking heats in which the soul of the sensualist ferments and rots.

Well-being comprising the two elements of character and happiness, we find again the two elements of righteousness and benevolence in the love which seeks universal well-being. And since the only worthy happiness is incidental to a right character, benevolence desires for men no other happiness, and thus is in unity with righteousness, seeking universal well-being only in harmony with the supreme law, only in the blessedness of the righteous.

Therefore without righteousness benevolence cannot realize its own ends; it deteriorates into a maudlin fondness, and rejoices in evil as good, until, transformed into the very opposite of itself, all its sweetness is fermented into acidity and corruption. Take away from love the element of righteousness, and you take away its self-consistency, its authority, its god-like majesty, and its power to bless. The benevolence which is left is a mere amiableness, a desire to please everybody, a jelly of good nature yielding to every pressure. The wicked man comes trampling into the presence of this amiable person, defrauding the ignorant, grinding the poor, crushing the weak, rising to office by intrigue, bribery, or oppression, and this amiable man only desires that this Nimrod be very happy, would have him indulged, humored, satisfied. Oh fond amiableness! oh vain benevolence! — benevolence defeating itself, desiring to make everybody happy, and thereby helping to make the ungodly more wicked and his wickedness more destructive.

What is thus obvious in the case of an individual is true of the universe at large. The universe being the expression of the law of reason, the *summum bonum* can be found only in conformity with that law. To attempt to realize the greatest good without righteousness would be an attempt to subvert the supreme reason, to break down the eternal laws of the universe, the "flammantia moenia mundi," which protect the rights and enforce the obligations of all rational beings, and make peace and blessedness possible throughout the worlds.

Therefore love cannot prompt even a desire that a sinner should be happy in his sin. On the contrary it meets him with indignant antagonism; an indignant antagonism, the absence of which is the absence of moral strength and grandeur of character, and marks the man as a sneak; an indignant antagonism justified by all that justifies the supremacy of reason, and the absence of which is the weak consent of the soul to unreason and misrule.

And this antagonism is essential in the very nature of love. Love is righteousness because it is love. It fills the world with blessing; yet it does so by virtue of its persistence in maintaining its own authority as law in antagonism to sin; does so, therefore, because in the last resort it utters itself in judgment and condemnation. Electricity commonly works quietly, diffusing blessings through all nature; but when its equilibrium is disturbed, and its silent and life-giving flow interrupted, then it is a thunder-bolt. And its power to bless arises from this very quality of its nature, which makes it, when disturbed, a thunder-bolt. If it could not smite in the red lightning it would be also powerless for good. The sun's light ministers to all life and growth, and sustains the forces of nature. But it could not do so were it not in its nature to burn; were it not, when disturbed in its diffusion, obstructed, accumulated, a consuming fire. So it is with love. The Scripture says, "God is a consuming fire." It does not mean that God consumes in his wrath all who approach him. He diffuses his love through all the universe to bless it, as the sun diffuses his light. But when that love is concentrated on a transgressor, the love itself is found to be a consuming fire. If this were not so, love would be unable to diffuse its benign influence, quickening life and joy throughout the universe.

4. *This antagonism is accordant with the common moral sentiment of mankind.*

Dr. Channing says: "We must not mistake Christian benevolence as if it had but one voice, that of soft entreaty. It can speak in piercing and awful tones. There is constantly going on in our world a conflict between good and evil..... That deep feeling of evils which is necessary to effectual conflict with them and which marks God's most powerful messengers to mankind, cannot breathe itself in soft and tender accents. The deeply-moved soul will speak strongly, and ought to speak so as to move and shake the nations."[1]

Nor should we wonder that faithful men, working and suffering for the kingdom of righteousness and seeing its progress opposed and hindered by the wicked, should pray sometimes for the intervention of eternal justice which

[1] Works, Vol. i. pp. 24, 25.

guards the world from crime, and pray with language so impassioned as to startle us in our peaceful time and our unsacrificing and genteel efforts to advance Christ's kingdom. Such prayers are wrung from the hearts of Christians when they see wickedness armed and in power, violating truth and justice, destitute of mercy, resisting human progress, crushing the defenders of righteousness, undoing the work of generations in behalf of truth, and thrusting society back into the darkness of the past. However in times of peace and indifference, men may think themselves more charitable than the participators in the conflict and suffering of former ages, whose piercing outcry against the powers of wickedness they commiserate as the illiberality and hardness of an unchristianized age, yet, when a similar conflict comes on them, in their anguish they find the need of similar expressions.

In this the sentiments of mankind concur. Children always rejoice at the overthrow of Pharaoh and the punishment of Haman. The savages at Melita believed that the viper on Paul's hand was God's messenger to punish murder. Epics, lyrics, and tragedy, philosophy and religion in all ages teach the punishment of sin. The source of perplexity and scepticism in all ages has been the fact that in the actual courses of human life God apparently does not punish sin; the wicked prosper and the good are depressed. From the days of Job until now the anxious question has been, "Wherefore do the wicked live, become old, yea, are mighty in power?" And always relief has been found in the same answer, "God will award them just retribution." What a grand chorus of the ages is here, the voices of children and savages, of poets and philosophers, of prophets aud apostles, — all generations standing with hands uplifted to God, crying that wickedness may not go on with impunity: "For the crying of the needy, for the oppression of the poor, for the sighing of the prisoner arise, O Lord, and render into the bosom of the wicked the reproach wherewith they have reproached thee." And from the holy and blessed heaven opened to John issues the voice of the martyrs slain by triumphant wickedness: "How long, O Lord, holy and true, dost thou not judge and avenge our blood on them that dwell on the earth"? How grand a chorus! How august a company! But here comes a solitary form, pale offspring of modern sentimentality, its consumptive frame nursed on what John Randolph called the ass's milk of human kindness, and lifts alone her contrary hands and voice: "To me the perplexity is that God does punish the wicked. Oh for a God that never smites the transgressor! Oh for a God of exceeding amiableness, who leaves wickedness unscathed in its triumph, and gives it without discrimination equal reward with the righteous."

III. Love must carry with it and express in Redemption the Element of Righteousness and its Essential Antagonism to Sin.

Otherwise love in redemption would cease to be love; for whenever righteousness is eliminated from love, love loses its essential nature and ceases to be love.

Otherwise sin would be not essential but only incidental evil, which under certain conditions love may approach with no expression of antagonism. Redemption is redemption from sin; thus the very act of redemption is the recognition of sin itself as the essential evil, from which the whole action of redemption seeks to deliver the sinner, and to which the essential antagonism of love must be exercised and expressed in the very act of redemption.

Hence in redemption the divine love must make atonement for sin. In redeeming the sinner the divine love cannot divest itself of its character as law. It must secure the sinner's redemption in such way as to maintain the authority of law, and to exercise, express, and satisfy the eternal righteousness of God; so that the essential antagonism of love to sin and the nature of sin as essential evil appear even in the act of redeeming the sinner. This law of love being a constituent element of rationality, being eternal in the divine reason and the constituting principle of the universe, must be equally a law in redemption; and the righteousness, which is the consent of the will to the law and without which love ceases to be love, must be exercised, expressed, and satisfied in redemption. And since redemption is wrought by God for the sinner, and not by the sinner for himself, this exercise, expression, and satisfaction of righteousness in redemption is made by God for the sinner, and not by the sinner for himself. It is therefore vicarious. And since this exercise, expression, and satisfaction have been historically made through the incarnation, in the humiliation, suffering, and death of Christ, it follows that these are historically the vicarious and atoning action of God for the sinner, wherein in redeeming the sinner God both *is* righteous and *declares* his righteousness.[1]

A vicarious atonement is, therefore, inherent in the idea of redemption from sin. Without it the history of the incarnation and the humiliation, sufferings, and death of Christ loses its distinctive significance. Without it, in the redemption of men from sin, love loses the element of righteousness and ceases to be love; law loses its supremacy; and any doctrine of eternal and immutable right becomes impossible.

It must be added that in all action, subsequent to Christ's atoning sacrifice, to extend the benefits of redemption through the world, love must show the same antagonism to sin. Redemption, as it is carried onwards to its consummation, is always a conflict. The love, which carries the glad tidings of redemption through the world, can never divest itself of its authority and severity as law. The hand which it extends to the lost is a holy and a sovereign hand, the blessing which it offers is pardoning mercy, its invitation to the sinner is to faith in the Redeemer, to repentance, humiliation, and self-surrender, and its approach to the sinner to save him is always with a commanding majesty, revealing "how awful goodness is."

The historical character of redemption makes it necessary that the conflict between Christ's kingdom and Satan's turn

[1] Rom. iii. 25, 26.

on the acceptance or rejection of Christ as Redeemer and King. Religious truths and moral precepts are a common heritage of man, and under various forms are to be traced in all history. If Christianity consisted essentially of doctrines or precepts, it would be one of the religions of the world, and on the same plane with them, and would lose all its distinctive characteristics. But Christianity is not primarily doctrine and precept, but history; God in Christ reconciling the world unto himself. Hence it must be exclusive. It must proclaim: "Neither is there salvation in any other." Therefore the conflict between Christ's kingdom and the world turns on the acceptance or rejection of Christ as Redeemer and Lord. So it is represented in the New Testament: "Whosoever denieth the Son, the same hath not the Father; but he that acknowledgeth the Son hath the Father also. Every spirit that confesseth that Jesus Christ is come in the flesh, is of God; and every spirit that confesseth not that Jesus Christ is come in the flesh, is not of God. And this is that spirit of antichrist, whereof ye have heard that it should come, and even now already is it in the world. Whatsoever is born of God overcometh the world; and this is the victory that overcometh the world, even our faith. Who is he that overcometh the world, but he that believeth that Jesus is the Son of God?"

The thought which we have now been considering is the one thought of the wonderful epistle from which these quotations have been made. That epistle is not an argument; it makes no progress. It is rather a lyric, reiterating in varied forms the thought that redeeming love and all that grows out of it are in warfare against sin. In Christ the word of God, the eternal life entered into humanity as a life-giving power, and was manifested among men. All who participate in it come into union with the Father, who is its source, and with the Son, who has made it a saving energy in humanity. Every one who thus is brought into fellowship with the Father and the Son is light, for God is light, and cannot participate in darkness; he is love, for God is love, and cannot participate in selfishness or hate; he is God's offspring and cannot sin; he is of God's kingdom and therefore in conflict with the world and overcoming it. Herein are the children of God distinguished from the children of the devil; for this very purpose Christ came, to destroy the works of the devil.

IV. The Antagonism of Christ's Kingdom to the World is, as to its Quality, the Antagonism of Love and not of Hate.

God loves the world, and in redemption his love goes out to save the lost. Sin cannot stop its efflux nor change its nature, though it may exclude its life-giving efficacy from the sinner's heart. But God's love still rolls on, filling every creature according to its capacity and disposition with the fulness of God, and flooding with its glory even the heart that shuts itself against it. God's love, converging on the sinner, must act like the sunshine on the seed, and, failing to quicken it, hastens its corruption. But the love remains pure love. All the sin in the universe is powerless to check its outflow, to lessen its fulness and extent, to vitiate its divine purity and sweetness, or to infect it with any taint of malignity or ill-will. When the Bible speaks of God's hatred of sinners, it only declares in popular language the righteousness which is essential in love as the real principle of law, and which is in unchangeable antagonism to selfishness and sin. When President Edwards says of lost sinners, "God never loved them, ..... but he hates them, and they will be forever hated of God; you will see nothing in God, and receive nothing from him but perfect hatred,"[1] he uses language seemingly denying that God loves the world, and dropping out from love its essential element of good-will. Christ weeping over Jerusalem expresses, under human limitations, the heart of God in condemning the wicked; the tears declaring his inextinguishable good-will, while the declaration of the inevitable doom declares his righteousness. His whole

[1] The End of the Wicked Contemplated.

action in redemption is action in antagonism to sin; this redemption itself implies; but his whole action is the expression of love: "God so loved the world."

The same must be true of all human antagonism to sin. It is necessary to the possibility of antagonism that there be some similarity of nature in the antagonists. A cannon-ball cannot be turned aside by argument or an appeal to compassion; an argument cannot be shattered by a bomb-shell, nor a conclusion overturned with a lever. The only possible antagonist of error is truth, and the only possible antagonist of selfishness is love. Love, then, is in Christ's kingdom the only fighting principle against sin. No other is legitimate or effective. The law of the kingdom is: "Overcome evil with good."

In the Christian character opposition to sin is not primary, but secondary. It is not the action, but the reaction of the love. Religion does not consist primarily in hating the devil, but in loving God and man. The opposition to sin, being a reaction of love, must be in its essence love. And love in every manifestation, whether by God or man, must absolutely exclude selfishness, ill-will, and hate, as light excludes darkness. While in approaching sinners it can never divest itself of its majesty as the real principle of God's law, it is still love.

And love in its conflict with sin, and seeking to save sinners is the highest and most truly divine love. Love to sinners is love in its furthest reach and greatest power; love which even vileness and defiant malignity cannot repel; love embracing sinners as the sunshine cherishes the reeking mould, in its own absolute purity incapable of defilement by the contact, and quickening life in the corruption. Love to sinners is the highest type of love; it is the love of Christ submerged in humanity and bearing the sins of men to save them, yet revealing the indefectible purity of love; declaring the majesty of the law, yet dying to redeem sinners from its curse. Love to sinners is love most distinctively imperishable and unconquerable; the vilest unable by his greatest sins to restrain the forthcoming of that love, or to check it as it goes on in its divine course of suffering and sorrow, or to prevent its opening wide to the sinner the golden gates of mercy, and proclaiming with infinite tenderness, "Whosoever will, let him come." Like Christ's is every Christian's love. It is love to sinners. However wicked a sinner may become, he has no power to quench Christian love to him, or to suppress it as, imperishable, like the love of Christ, it breathes in prayer, it prompts to efforts, to suffering, and sacrifice, to save the sinner from his sins.

Love is spiritual life. Its processes in its antagonism to sin are analagous to those of life. Life subdues foreign matter by transforming it into its own organization. When an acorn falls into the ground it may be said to enter into conflict with all around it. Yet the conflict is not the primary idea, but secondary, and incident to the life. And the living seed is continually conquering in the conflict, not by destroying its opponents, but by transforming them into its own organization. Thus the slender germ shoots into the upper air, and lifts itself in victory over gravitation, and builds its great trunk and boughs, and crowns itself with leaves, transforming the soil, the air, and the rain into organic strength and beauty. Such is the kingdom of God; a mustard-seed growing into a tree, a vital power from God transforming the world into a kingdom of righteousness.

And in this its strength lies. The earth which lies heavy on a seed cannot suppress its pale and tender shoot rising with the force of life into the air. So it is with the growth of the kingdom of God. However ancient and solid any institution of evil, it cannot suppress the vital force of love quickening any seed of truth. Any reformation, which is thus the bursting into growth of this vital force, will prove itself irresistible.

When a vital organ is invaded by a foreign substance which it cannot transform or expel, its resistance is uncompromising and persistent unto death. When a speck of dust enters the eye, the eye resists and expels it with weeping;

and will itself perish, resisting and weeping, if it cannot expel the intruder. So prompt, uncompromising, and persistent is the resistance of love to sin, resistance with weeping and suffering, and, if it does not prevail, persistent unto death.

V. The greater the Energy with which Christian Love acts, the more energetic will be the Antagonism against it.

Christ's word is always a fan winnowing the wheat from the chaff. The power of redemption is necessarily a power of separation. It must separate that which it renews and vitalizes from that which it cannot assimilate. The Saviour's voice calls out into a separate flock the sheep that know it and follow him. The mustard-seed separates from the soil the matter which it transforms into itself and by which it grows. The kingdom of heaven is a net gathering of every kind, the good preserved, the bad cast away. It is the wheat mixed with the tares, distinct already in nature, and to be separated in the harvest. Jesus said: "God sent not his Son into the world to condemn the world, but that the world through him might be saved." He also said: "For judgment I am come into this world." There is no contradiction here. Christ's work is primarily redemption; but because it is redemption, it must be judgment (*κρίσις*), primarily, separation, — the separation of all that come to him from all who reject him — ultimately, judgment, the condemnation of those who reject him. Therefore Jesus declares that the work of the Holy Spirit, renewing human hearts and transforming the world into the kingdom of Christ, is a perpetual judgment of the prince of this world. The final *κρίσις*, separation, or judgment, will only declare the separation of which redemption had already been the occasion; the sentence, "Depart," will only declare as irrevocable that departure from Christ and his salvation which the sinner has already made a fact by refusing him.

This separation being incidental to redemption, the more energetic the action of Christian love the more rapid must be the process of separation, and the more marked the antagonism of the kingdom of light and the kingdom of darkness.

In times of indifference truth and error may slumber side by side. But Christianity has always the power of revival; God breathes into the slumbering community a new power; men become sensitive to the difference between sin and holiness; truth is spoken with explicitness; God's law is proclaimed in its breadth, its purity, and its particularity. Thereby evil is both discerned and aroused. Thus the more vigorous the action of Christian love, the more marked the antagonism to it of sin. The great epochs of history are said to be times that try men's souls. Every period when Christian love acts with energy is a time that tries men's souls; it puts men to the test; it discerns between the righteous and the wicked; it compels an answer to the question: "Who is on the Lord's side?"

Hence the great epochs of human progress are often epochs of great darkness. They often seem for the time to be epochs of the triumph of evil. When Christ was on earth demons thronged the scene of action in numbers never seen before or since. When he was about to offer the great sacrifice of redemption, he exclaimed, "This is your hour and the power of darkness." The hour of the world's redemption was emphatically the hour of the power of darkness. So that it may be considered as a law in the progress of Christ's kingdom that every epoch of its advancement is also an epoch of Satanic achievement. Of every such epoch we may say, not only, "Rejoice, ye heavens, and ye that dwell in them," but also, "Wo to the inhabiters of the earth! for the devil is come down unto you having great wrath, because he knoweth that he hath but a short time."

### VI. Every Christian life is a Battle against the Powers of Darkness.

In the long course of education preparatory to the Christian ministry, a young man is in danger of forgetting this aspect of life. Living for years in a literary atmosphere and occupied in intellectual pursuits, he may come to regard intellectual attainments as the great object of life and the ministry as a profession subordinate to this end. In preparing sermons his chief aim may be to produce a finished and able oration, and his highest ambition may be satisfied with the admiration of the more cultivated of his hearers; thus he makes his sermon an end not a means, and his ministry degenerates into a contemptible dilettanteism. This is not the warfare against Satan's kingdom.

Nor is the battle merely against inward corruption, the ghastly conflicts of the cloister and the desert. Religion is not a dream, but an action. It is not meditation, nor excitement, nor emotion, nor worship terminating in itself. It is a fight with the falsehoods and sins of human life. Every Christian is a Hercules slaying monsters.

As Jesus put himself into actual contact with humanity, entered into it, so as to be in quick sympathy with its life and "touched with the feeling of our infirmities," as he bore its sorrows and its sins, and virtue was always going out of him to save, so every Christian, and especially every Christian minister, with whatever knowledge, culture, spiritual power, lives in immediate contact with humanity, *touched* with the feeling of its infirmities, in sympathy with its sorrows and its joys, meeting its wants, its errors and its sins, and constantly with virtue going out of him to help and save.

The battle is against the kingdom of darkness, not in the abstract, but in the actual sophistries, temptations, and sins, the actual evil opinions, customs, and institutions, by which the powers of darkness are deceiving and destroying men.

It is important to be sure that our warfare is in reality, and not in name only, against the kingdom of darkness. In addressing an assembly of students for the ministry it may not be amiss to say that ministers have usually been sufficiently given to controversy and warfare; but it is often internecine, for differences in philosophy and forms, against faithful servants of Christ; so that there needs to be a moral parallelogram of forces to determine what small resultant bears on the object to be moved. It has even been urged, to their discredit, that exhausting their strength in these feuds they have exerted no earnest and effectual influences against the rapacity, dishonesty, and oppression, which are corrupting society. It must be added that in the present unsettling of thought and confusion and conflict of opinion respecting reform and progress, when the advocacy of the pope's infallibility and temporal power goes on side by side with the advocacy of woman's suffrage and of agrarian rights for working-men, it demands spiritual discernment to know the truth and to escape being found fighting against God. The security is, that the soul be in fresh and living sympathy with the living Saviour rather than with the *hortus siccus* of creeds and systems, and in living sympathy with humanity in its actual life. The Saviour says: "My sheep hear my voice." It is only as we are in sympathy with him, receiving through the Spirit his thought and life into our own, and in sympathy like him with man, that we shall know his voice amid the babel of voices in this age: "I understand more than the ancients because I *keep* thy precepts." Spiritual discernment and far-sightedness come from keeping God's precepts. When statesmen, having no affinity for the law of God and the spiritual life of love, recommend measures for the welfare of the state which assume that selfishness is the only power to be considered in human affairs, and so fatally mistake the drift and movement of human thought and miss the measures needed for the welfare of society, the spiritual mind discerns the spiritual forces which the carnal mind knows not, and proclaims with prophetic far-sightedness the principles of justice in which alone safety can be found. This is the "poor wise man" who delivers the city.

The fact that life is a battle demands of every Christian the spirit of martyrdom. There cannot be a Christian life without it. He who has not learned to value duty, fidelity, the kingdom of Christ, more than property, reputation, or life, has not learned the first lesson of Christian living. He whose end in life is only to attain ease, comfort, fame, culture, the gratification of taste; he who does not accept life as a warfare, demanding the endurance of hardness for Christ, has not yet accepted the Christian idea of life. But if any Christian sacrifices his ease, or suffers persecution or reproach for Christ, Christ with his own hand writes his name in the glorious catalogue of the martyrs, saying of him: "So persecuted they the prophets." Thus the most common-place soul becomes luminous with heavenly glory, as a lump of coal at the touch of fire bursts into flame, and is glorified with brightness while it is consumed.

Paul animates the suffering Christians of his day by pointing to those who had been faithful to God in preceding ages, who now, a great cloud of witnesses, look down as in an amphitheatre on them in their conflicts. In that assembly of spectators Paul himself and the apostles and innumerable faithful ones in the ages since, have already taken their places. They have transmitted the great conflict to us to hold and extend their victories. In their presence we are fighting the good fight of faith. Their plaudits do not break the silence of eternity and fall on mortal ears; but "there is joy in heaven over one sinner that repenteth." In times of declension when Christ's kingdom is overborne by the world, the ear of faith can hear the cry of the martyrs wailing the triumph of wickedness: "How long, O Lord, faithful and true"? And the great cloud of witnesses exult in the grand and solemn joy of eternity for every instance of fidelity, for every heroic achievement of love, and send to the combatant their words of cheer: "Be thou faithful unto death, and thou shalt receive the crown of life."

# LECTURE III.

## THE PECULIARITY OF CHRISTIAN VIRTUE INVOLVED IN THE FACT THAT IT IS THE RESULT OF REDEMPTION.

At the banquet in Boston to the Chinese embassy, a distinguished literary man quoted the maxim of Confucius: "Do not to others what you would not that they should do to you." On that remarkable occasion when heathenism and Christianity were confronted before the world, he evidently intended to intimate that the morality taught by heathen philosophy is the same with that taught by Christ. This represents a type of thought which has acquired currency as an argument against Christianity. The argument is, that all the more profound philosophies and religions of the world recognize with more or less distinctness the same principles of morality; that therefore Christianity is merely one of the religions of the world and has no pre-eminent claim to a divine origin.

The first reply is that the New Testament explicitly teaches that conscience gives all men a knowledge of moral law, so that they are without excuse for sin.[1] Without this, Christianity would have no basis; a universal religion, and even a universal community of moral sentiment, would be impossible. The defenders of Christianity have been earnest to vindicate this against sceptics, who have endeavored to establish atheism by denying man's moral nature and the universality of moral principles. Christian apologists have cited the common moral sentiments of different literatures; and have met the objection, founded on the conflicting judgments of different peoples respecting the moral character of outward actions, by showing that they all appeal to the same

[1] Rom. i. 18–32; ii. 12–16.

principles in justification of these diverse actions. The heathen woman who religiously throws her child into the Ganges, the slaveholder, the despot, if they attempt to justify their actions, appeal to the same principles to which we appeal in condemning them. We welcome the concession of this point by Comte, Buckle, and writers of their school, and rejoice in the research which has established the Christian doctrine beyond further controversy.

A second reply is, that Jesus was not distinctively a teacher of philosophy or of ethics, nor even a lawgiver; but he was the Redeemer of the world. He assumes that God's law is already known and already transgressed. He comes to redeem men from sin and guilt of which they are already conscious. He presupposes and takes up into his teaching the religious and moral truths acknowledged in the religions and philosophies of the world; but he himself is the Redeemer, bringing God's love into human history as an energy of redeeming grace, making propitiation for sin, and quickening sinners into the life of faith and love. He speaks the word of promise and of hope to man, quickens in sinful humanity the germinant forces of a new and spiritual life, establishes his kingdom of righteousness, and sets humanity forth in a progress to realize the ideals of moral and spiritual perfection both in the life of the individual and the civilization of society. To whatever extent it may be possible consistently with historical facts to demonstrate an agreement between Christianity and the religions and philosophies of the world, the demonstration has no force against the distinctive claim of Christianity to divine origin and authority.

The English writers of the last century on the Evidences of Christianity, in urging the superior morality of the New Testament, sometimes wrote as if they regarded Christianity as simply a system of ethics. They thus unwittingly admitted rationalism into the very defences of Christianity, and betrayed their position to their adversaries; they invited the objection under consideration and others of a similar character, which have no force against Christianity as an historical redemption.

But, for the very reason that Christianity is distinctively redemption, Christian virtue must have certain distinctive peculiarities; the Christian conception of virtue must be distinct from and superior to the conception of virtue in the mind of one who is ignorant of redemption, and knows only the moral law. This is our present subject: The Peculiarity and Superiority of Christian Virtue involved in the fact that it originates in Redemption from Sin.

I. Christian Virtue springs from the Consciousness of Sin through Consciousness of Justification or of Reconciliation with God.

Christianity does not create the sense of sin and guilt. It has been powerful in all religions. We look with awe on the human race, bound and writhing through all history in the sense of guilt, like the Laocoon in the embrace of the serpents, the marble anguish unchanging through all the ages.

The consciousness of guilt is not ennobling, but the contrary. It involves a certain abjectness. In its nature it is the consciousness of failure, of unworthiness, of ill-desert. It compels the substitution of self-loathing and self-condemnation for self-respect. It is the consciousness of having no claim to the approval of either God or man. It depresses with fear; it overshadows with superstition; it crushes in despair. It makes life a dread of the future, a despair of the present, a lament for the past. The whole consciousness becomes concentrated in the one daily and doleful cry: "We are all poor creatures."

Both the ethnic religions and the ethnic philosophies fail in the presence of this terrific fact — the consciousness of sin. Neither can evoke a life of virtue from it. Their failures, however, are in opposite directions.

All religions necessarily intensify the sense of sin. They quicken the moral nature; they bring God and the unseen world and retribution close to the soul. The first effect is depressing. The greatness of God overpowers, and his holiness terrifies. The presence of an unseen, mysterious, everywhere-present Being, whom no cunning can deceive, no art elude, no speed evade, and no power resist, paralyzes the soul; his burning inquisition for sin scorches it. It is only as God is known in his redeeming love that his presence inspires and quickens. The defect of all ethnic religions is, that while they bring God near to the soul, they bring only the depressing influences of his presence; while intensifying the sense of guilt, they leave the soul scorching in its fiery heat. The service to which they impel is sacrifice and penance to appease the divine wrath, not the life of love which ennobles the man. The service itself is a superstition which abases. We cannot respect the man whose life is a prolonged abjectness and terror in the sense of guilt, a continued suppression of the joyousness and freedom of the spirit, whose loftiest meditations are on a skull and cross-bones, and whose greatest deeds are the infliction of torture on himself or compelling his sons to go through the fire to Moloch. Hence in heathen civilization the highest nobleness of character has not ordinarily been the outgrowth of the popular religion.

Philosophy, on the contrary, turning away from religion, refuses to take notice of sin. It develops virtue from self-respect. It develops a right character, not from the sense of sin, but from the pride of virtue. Such was stoicism, the best type of Greek philosophy. At the first glance heathen philosophy seems to have taken the better side of human nature, and to have realized a higher result than the heathen religions. But philosophy reaches only a few. Even with the few whom it reaches, it is as one-sided as the religions. It gets rid of the sense of sin only by ignoring it. But it can ignore sin only by ignoring God. Man cannot know God without the consciousness of sin. But when the consciousness of sin is awakened, self-respect ceases and a virtue founded on self-respect is no longer possible. Heathen philosophy, therefore, leads away from God; or, if the idea of God is retained, it is so abstract, so difficult to be grasped, so impersonal, as to be divested of moral power. Thus excluding God and the sense of sin, self-respect, which philosophy presents as the essence of virtue, becomes pride or self-sufficiency, which is the essence of sin. Philosophy preaches the very gospel which the serpent preached in paradise: "Ye shall be as gods"; it inculcates the very self-sufficiency which was the original germ of human sinfulness, and which is declared by Paul to be also its culmination in the anti-Christ, "who, as God, sitteth in the temple of God, showing himself that he is God." Besides, the sense of sin springs from the facts of human history and character; philosophy ignores it, but does not remove nor heal it. Therefore, in spite of philosophy, it perpetually re-asserts itself.

Christianity, more than any other religion, by its clearer revelation of God and of his law, declares his holiness and justice, and intensifies the sense of sin and guilt. At the same time, by its revelation in Christ of God's redeeming love to sinners, it takes from the divine presence its power to terrify and paralyze, and makes it the source of inspiration and hope; the sinner looks in God's face and sees a Father hastening to the returning prodigal to fall on his neck and kiss him. It takes from the sense of sin its power to depress and abase, frees from the abjectness of self-contempt, terror, and despair; and creating instead the consciousness of justification and of sonship with God, quickens a new life of free, joyous, and loving service. Thus quenching the consuming fire of conscious guilt, and transforming the sense of sin into dewy and refreshing penitence, it calls forth virtue from the consciousness of sin, life out from death. The religious life is no longer a life of penance and sacrifice to appease God's wrath, but it is the budding and blossoming and fruiting of the soul in faith and love beneath the outpouring of God's love, like the opening life of spring beneath the returning sun. Christianity thus combines the otherwise separate and incompatible ideas of religion and philosophy; and in a Christian excellence distinctively religious and growing out of the sense of sin, realizes the nobleness of character which philosophy abortively attempts to develop from the pride of virtue.

This origin of Christian virtue gives it the following peculiarities. The sense of sin is deepened by the thought that the sin is against God's love. Thus is brought into it an element of tenderness and penitence, as if God's love had melted the sense of sin and guilt into its own nature as love. Hence is also developed in Christian virtue a peculiar delicacy of spiritual sensibility to the difference between right and wrong; the soul is sensitive to sin, as the eye to a speck of dust. Another characteristic is aspiration. The sense of sin, healed through God's redeeming grace, issues in the most intense aspiration to be free from sin and to be like God. The aspiration is lofty as well as intense. God in Christ is not only the Redeemer of man, but his ideal. He dares to aspire both to live in intimacy with him and to be like him. His whole life becomes an aspiration, a prayer to be morally perfect as God is; to live and love like Christ. Here the Christian character takes up into itself all the virtues which cluster around self-respect and constitute nobleness, no longer as philosophy presented them, as pride and self-sufficiency, but transfigured by the knowledge of redemption, of intimacy and sonship with God, and of the promise of being like him. The incitement to a noble life now is, "See that ye walk worthy of your high calling, that ye walk worthy of God."[1] Also the Christian's belief that the Holy Spirit dwells in him — so much above the inspiration by which Socrates thought himself restrained from evil — gives courage to attempt great things and joyous confidence in the realization of the highest ends. And, further, on account of his own deep sense of sin, a Christian, in doing good, will seek first, and as indispensable to blessedness, the deliverance of men from sin by bringing them, through the consciousness of sin, into reconciliation with God by faith in his redeeming

[1] J. S. Mill is singularly at fault when he suggests the perfecting of ethical science by the recognition of *Nobleness* as a *new* constituent.

love. He stands, therefore, in uncompromising antagonism to sin. No fondness for the sinner can beguile him into consent to the sinner's transgression. A Christian must indeed be meek and forgiving. But a man can forgive only personal offences. Sin is not a personal offence against the Christian ; it is an offence against reason, against the universe, against God. "Who is this that forgiveth sins also? Who can forgive sins but God only?" At the same time his own consciousness of sin takes away from his uncompromising antagonism to sin, all ill-will, arrogance, and self-righteousness, and creates the tenderest compassion for sinners and Christ-like earnestness to save them from their sins.

Since Christianity, more than any other religion, intensifies the sense of sin, while bringing with it justification and deliverance through God's redeeming grace, it is not surprising that the Christian experience often moves the soul to its depths, passing from profound sorrow and darkness, through many fears and struggles, to the joy of forgiveness and the enthusiasm of faith and love. Such was the experience of Paul, Augustine, Luther, Wesley, Edwards. Such an experience has been familiar in all ages. This type of experience, and the sense of sin out of which it grows, are less noticeable now than in some former ages. This does not necessarily prove a decay of religion. One may grow up with faith in God's redeeming grace healing the sense of sin, and so the whole life may pass peacefully beneath the sunshine of God's love. This type of the Christian life has never been wanting. As Christianity shall prevail this will be more and more the prevalent type. On the other hand, the infrequency of this type of experience may indicate the decay of religion. The placidity may not be the peacefulness of faith and hope joined with earnestness and energy of love; it may be the placidity of indifference. If your soul has never been moved to its depths in an experience like that of Paul and Augustine, you have no reason to look down on them as from the superior heights of a serenity above the storms. Your placidity may indicate the superficialness of your life. You may never have sounded the depths of your own being, nor known the grandeur of its relations, obligations, and possibilities. It is a fatal exchange to escape the consciousness of sin by losing the consciousness of God.

We ought to look with suspicion on speculations which tend to destroy the consciousness of sin and to stigmatize as fanaticism and superstition the deeper emotions, the more severe inward struggles and the more extatic joys of religious experience. Such is the rationalism now gaining some currency, which regards Christianity as one of the religions of the world, in the same plane with the heathen religions, and, like them, partial, imperfect, and destined to pass away, and which offers itself as containing the essential truths of all religions and worthy to supersede them all. This rationalism starts from the pride of virtue, and ignores the sense of sin. It is a philosophy, not a religion. We see in it, what has been often seen in former ages, philosophy striving to thrust out religion and to usurp its place.

For the antagonism of the ancient philosophers to religion an apology is possible. Even in that antagonism the philosophy commands respect as a legitimate outgrowth of human thought. When religion intensified the sense of sin only to abase the soul in terror, when the religious service was itself a superstition, it is not wonderful that the best minds should reclaim the nobler elements of humanity, even at the expense of religion. But now that Christ has come, reconciling man to God, and quickening the noblest growth of humanity out of the sense of sin, there is no longer an apology for philosophy in maintaining its antagonistic position. And this modern rationalism has no right to disown its own parentage and family, and to baptize itself as a religion. It has no right to teach as its own the love of God to man, seeking to bring man into friendly relations to himself, the right of man to loving intimacy with God, the divine promise of the progress and renovation of society, and the human hope of its realization through the energy of God's love acting as a life-giving and renovating power in human history, nor the privilege and duty of man to be a worker with God for this end, as Jesus was, and with love as all-embracing and as self-sacrificing as his. For these are truths for which the world is indebted distinctively to Christ. It is a historical fact that, aside from Christ, religion has been too great for sinful man, and has crushed him by its greatness; the approach of God to the sinful soul has terrified and paralyzed it. Christ alone has brought God in his majesty, the law in its purity and supremacy, eternity in its grandeur and glories close to the human soul as a power of inspiration and of life. When modern rationalism appropriates to itself Christian ideas, christens itself religion, and offers itself to supersede Christianity, it is still only a philosophy disguised in what it has appropriated from Christianity.

II. Christian Virtue springs from Faith in God.

Philosophy fails to recognize this, or positively denies it. Thus Cicero makes Cotta urge, as an indisputable maxim, that men do not look to God for help in leading a virtuous life: "All men regard outward advantages, fruitful harvests, and the comforts of a prosperous life as received from the gods; but no man ever referred his own virtue to God as a divine gift. And this is right; for we ourselves are justly praised for our own virtue, and properly glory in it; which could not be, if virtue were a gift from God. But when we obtain honor or wealth, or escape calamity, then we give thanks to the gods, and take no credit to ourselves. Who ever gave thanks to the gods for being a good man? We give thanks only that we are rich, honored, in health; and for these things we pray to Jupiter optimus maximus, but never that he would make us just, temperate, or wise."[1] The ethical philosophy of the stoics involved in its fundamental principle the sufficiency of man for himself in a life of virtue.

Since, as has been already said, the heathen religions

[1] De Natura Deorum, Lib. iii. cap. 36.

present God as a power to menace and alarm, since the sentiment which they awaken is superstitious fear, and the service to which they impel is sacrifice and penance to appease the divine wrath, they neither present God as the object of faith, nor make that faith an inspiration to a life of virtue.

Christianity teaches, on the contrary, that virtue springs from faith in God. The doctrine of justification by faith does not mean, as it is often misrepresented, and sometimes by Christians themselves misunderstood, that God is induced to pardon a sinner on account of an act of faith which the sinner performed one day. This misconception makes faith an isolated act, and not the inspiration of a life; and implies that its efficacy consists in its persuasiveness with God, not in quickening and inspiring the man. Even the sense of pardon thus viewed is not ennobling; for it is only the criminal's gladness that he has escaped penalty, not the consciousness of sonship towards God. Religion thus becomes a hope of heaven, instead of a divine life on earth, and the religious life is sundered from the secular. The gospel is distinctively God in Christ reconciling the world unto himself. God loves the sinner, and seeks him in his sins to bring him back to himself, as the shepherd seeks the lost sheep. He encompasses the sinner with his love, as the sunshine encompasses every earthly thing with its quickening and invigorating beams, grace sufficient for him in every need and every emergency of his life. Faith is the sinner's trust in God as thus revealed in Christ, the Redeemer of men from sin. Faith does not make God a Redeemer, nor induce him thus to love and seek the sinner; it simply trusts God as being thus the Redeemer of sinners, and revealed as such in Christ. Christian faith is distinctively faith in Christ, because, while without Christ God is known as a holy God, as a Lawgiver, a Judge, a God who inflicts just retribution on sin, it is only in Christ that God is clearly known as loving even sinners, and extending to them grace always freely offered and always sufficient for them. Faith is the sinner's confidence in this divine love. The life of faith in God is, therefore, a life of filial trust, of loving service, of confidential intimacy. Faith thus becomes an inspiration, at every moment quickening to a life of love.

This origin of Christian virtue causes in it certain peculiarities.

It brings into virtue the element of personal love to God. Christian faith is not primarily the intellect's belief of a truth; but it is the heart's trust in a person. Trench says: "There is a natural gravitation of souls, which attracts them to mighty personalities — an instinct in man which tells him that he is never so great as when looking up to one greater than himself, that he is made for this looking upward, to find, and finding to rejoice and to be ennobled in, a nobler than himself." In the emergencies of life men feel the need of a wisdom, a goodness, a power superior to their own. When they find, or think they find, the possessor of these superior endowments, they trust him; and him whom they trust they follow. In a village, a college, a political party, in every association of men are leaders who thus draw to themselves a following. The man who thus trusts a leader surrenders himself to him, thinks his thoughts, adopts his policy, is his man. When, in addition to superior endowments the follower sees in his leader intense love to him, attested by disinterested and self-sacrificing services, and when he has thus received from him the most signal benefits, the self-surrender of the follower glows with enthusiastic loyalty to the leader. Such is the nature of Christian faith. When we feel our ignorance, weakness, and sin, and then discover both God's greatness and his love in Christ, we are drawn to him, we trust him, we surrender ourselves to him, we think his thoughts, we do his bidding, we are his men. Thus there enters into Christian virtue the element of personal trust, affection, and loyalty. We respond to the call of Jesus: "Do it for my sake." For his sake Christians attempt the great things of Christan heroism, and patiently do the little things of a righteous and loving life. Thus a Christian life is lifted up, not merely to obey an abstract command, but to please the loving God, the Redeemer.

This personal element inspires Christian virtue with a peculiar enthusiasm. Christianity goes even beyond philosophy in teaching the eternity and immutability of right, the supremacy of law, and the sternness of duty. Even more than philosophy it clarifies and quickens the conscience and makes its voice terrible. But in quickening trust in God's redeeming grace, it warms and vitalizes duty with the enthusiasm of personal affection and loyalty. It tints the cold precepts of reason with the glow of sentiment. Thus it combines the two mightiest principles of human action, the clear truths of reason, and the inflexible commands of conscience with the glow, enthusiasm, and passion of personal confidence and love.

Thus the moral element acquires a prominence and power in the life of the individual and the civilization of Christian nations which neither philosophy nor any heathen religion has been able to give. The life of the individual becomes an aspiration and a prayer for moral perfection; and society concentrates its thought and action on the removal of moral wrongs and the realization of moral ideals.

Since virtue originates in faith, the converse is also true, that faith unfolds into virtue. "Faith worketh by love." Thus morality and religion are brought into unity. Virtue grows out of religion, and religion unfolds into virtue. Thus the secular life is no longer separated from the religious, but is lifted into the religious, and ennobled as being itself a service of God. So long as religion is conceived of only as an action of man to propitiate the offended God, men offer their sacrifices, perform their penances, and commit their crimes. It is only when Christianity reveals God in Christ reconciling the world unto himself, and proclaims: "There remaineth no more sacrifice for sin," that religious service ceases to be sacrifice and penance, and becomes a service of universal love. Then its very garment is light.

It is a remarkable fact in history that wherever Christianity has not come in its purity, an impassable gulf has separated the secular thought and life from the religious. In the sphere of thought philosophy and religion remain irreconcilable. Philosophy either turns away from religion, as a sphere with which it has no concern, and constructs some fine theory of virtue without God; or it turns against it in avowed scepticism. Religion either turns away from philosophy as a sphere of thought so alien that its truths cannot be antagonistic to religious doctrine, as two bodies moving on different parallels cannot meet, as the university of Paris is said to have decided that a certain proposition was true in philosophy but false in theology; or religion assails philosophy as infidel and usurps the whole domain of thought.

The same antagonism appears in practical life. Religion either abandons the secular life as essentially worldliness, and withdraws to the desert or the cloister; or it attempts to crush the native instincts, and to occupy life with a saintliness which is ascetic, dehumanizing, and ghastly; or else taking up both spheres into one life, it gives us the Pharisee, making long prayers in his religious life and devouring widows' houses in his secular life, tithing mint and anise to the Lord but driving hard bargains with men, lengthening his own face in sanctimoniousness while grinding the faces of the poor.

But when the gospel of salvation by faith in God is received, this antagonism disappears. Philosophy acknowledges God; morality finds its root and vitality in faith; the whole action of life goes on religiously in filial trust and loving service towards God and confidential intimacy with him. Thus while scope is given to the loftiest enthusiasm and heroism of Christian love in the service of man, the humblest life and the most petty duties are ennobled as a service of God — lifted and luminous in the divine love, like a speck of dust floating and shining in the sunshine.

III. The Christian Law of Love is distinguished by superior Clearness and Comprehensiveness in the Enunciation both of the Principle and its Applications.

In comparing the moral teachings of heathen philosophy with those of Christ, it is necessary to suggest the caution that some recent writers overstate the merits of the former, and depreciate, and sometimes even misrepresent, the latter. In their obvious partiality to heathenism they become its eulogists rather than its critics. If they find a fine moral sentiment they expand and display it, as the optician expands a ray of light in all the colors of the rainbow. From their own knowledge of Christianity they interpret into an isolated sentence of a heathen author a meaning which the connection does not warrant, and which the author did not design to express. They gather fragmentary truths scattered through the heathen literature of all ages to obtain material to compare with the teachings of Christ. They give niggardly recognition of the beauty and completeness of his teachings. One recent writer has even put forth the gross misrepresentation that the morality of the New Testament is entirely negative or prohibitory, and disparages it as such in contrast with the positive requirements of heathen ethics. Others misrepresent it as in its tendencies wholly antimundane and ascetic. Therefore, while admitting a universal moral law cognizable by human reason, truth still requires the assertion that the law of love, as declared and applied in the New Testament, is superior to any heathen exposition of that law and its applications. To exemplify this thought the following distinctive peculiarities of Christian love may be mentioned.

The enunciation of the law is more clear and comprehensive. Especially is this apparent when we know that the sacrificial love of Christ in his humiliation, sufferings, and death to redeem man from sin, is itself the expression of the true nature of love in God, and the type and measure of all love in man.

Since Christian love grows out of faith, it involves the unity of religion and virtue. Christianity implies communion with God not less than service to man. The communion with God gives quickening, guidance, purity, and efficacy to the service of man. Worship does not terminate on itself; is not a self-friction to induce a glow of emotion; it is the soul coming to God for his help in doing the work of a Christian life. In this particular, also, Christian love has a superior comprehensiveness and completeness. While it manifests itself in the two opposite poles of faith and love, it completes the electric circuit of the Christian character.

In its applications it becomes philanthropy. It manifests itself in reverence for man, a sacred regard to his rights, a zeal for his highest welfare. And this love to man becomes universal, as opposed to all clannishness and all enmities of race.

It also inspires hope for the future of society and quickens the progress of man.

It is not necessary, however, to delay on the question whether, in the enunciation of moral principles, Jesus declared anything absolutely new. The grand distinction of Christianity is that it has made its ethical principles powers of life and of civilization. When we pass from heathen literature to Christian, the change in the tone of thought and feeling is like a change of climate. And a similar change affects us in the transition from the study of heathen life and civilization. The Christian church in the outset conquered the world by Christ-like love. When in the Decian persecution the plague desolated Alexandria, and the heathen in terror abandoned their sick and dead, the Christians formed themselves into classes, and devoted their personal services and contributed of their property to the care of the sick and the burial of the dead of their persecutors. The same was their action in the plague at Antioch and elsewhere. And in the progress of Christ's kingdom the law of love is slowly but irresistibly gaining for itself assertion and realization, not only in the enthusiasm and heroism of individuals, but in the constitutions and laws of states, and the customs and civilization of society. Lecky, alluding to the reconstruction of society after the dissolution of the Roman Empire, says: that after making the fullest allowance for other influences, it remains "an undoubted fact that the reconstruction of society was mainly the work of Christianity. . . . . . It did this in three ways; it abolished slavery, it created charity, it inculcated self-sacrifice."[1] The reverence for man, the regard to his rights and welfare, the broad philanthropy characterizing modern civilization, are the outgrowth of Christianity, of the life and love of Christ penetrating the life of humanity.

IV. A Distinctive peculiarity of Christian Virtue is Spiritual Freedom.

From the ancient Pythagoreans, who defined virtue as "a habit of duty," to Reid, who defines it as consisting "in a fixed purpose or resolution to act according to our sense of duty," ethical philosophy has recognized no principle of virtue higher or more effective than the sense of duty. This is, indeed, a grand principle; and its presentation by some philosophers rises to the sublime.[2] Christianity does not reject it. Christianity broadens and spiritualizes the

[1] History of Rationalism, Vol. ii. pp. 227–229.

[2] "Duty! thou great, sublime name! thou dost not insinuate thyself by offering the pleasing and the popular, but thou requirest obedience; although to move the will thou dost not threaten and terrify, but simply settest forth a law, which of itself finds entrance to the mind, which, even though against the will, wins approval and reverence, if not obedience, before which the passions are silent, even though they work secretly against it. What origin is worthy of thee, and where is the root of thy noble pedigree, which proudly disowns all relationship with the passions, and descent from which is the indispensable condition of that worth which alone man can of himself confer on himself? It can be nothing less than that which lifts man above himself as part of the world of sense, which unites him to an order of things which the understanding can only think, and which subjects to itself the entire world of sense, and the empirically determined existence of man in time. It is nothing less than personality; that is, freedom from and independence of all the mechanism of nature, which implies the subjection of the person considered as belonging to the world of sense, to his own personality so far as he belongs to the world of intelligence. No wonder, then, that man, belonging to both worlds, in regard to his highest destiny, must regard his own being with reverence and its laws with the highest veneration." — *Kant, Kritik der Praktischen Vernunft, p.* 214.

law, and emphasizes its authority, its immutability, and its sanctions. It quickens the conscience, and adds to the delicacy of its discernment and the authority of its commands. It makes the voice of duty to be nothing less than the voice of God. But the voice of duty is the voice of God proclaiming his law; it is in its nature regulative, not impulsive; it carries in it the constraint and restraint of authority, not inspiration; it is like the balance-wheel in machinery, regulating, but not originating, the motion. Christianity makes virtue consist in love inspired by faith in God's redeeming grace. Love outstrips the sense of duty; it moves with the quickness of the lightning, which the thunder of the law follows, but cannot overtake. Before conscience can utter its "categoric imperative," the willing work of love is done. A virtue driven only by the sense of duty, and never quickened by love, is imperfect. "Though I bestow all my goods to feed the poor, and though I give my body to be burned, and have not love, it profiteth me nothing." In ethical philosophy moral power is presented as regulative and restrictive; in Christianity, as motive, inspiration, life. The former gives us only law and government; the latter gives us also gospel and redemption.

Therefore freedom, spontaneousness, joyousness, are distinctively and pre-eminently characteristic of Christian virtue. It is a new life — faith working by love, and spontaneously unfolding in all the beauty and fruitfulness of a Christian life. It is an entire misapprehension and misrepresentation of Christianity to say that it restrains the freedom and development of humanity, and suppresses the spontaneousness and joyousness of life. There may be a propriety in bringing this charge against ethical philosophy which presents nothing higher than the restraints and constraints of the sense of duty; and still more against the ethnic religions, which make the fear of the divine wrath for past transgressions more urgent than the sense of duty commanding to obedience. But the contrary is true of Christianity. It reveals to the sinner God's redeeming love in Christ; and faith in God the Redeemer becomes the inspiration of a new life. It is precisely this Christian faith which creates in man the true consciousness of his own greatness and worth, quickens irrepressible aspirations to realize the highest possibilities of his being, delivers him from the bondage of passion and desire, quickens him to obey the lofty commands of reason, and to aim to realize the ideals of truth, right, and perfection, makes his obedience spontaneous, and gives him in obedience the consciousness of freedom. This is the service of filial love, as distinguished from the servile spirit of bondage. It is the freedom wherewith Christ maketh free.

# LECTURE IV.

## THE DIVINE AGENCY IN THE ESTABLISHMENT, ADMINISTRATION, AND TRIUMPH OF CHRIST'S KINGDOM.

THE kingdom of Christ is not originated and advanced by the spontaneous development of humanity; but a redeeming power comes down upon humanity from God, and enters into human history as an always-working energy, quickening men to spiritual life and transforming society into the kingdom of God. This thought is repugnant to the rationalism and naturalism of this age; but it is distinctive and essential in Christianity, and must be recognized in any truly rational philosophy of human history. It is the subject which is now to be considered: The Divine Agency in the Establishment, Administration, and Triumph of Christ's Kingdom.

The historical course of the divine action in redemption, as set forth in the scriptures, is familiar, and needs only to be indicated. The divine energy of redemption enters human history at its very beginning and declares itself in promise. It appears in the call of Abraham and the promise to all the world through his seed, giving a distinct organization to God's kingdom in the call of a chosen people, to be his, as the prophets continually insist, not by outward descent, but by his covenant and promise, and their faith and obedience; a kingdom, as Paul explicitly demonstrates, differing in form, but the same in essence with the same kingdom as it afterwards appeared in the Christian church. Centuries after the call of Abraham the Jewish state appears, itself a Theocracy, within which the germinant kingdom is secluded and protected, as a chestnut in its prickly bur, until it is ready to drop and become the germ of a great tree. Then God is in Christ, makes propitiation for the sins of the world, subdues the power of darkness and death, and makes world-wide the power of attraction by which, from the Saviour's cross, he draws all men to himself. This saving power is perpetuated in the Holy Spirit "poured out on all flesh." Christ at the right hand of the majesty on high, administers his kingdom by the invisible agency of the life-giving Spirit. By this the energy of redeeming grace widens its scope, intensifies its action, multiplies its agencies, and makes itself more and more manifest as a spiritual power established in human history, quickening a spiritual church, directing human thought and action, guiding the forces of civilization, and transforming society into Christ's kingdom. Finally, Christ will come a second time to judgment and will present his kingdom, completed and glorious, to the Father.

Here is a divine action running through human history, working the redemption of man from sin. We will confine our attention to some of the general characteristics of the divine agency in the establishment, administration, and triumph of Christ's kingdom.

I. The Divine Agency is Historical.

Here is the starting-point of the difference between Christianity and Rationalism.

Christianity, being essentially redemption, is necessarily historical. It is the promised Christ of the Old Testament, the living Christ of the New Testament, the Christ reigning and life-giving in the dispensation of the Spirit. Christianity, therefore, is not primarily doctrine, but history; not philosophy or ethics, but the historical action of divine love redeeming man from sin. It is history in the past, life-giving energy in the present, promise for the future.

Rationalism, on the contrary, is the doctrine that human reason, without supernatural intervention, is sufficient for all man's spiritual needs. God moves above and before man in the undeviating and majestic movement of nature. Man stands beneath, gazes on the grand panorama, and learns all respecting God that is needful for his spiritual welfare.

Rationalism is in agreement with Christianity in acknowledging the spirituality and personality of man, the endowment of man with reason, by which philosophy is possible, the existence of a personal God and of his moral government. In the same particulars rationalism is in antagonism to the naturalism which resolves mind into physiological phenomena, and thought and volition into forms of mechanical force, which confines the sphere of inquiry to phenomena and their uniform sequences, which denies that man is "the interpreter of nature," able to explain its phenomena by their rational principles, laws, and ends, and which acknowledges no personal God. Christianity presupposes theism and all the moral and religious truths which reason discovers. In respect to these truths it is not antagonistic to rationalism, but takes them up into itself. Christianity is itself the true rationalism, because it presupposes all the religious and moral truths which reason discovers, and because it claims to be itself the rational explanation of the facts of man's nature and history. Christianity has no conflict with reason; it is in itself the highest rationality, and it always appeals to reason as the arbiter of its own claims.

Notwithstanding this agreement, rationalism is in sharp contrast with Christianity. It teaches that the knowledge of God gained by human reason from the divine action in nature is sufficient for man's welfare. The difficulty with man is, therefore, his ignorance, not his sin. He needs instruction, not redemption. He is himself the originator of his own progress and perfection; and intellectual acquisition and culture make the only factor in human progress. Man is to think himself into the kingdom of God. Rationalism, therefore, is abstract and speculative, not historical. It is a philosophy. It coincides with dogmatism in insisting on intellectual belief of doctrine rather than on spiritual life; its gospel, its glad tidings of great joy, will be found somewhere in metaphysical speculation. Hence it rejects Christianity, and becomes antagonistic to it. It values Christianity only as Christianity enunciates ethical and philosophical truths, not as the historical action of God's redeeming grace. The permanent in it is the abstract truths, common to the religions and philosophies of the world. The historical facts are transient and unimportant. Jesus sinks to the level of Socrates and Confucius. When we have extracted from his story the truths which he taught, the history may be thrown away, as a merchant throws away the broken boxes after the goods are taken out, or as a chemist destroys a plant in distilling from it a drop of essential oil.

The chief priests and elders had the effrontery to say before the crucified Jesus: "Let him now come down from the cross, and we will believe him." Let him leave the sacrifice of redemption unfinished, and conform to our ideas of the Messiah, and we will receive him. The same is the challenge of the rationalist to-day: "Come down from the cross; cease to offer thyself as the world's Redeemer and Lord; accept our ideas, and present thyself as one of the philosophers, — as one of us, for we also are philosophers, — and we will receive thee. Humanity is wiser than any individual; and we have the light of nineteen centuries which thou hadst not, and have surveyed all the philosophies and religions of the world, of which thou wast ignorant. Abandon the pretence that thou art the Redeemer of the world, and we will receive thee among the enlightened minds of human history, such as we are." There is a spice of self-appreciation here analogous to that which Goethe hits in his epigram on the pantheist: "What is the use of your jeers about the All and the One? The professor is a person; God is not."[1]

Rationalism, allying itself with Christianity in opposition to naturalism, aims to establish intermediate between the two a rest for the intellect and the heart. But, denying historical redemption, by the necessity of its own principles it gravitates steadily towards naturalism; it builds its half-way house within the line of perpetual frost, and the glacier

[1] Werke i. p. 198. Sprüche in Reimen.

on which the structure rests bears it steadily downwards, and buries its fragments in the fields of eternal ice. It needs but a slight scrutiny to demonstrate this tendency; for rationalism involves irreconcilable inconsistencies, and does not admit a logically complete and systematic statement.

1. In rejecting miracles on the ground of their impossibility, it is precluded from admitting the existence of a personal God.

A miracle is always possible, if there is a personal God. This J. S. Mill affirms: "A miracle is no contradiction to the law of cause and effect; it is a new effect, supposed to be produced by the introduction of a new cause. Of the adequacy of that cause, if it exists, there can be no doubt; and the only antecedent improbability which can be ascribed to the miracle is the improbability that any such cause had existence in the case."[1] The argument against miracles founded on their impossibility has force only as part of a naturalism which rejects God. Trench compares it to the giant Antaeus, "unconquerable so long as permitted to rest on the earth out of which it sprung, but easily destroyed when once it is lifted into a higher world."[2] Rationalism, assuming as an axiom the impossibility of a miracle, suddenly drops into naturalism.

2. The same tendency is inherent in the rationalistic doctrine of the sufficiency of human reason. God acts in nature. Man, observing God's action in nature, attains knowledge of him, and that knowledge is sufficient for man's spiritual welfare.

But here is a God submerged in nature, imprisoned in its uniform and necessary sequences, incapable of acting outside of nature to quicken by his grace the heart of man. God is shut out from man, and cannot communicate his grace. Man is shut out from God, and cannot commune with him. Prayer becomes impossible; for it cannot alter the fixed courses of nature, in which alone God can act. The familiar illustration is, as a man in a boat by pulling on a line may draw

[1] Logic, p. 376. [2] Miracles, p. 62.

himself towards the wharf, but cannot draw the wharf towards him, so prayer may lift the soul towards God, but cannot draw God to the soul. But, if so, an honest man will cease to pray. He will not practise on himself by offering petitions which he knows God cannot answer, merely by these spiritual gymnastics to gain strength to his own soul. It will be replied that the worshipper will conform his worship to his belief, and omit all petition. What, then, is left? Thanksgiving? But he has received no grace from God; his own reason is sufficient for his spiritual needs. Confession? But God gives neither pardon for the past nor grace for the future. What, then, is the worship? An empty rhapsody, a pale meditation. But this conception of God takes from meditation itself its warmth and power. If he heeds not your prayers, he equally heeds not your meditation. You pour your confessions and praises into empty space, not into the heart of God. You have fundamentally changed the Christian conception of God. He is no longer a Father and Redeemer, with heart warm to help his supplicating creatures, but a stone colossus, moving no finger in sympathy for his wretched creatures, who cling with their tears and entreaties to his stony feet. Nature is above God; and wretched men cry in vain to insensate forces that cannot hear, to unknowing laws that cannot answer, to a universal mechanism that rolls blindly and inevitably by the necessity of its own being.

These are legitimate inferences. For if God, transcending the courses of nature, acts in the hearts of individuals and in the courses of human history, communicating his sufficient grace to quicken and to sanctify, to help men in their ignorance, their sorrows, and their work, then man's reason is no longer regarded as sufficient for his spiritual needs; but God's gracious action, coming down upon humanity and superadded to the action of human reason, is admitted. This divine action, transcending the courses of nature, is supernatural, and thus is open to the objections which are urged against the possibility of miracles. Lastly, this gracious action of God is necessarily historical. Rationalism is no longer a mere philosophy, a mere knowing; it admits the historical element as really as Christianity, and must proceed to tell us what and when and where this supernatural action is, and what are its historical results.

Rationalism, in some of its forms, admits the gracious action of God on the hearts of individuals and in human history. It even claims a certain superiority; it expresses impatience with Christianity, as needlessly bringing the revelation of prophets and apostles and the mediation of Christ between man and God, and exalts its own superiority as teaching the immediate communion of every man with God. It is impatient with the narrowness which limits inspiration to prophets and apostles, and vaunts its superiority in admitting that all genius is inspired. It is impatient with the exclusiveness of Christianity, and boasts its breadth in accepting the truths of all religions. All these claims, if clearly scrutinized, may be found to resolve themselves into naturalism. If not, rationalism, in making these claims, is inconsistent with itself.

3. The fundamental principle of rationalism necessitates not only the denial of redemption, but also the ignoring of sin. Since reason is sufficient, and man's spiritual welfare is attained by knowledge, the evil under which he suffers is not sin, but ignorance, and what he needs is not redemption, but instruction. Rationalism is now claiming to be the universal religion, dropping the historical and transitory, and gathering into itself the truths common to all religions. But all religions begin in the sense of sin and the conscious need of reconciliation to God. Rationalism excludes these. Therefore, instead of being the universal religion, it is not a religion, but only a philosophy. It will eventually appear that as a philosophy it is a philosophy falsely so called. Finding no place for the ideas and sentiments essential in all religions, it fails to declare the full-orbed truth of reason, and usurps the title of rationalism. It is, therefore, incapacitated to give a permanent resting-place either to the intellect or the heart.

We come back, then, to our starting-point, that God's action in establishing his kingdom is historical. Any divine action which is to be a power of renovation must be performed in contact with man and in the courses of human history. Otherwise it would be powerless on man as a revolution among a people in the stars. It is not possible to say *a priori* that the divine action must have been just what it is recorded in the Bible to have been. But, if God is to redeem men from sin, the redemptive action must enter human history at some point, and go on in some definite line of events to its consummation. Otherwise the facts of redemption and of sin must be rejected; and for the historical redemption must be substituted the bald rationalistic idea of religion as a knowledge of God and a consciousness of virtue, and of man's sufficiency for himself to realize the highest possibilities of his being.

Therefore objections against the scriptural history of God's action in redemption are equally pertinent against any other line of history in which the redemptive action may be conceived to have proceeded. If they have any force, it reaches to the extent of subverting the idea of redemption as contrary to reason, and impossible. All must admit that, if the Christian history of redemption is false, no other redemption has been or will be in human history, and the very idea of redemption must be abandoned. Accordingly Strauss and other rationalists start with the assumption that a supernatural and historical action in redemption is impossible. Their historical criticism of the Gospels is not for the purpose of ascertaining whether the narrative of redemption is true; but, assuming its falsity, the criticism aims only to explain how the wonderful history came into being and obtained credence, and what residuum of merely natural events may underlie it. It is a point gained to know that the historico-critical questions are secondary. The main question between the rationalist and the Christian pertains to the possibility of redemption. If the very conception of redemption in any form is not absurd, the historico-critical objections to Christianity lose their force. In fact, historical criticism then supports Christianity. For the unresolvable difficulty to the rationalist has always been, that both the external and the internal supports of the credibility of the gospel are so strong that it is impossible to explain the existence of these narratives, and their acceptance and power, on the supposition that the fundamental fact of the narrative is impossible.

It must be added that since God's action in redemption is in human history, it must not only be consonant with the constitution of the human mind, but also be at every time and place consonant with the existing condition of the minds on which it acts. If God acts on a child or a savage, the action can be effective only so far as it is adapted to their capacity. A human element, therefore, enters everywhere into God's action in redemption, limiting its action and modifying its results. It is sufficient for our present purpose distinctly to state this principle.

## II. God's Action in Redemption involves the Miraculous.

The incarnation, resurrection, and ascension of the Son of God are miraculous. These are essential in redemption. The whole conception of the Messiah and his kingdom implies the miraculous. The denial of miracles is the denial of that which is essential in Christianity. The attempt to retain Christianity after eliminating all that is miraculous is futile. If the residuum of speculative and ethical truth may be called a system of religion, it certainly has no claim to be called Christianity, and those who receive that system have no claim to be called Christians.

A single thought on this great subject is all that our space permits. It is involved in the very fact of sin that if God acts to redeem the sinner, the action must be special, varying from the action which would normally have expressed the divine perfections, if no creature had ever sinned, and varying also from the normal expression of the divine perfections in the punishment of sin. This speciality of the divine action seems to involve all that is essential in the miraculous.

10

The idea of atonement, as averting the punishment, which would normally express the divine perfection, by a divine action which equally expresses the same divine perfection in pardoning, seems to include within itself a specialty of divine action which is essentially miraculous.

The same specialty of the divine action in redemption appears to be involved in the very idea of sin. Jesus says: "If any man will do his will he shall know of the doctrine." He here teaches that light and influence sufficient for him whose heart is right are insufficient for him whose heart is wrong. If the sinner is to be saved from sin, the redeeming energy must transcend all that is necessary for those who do not sin. The abnormal action of the sinner must be met by extraordinary action of God. He cannot be reclaimed by the same action of God's love which he has already resisted in his transgression.

The great revelation of nature is open to the sinner not less than to those who have not sinned. "He maketh his sun to rise on the evil and on the good." God reveals himself to sinners as really as to the righteous in their own reason, and conscience, and spiritual wants. On the one as really as the other shines the light which "lighteth every man that cometh into the world." To sinless ones the external revelation becomes an inward light. The spiritual mind discerns that which the carnal mind knoweth not. But the same revelation to a sinner is inadequate, not through a defect of the revelation, but through the blinding and hardening caused by sin. The light, so far as it enlightens him, is a lurid illumination of his guilt, driving him to superstition. His degeneracy is not through the want of light, but through the power of sin perverting it. So Paul explicitly teaches in the opening of his Epistle to the Romans.

Evidently, then, if sinners are to be saved, the action of God in saving them must transcend all his action in the uniform sequences of nature, and through the human reason and conscience. The abnormal condition of the sinner requires special action of God for his redemption — action which would itself be abnormal if there were no sin; and is in that sense a suspension of uniform law; but which is the normal action to meet abnormal conditions. And this is action which is miraculous. Miracle, then, is involved in the very idea of redemption. And the abnormal condition of the sinner is the occasion and antecedent probability of the special and therefore miraculous intervention of God in redemption. Miracles are reasonable because sin is unreasonable. Miracles are normal because sin is abnormal.

And since redemption is essentially miraculous, it is impossible to determine *a priori* how far or in what ways the redemptive energy entering into human history may transcend the ordinary sequences of nature, and no objection against any miracle recorded in the Bible is valid on the ground of the impossibility or antecedent improbability of miracles.

The argument against miracles is, therefore, an argument against redemption, and finally against the existence of sin, which is the occasion of redemption. Precisely accordant has been the history of rationalism, beginning in the denial of miracles, proceeding to the denial of redemption, and issuing in the denial of sin.

III. God's Action in Redemption constitutes a Revelation.

1. God's revelation of himself is primarily by his action, and especially by his action in redemption. God reveals himself by his action in nature. Suns and planets and cosmic forces are the words in which his thoughts are written, and the secret of his being revealed. So in redemption he reveals himself by his actions. He makes known what he is to sinners by what he does to sinners. The expulsion from Eden, the call of Abraham, the preservation and education of the Jews, the incarnation, the life, death, resurrection, and ascension of the Christ, the outpouring of the Spirit, the rise of Christ's kingdom on earth under the ministry of the apostles, and the continued intercession and reign of Christ

in the dispensation of the Spirit constitute God's revelation of himself to men.

2. The revelation by words, oral or written, is secondary and subordinate to the revelation by actions. Thought and character must be expressed in action before they can be symbolized by words. A mother cannot reveal her love to her child simply by taking it on her knee and saying: "I am your mother." The word is a mere articulate sound; it has no meaning. It is only by the service of motherly love, caring for the child and encompassing it through all its life, that she can reveal herself to her child. So revealing herself she makes the word *mother*, a life-long power to her child. So it is impossible for God to reveal himself primarily by words. Were it written across the sky, with letters made of stars, "GOD IS LOVE," it would be a meaningless emblazonry, unless God by his action had first given meaning to the words. This he does in redemption, revealing his majesty, his holiness, his authority, his patience, his immeasurable love, as pure as it is tender. So he puts meaning into words. The revelation, "GOD IS LOVE," is written not in letters on the sky, but in redeeming grace acting in the history of man. Thus the name of the Redeemer is above every name, a power to subdue, to quicken, and to inspire the sinner's heart.

It may be objected that after we have acquired the meaning of words, God may reveal himself through them. True. But the very point we are making is that thought and character must be expressed in deeds before they can be symbolized in words. In the revelation, "God is love," the word God, would have no meaning if God had not first manifested himself in his works; men would never have had occasion for the word if they had not first found the Infinite Being through his works; and the word "love" would have no meaning except such as is derived from the action of selfish men. In theology we are always at this disadvantage, that the thought and character of God must be expressed by words which primarily derive their meaning from the actions of men. But the words which declare the mind and heart of God must be interpreted through the action of God, and not through the action of men. Thus God's action in redemption gives significance to the words of revelation which are to be interpreted by God's action rather than by man's. It is God's action in redemption in Christ and in the Holy Spirit by which we are to learn the meaning of God's love.

Hence Christ is emphatically the Word of God. In him is spoken the great Word of revelation. His person, his life, death, resurrection, ascension, intercession, and continued reign are the true revelation of God. The revelation by words is secondary and subordinate.

3. When God has revealed himself by actions, a revelation by words is possible, supplementing the revelation by action. A mother, revealed already to her child through acts of love, can take the child on her knee and explain its filial duties; and every word is now powerful with the power of a mother's love. So God, entering into human history with the energy of redeeming grace, may inspire individuals with knowledge to be communicated to others. But these private revelations must always be dependent on and subordinate to the public acts of his redeeming love. A general reveals the plan of his campaign by his acts in prosecuting it. But, as incidental to it, he gives sealed orders to this general and that, sends despatches to this one and that, takes some into his counsels, and declares, explains, and vindicates his plans. These private communications are afterwards of great use in throwing light on his plans. But they are incidental and subordinate to the grand revelation which he makes in the action of the campaign. So we have inspired communications from prophets and apostles, but all incidental and subordinate to the grand revelation in the divine action in redemption, and pre-eminently in Christ, the Living Word.

4. Revelation, therefore, is not an end in itself, but an incident to the divine action in redemption. A mother in her care of her child, a general in the conduct of a campaign, a statesman in the administration of government, reveal

themselves; but the revelation is incidental to their main purpose, and is not itself the end for which they act. So God's action in redemption is incidentally a revelation; but the revelation is not the end for which he acts.

All God's action must be sincere and hearty. It must be the expression of what God is. He cannot act merely for show or for effect. His action is the expression of what he is; it carries in it all the earnestness and energy of God. So the blessed sunlight, which reveals the sun and illumines all things, is the outpouring of the light and heat which burn with energy inconceivable in the sun, raging in cyclones of fire, bursting in volcanic eruptions which might throw up the earth as a stone into the air, streaming in cones of flame eighty thousand miles into space, and in a few minutes falling back into the burning mass. So God's love, glowing with the infinite energies of the Godhead, and pouring through all space with blessing, will certainly reveal itself; but the revelation is not the end for which he acts.

If the revelation were the end of the action, the action itself would cease to be the action of love; the revelation would cease to be a revelation of love; and the whole manifestation would cease to be a moral power quickening love in man. Any theory which represents the incarnation or any divine action as designed only to show God, and so to produce a moral impression on his creatures, is void of meaning; for God's action can reveal God and become a moral power upon man only as his action is the sincere and hearty expression and outshining of what God is. The supposition that revelation is an end in itself drives us into this erroneous theory — a conception derogatory to God, and making his action not real and hearty, but scenic and sensational. It also leads legitimately to the fundamental error of rationalism — that the evil into which man has fallen is not sin, but ignorance, or at the worst error, and therefore that he needs not redemption, but instruction.

Writers on the Evidences of Christianity often argue as if the grand design of God in all the divine action recorded in the Old Testament and the New was to prepare the Bible as an authoritative revelation of his will, and leave the Bible in the world to effect its renovation. But it is not the written word, but the living Word; not the Bible, but God's grace in Christ and in the Holy Spirit, which is the power of salvation to men.

5. It follows that miracles are not to be regarded simply as seals of the truth of revelation, as credentials of inspired messengers, certifying their authority to reveal God's will, but as a part of the divine action in human history redeeming men from sin. As the divine love worked its way into human history, its divine energy could not always be contained in the ordinary courses of the divine action, but leaped from its overcharged conductors, and scintillated and flashed and electrified in miracles. It sometimes encountered obstacles which could not be removed by ordinary action, and which were miraculously swept away. Especially, in entering humanity in Jesus Christ, and offering the oblation of sacrificial love in the redemption of man, the action was necessarily and in its very essence miraculous. Therefore we no longer point to miracles as simply the external evidences of the divine authority of a book; we no longer draw the internal evidences of the divine authority of that book from its superior morality alone, thus sinking Christianity to the level of rationalism; but we regard Christianity as the action of God redeeming man from sin — an action which is primarily redemption, necessarily historical and supernatural, and incidentally a revelation. And we claim that Christianity is true on the grounds that it is the only rational and satisfactory exposition of the condition, history, and destiny of man in his relation to God, and the only manifestation of God which in every age meets man's spiritual necessities.

6. The objection of F. W. Newman and others, that a book-revelation is impossible, is now seen to be without force. It is founded on the supposition, itself rationalistic, though apparently accepted by some writers on the Evidences, that the Bible is simply a revelation of moral truth and duty,

and that the end of all God's supernatural action was to make and authenticate this revelation. To this it is objected that moral truth and law must always be judged by man's moral or practical reason, and therefore cannot be substantiated by outward authority, not even by miracles. Certainly, a miracle cannot prove that it is right to hate one's neighbor. But the objection is of no force against God's supernatural action in redeeming men from sin, and the revelation of his love incident thereto.

IV. The Knowledge of God revealed through his Action in Redemption is a Moral Power in the Establishment and Administration of his Kingdom.

Every action spreads its influence beyond the time and place in which the power is exerted, as a candle shines far beyond itself into the darkness; as the cholera, once when it swept around the world, originated in the filthiness and other unwholesome conditions of certain crowds of pilgrims in the East. This is true of all action, but especially noticeable in respect to memorable acts. A mother's love continues to be a moral power on the son, though he dwells in another hemisphere; and after her death it is purified and intensified into a heavenly power. The memory of the martyrs is an inspiration in every age. At the stake Latimer said to his companion: "Fear not, Master Ridley; we shall this day light such a candle by God's grace in England as, I trust, shall never be put out." The young men praying near the haystack in Williamstown are still missionaries to the heathen. Howard still inspires to benevolence. The great name of Washington still overshadows and protects his country. "Stat magna nominis umbra." Every heroic life is a power so long as its history is read.

These are analogous to the moral influence of God's historical action in redemption. Of his propitiatory sacrifice Christ said: "It is finished," and died. His earthly life ended, and became a part of the history of the past. But in that life and death he made propitiation for our sins, and opened the way of deliverance from their power; he triumphed over death; he disclosed the infinite love of God our Redeemer; and in all the ages his name is above every name; and his appeal: "Do this for my sake," finds a willing response. The same moral power, though less marked, is inherent in the action of God in the history of the Jews. It is a study and a guide to all generations. Thus God's past action in history is a moral power in all subsequent generations; and this must not be overlooked in considering the divine agency in the establishment, administration, and triumph of Christ's kingdom.

Here, however, it must be observed that the moral power of God's past historical action is an incidental result of that action, not its primary end. An action of which the primary end is to make itself a moral power is an action from which the essence of the moral power is left out. It is a revelation that reveals nothing. The very conception breaks down, like the conception of motion in which nothing moves. There would be no moral power in a martyrdom suffered for the purpose of creating moral power. The martyr would be a witness testifying nothing. The moral power is not in the dying, but in the character manifested in the dying, and which, under the circumstances, would equally have necessitated the dying if it were to be forever secret.

So Christ did not come into the world and die primarily to create a moral power. The supposition eviscerates itself. It has been already said that all God's action is the sincere and hearty expression of what God is. Its moral power does not lie in the action, but in the divine thought and character expressed in the action. If we leave out of Christ's work the idea of atonement, — if he did not suffer for us, the just for the unjust, to bring us to God, and was not the propitiation for the sins of the whole world, — then we leave out the essence of his moral power. God in redemption reveals his entire character in harmony. God is not a nature having instincts and wants seeking gratification. His action is not the development of a nature according to necessary impulses.

His action is the expression of reason. His love itself is the expression of reason in acts of will. Redemption, then, does not merely express a divine compassion for sinners, but also the supremacy and majesty of the eternal reason, the unchangeableness of its truth, the authority and inexorableness of its law, the grandeur of its ideals, the blessedness of conformity to it, and the impossibility of blessedness without that conformity to it. If it expressed only the fond impulses and cravings of a nature seeking its own happiness or that of others, it could not be a spiritual power potent to lead men to God.

In this line of thought we see the moral power of the Bible. It is the inspired record of God's supernatural and providential action in redeeming the world in Christ and founding his kingdom under the dispensation of the Spirit. It contains the private revelations of his will to prophets and apostles incident to his redeeming action. It reveals God as the providential and moral Ruler of the world and as the Redeemer of men from sin. It necessarily carries in it the highest moral power; it must always be the instrument in advancing Christ's kingdom; and intimacy with it and reverence for it must always be the condition of a pure, strong Christian character in individuals and in nations.

### V. God's Action in the Establishment and Administration of his Kingdom is continued through all Generations in the Holy Spirit.

The energy of God's redeeming grace did not cease to act with the events recorded in the Bible. Redemption is present, not less than past.

The divine agency now is not merely the moral power of the revelation already made, but it is also the present, personal influence of God through the Holy Spirit. The analogy here is not to the memory of a departed mother, but to the mother present with her child, always ready to counsel and help, impressing her influence on it every day, and thus accumulating her moral power. The Christian life is not sustained merely by knowledge of the truth and meditation on God's action in the past, but by the present action of God upon the soul through the Holy Spirit.

This doctrine is opposed to the doctrine of Romanism, that divine grace comes to men through the *opus operatum* of the church. It recognizes every Christian as in immediate communion with God, a recipient of God's grace. It is opposed to a certain rationalistic element which has shown itself even in the best forms of Protestantism ; the impression that truth and meditation on the truth are the sole agencies in spiritual life and growth ; the Lord's supper, for example, is profitable as an occasion for meditating on the love of Christ, not as an ordinance appointed to convey the influence of the Spirit to him who receives it in faith. This type of thought gives whatever ground there has ever been for the charge of Bibliolatry — a charge brought by rationalism against the churches, the only ground for which is the admission by the churches of a rationalistic type of thought. The doctrine of the Spirit is opposed to the rationalistic tendency alleged to be inherent in Protestantism. If the allegation is true, it is only because Protestantism is a protest against errors and abuses; the tendency is not inherent in Christianity, nor in the affirmation of spiritual and historical Christianity which Protestantism makes. Finally, the true doctrine of the Spirit is distinguished from the fanatical by the facts, that the work of the Spirit is the continuance and world-wide extension of God's work of redemption; that it avails itself of the moral power accumulated by God's antecedent redemptive action and the revelation which he has made of himself in the same; that, as the progress and extension of that same redemptive action, it must be in harmony with all the work of redemption which has preceded and with the revelation of the same in the word of God. So Christ explicitly teaches: "He shall glorify me; for he shall receive of mine and shall show it unto you."

In the action of God recorded in the Bible he makes an entrance into human history; educates the race for the coming Christ and the establishment of his kingdom; makes atonement; creates the moral power of the name that is above every name. In the Holy Spirit the redemptive energy becomes a world-power, and the life of Christ flows out into humanity as a life-giving and sanctifying power.

Thus the Spirit brings us into immediate connection with Christ. His presence on earth is a token that Christ lives and reigns, administering and extending his kingdom. If a friend, going to a distant country, promises to send you on his arrival some curious product of the country, and if, in due time, the promised present is brought to you, you have in hand a pledge and token that he has safely accomplished his journey, and in that distant land remembers you and has kept his promise. So the descent of the Spirit on the day of Pentecost was the present token and pledge to the disciples that Jesus, according to his word before his death, had ascended to the right hand of the majesty on high, that all power was given him in heaven and on earth, that in his exaltation he remembered his disciples and kept his promise. And wherever the Spirit touches any human heart, it is in all ages the present token of the same. The Spirit, also, continues the work of redemption. He proceeds from Christ. In him Christ acts, administering his kingdom and advancing it to its triumph. In him the life and redeeming power of Christ, confined while he was on earth to his bodily presence, diffuses itself through the world and courses through human history, more effective than his bodily presence could be: "It is expedient for you that I go away; for if I go not away the Comforter will not come to you."

Thus in the action of the Spirit the redeeming energy of the Son of God is brought immediately upon us. We are brought into immediate contact with the Son of God, and thereby into contact with the Father, in whose love to the world redemption originates; whose love in redemption through Christ and the Spirit floods the earth with its glory and pours through the history of man. It is just as by the sunbeams we are brought into immediate contact with the sun. So the Spirit touching human hearts with light and quickening, brings us into immediate connection with the Son of God, who is "the outshining of the Father's glory," and who reveals the otherwise unknown Father, and reveals him by flooding us with his love. Thus through the Spirit "God, who commanded the light to shine out of darkness hath shined in our hearts, to give the light of the knowledge of the glory of God in the face of Jesus Christ." Thus redemption, with all its glory, comes upon us — redemption from the Father, through the Son, and by the Holy Ghost.

Thus redemption is the channel in which all the fulness of the Godhead has been poured through human history, widening and brightening from the first promise to Adam until now. So Ezekiel represents it, a fountain bursting forth from beneath the threshold of the sanctuary, at first only up to the ancles, farther on to the knees, then to the loins, and afterwards a river too great to be crossed. We cannot originate that river of life; but we can embark on it as it flows by our doors, and be borne by its shining waves on into the ocean-fulness of God's eternal love.

# LECTURE V.

## THE CHURCH THE ORGANIC OUTGROWTH OF THE LIFE-GIVING AND REDEEMING GRACE OF CHRIST PENETRATING HUMAN HISTORY IN THE HOLY SPIRIT.

JOHN in his first epistle, presents Christ's life as penetrating humanity and manifesting itself therein by a growth vitalized by that life and having its character; as the vital force of a seed penetrates inorganic nature and creates a growth "after its kind." The eternal life which was with the Father is in his Son; by him, the Word of Life, it is manifested to men. He that hath the Son hath the life, and participating in his life, is like him. The life penetrating human history, creates a growth after its kind. That life in God is light, and as it unfolds in man it is light, and in it is no darkness at all; in God it is love, and unfolding in humanity it is love, excluding all selfishness and hate; in God it is absolute purity, and among men whosoever hath this hope in him[1] purifieth himself even as he is pure; this life entering the human heart effects a new birth, and "whosoever is born of God doth not commit sin, for his seed remaineth in him, and he cannot sin because he is born of God." The "fellowship" on which the apostle insists is more than communion in meditation and worship; it is participation in the life that was in Christ, as a plant participates in the life of the seed. The apostle proceeds to teach that it is by the Holy Spirit that Christ abides in us. The criterion by which we discern the Spirit of God is that he is the Spirit

[1] *In him. Him* refers to God: whosoever hath this hope in God purifieth himself.

of Christ, confesses him as the life of the world, and creates an outgrowth of the life that is in him.

Since the life that was in Christ is thus penetrating and vitalizing humanity, it must manifest itself in effects which can be historically traced. In some form the kingdom of heaven must reveal itself in human history rising from the ruins of humanity and shaping itself in its divine beauty. Somewhere must appear the living tree into which the mustard-seed is growing. Goethe calls nature the living garment which is always weaving for Deity in the whizzing loom of time, and by which we see him. So the kingdom of heaven, forming itself in human history, is the garment which God is weaving by which we see him as the Redeemer and the life of men.

The more spiritual and profound historians of the church recognize it as the manifestation of this divine life flowing into human history. But this is true of the organized church only with important qualifications. The life must manifest itself in an organization; but the organization is neither the only nor the complete exponent of the life. The kingdom of heaven is organizing rather than organized. It creates for itself an organization, yet the kingdom of heaven is not the organization, but rather the life which produces it. The life which creates the organization, penetrates and purifies also the family and the state, renovates individuals, and blooms and fructifies in Christian civilizations; and these also are its historical manifestations. Always the kingdom of heaven is within you. In the variously organized churches of history, without doubt, the life has been revealed and organized. But no one has been the only and complete outgrowth and manifestation of the life. The kingdom of Christ is neither identical nor co-extensive with them.

These qualifications must be kept in mind as we proceed to consider the church as the organic outgrowth in human history of the life that is in Christ.

There are two maxims which express what is essential in the two conflicting theories of the church. The first is:

"Where the Spirit of God is, there is the church." The second is: "Where the church is, there is the Spirit of God." All organizations of the church fall into two classes, according as they express the one or the other of these principles.

According to the first of these principles, the Spirit of God is always originating and sustaining the new spiritual life, and the church is the constant and spontaneous development of this spiritual life into outward organization. The Spirit and life are primary and originant; the organization secondary and dependent. The church is not perpetuated by the cohesiveness of the organization, but by the indwelling Spirit. If Christianity is introduced into a heathen country, those whom the Spirit renews become a church through their fellowship one with another in that new life. If in any country the church becomes corrupt, any whom God's Spirit renews, withdraw from the corrupt organization and originate the visible church anew. The organization, forsaken by the Spirit, is no longer a church, but a carcass needing to be buried. The organization developed from the pre-existing life and perpetuated by the vitalizing and ever-present Spirit is subordinate to the life, and exists to promote the edification of its members and to facilitate the performance of their Christian work.

According to the second principle, the church came forth as an organization from Christ's hand to stand unchanged to the end of time. The organization is the vehicle through which God's grace and Spirit are conveyed to men. The organization is primary and originant, the Spirit and life secondary and dependent. The organization perpetuates itself by its own strength and cohesiveness. If Christianity is introduced to a heathen land, the church must be imported. If the church becomes corrupt, true believers may try to reform it; but to withdraw from it is schism. The life is subordinate to the organization. The church stands between the individual and Christ, to convey God's grace to him by its action in his behalf. And the church, speaking officially, is infallible, and its dicta binding, as the voice of God, on every individual's conscience.

The first of these conceptions of the church is from Christ. The second is historically from heathenism. The Christian church, first constituted as Christ willed, gradually took up into itself the principle of Roman imperialism and was corrupted into a hierarchy. Romanism is the logical result. Protestantism acknowledges the first principle. Yet Congregationalism is the only polity which carries out the principle, "Where the Spirit of God is there is the church," to its legitimate results.

In the light of this maxim, consider, next, in some details, what is the true idea of the church as the outgrowth in human history of the life which was in Christ and is manifested among men.

I. The Spirit acts primarily on Individuals, and the Life manifests itself primarily in them.

The divine action in redemption is directed primarily upon individuals, and not upon organizations and institutions. It is not a diffused daylight, an all-pervading electricity, acting equally and indefinitely on society as such, through institutions, public sentiment, and the spirit of the age, and lifting society in mass to a higher level. Its aim is not primarily the promotion of general culture, and refinement, and the advancement of civilization. It is the direct action of God on individuals to bring them into reconciliation with himself. Redemption aims to save souls. It is becoming fashionable in some circles to ridicule this phrase. A writer in a leading Review has even said that the idea of missions "to save souls" is becoming obsolete. The phrase, like any other, may degenerate into cant. But rightly understood it is the doctrine of Christianity, that redeeming grace is acting in human history to save souls. Christ came "to save the lost." The "faithful saying and worthy of all acceptation" is, that Christ came "to save sinners." They who are offended at this are offended at Christianity itself.

This individualism attaches to the redemptive agency in all its forms. Christ tasted death for every man — the singular number, the distributive pronoun. The attraction of the cross fastens immediately on every soul, as the attraction of the sun fastens with undivided power on every planet. Every one is invited to equal intimacy with God, each in the secrecy of his own closet. Every Christian, born of the Spirit, is the child of God and not removed by any intervening agency to a remoter relationship. Justification by faith gives to every sinner free access to God without priestly mediation.

Accordingly the Spirit is represented in the Bible as dwelling in the individual, not in the church. The temple of God, which Paul admonishes the Corinthians not to defile, is not the organic church, but the body of the individual.

Thus Christianity is characterized by intense individualism. This has originated the individualism which characterizes modern political institutions. But all experience confirms, what reason teaches, that political welfare is not attainable by that one-sided individualism which prompts every one to regard only his own liberty and rights. This is an individualism which is identical with selfishness. It must be supplemented by a regard to society. And it is remarkable that, while Christianity teaches an intense individualism, it insists on individual responsibility, duty, and love, rather than individual liberty and rights. Thus, while vitalizing the grand movement of society against oppression and slavery, and in favor of equal rights, it supplies the needed check to selfishness and the needed impetus to live for others and to guard and promote the interests of society.

## II. A Church is an Organized Association of Persons Renewed by the Holy Spirit.

This follows directly from the principle, "Where the Spirit is, there is the church." When Christ's sheep hear his voice and follow him, they are thereby separated from others and united to Christ; and in their union with Christ and following of him, united also to each other. Thus the church comes into being. It is an association of persons effectually called to Christ by his voice speaking through the Holy Spirit. They are united not by force or external authority, nor by the tie of birth; but by their own free act and covenant in the fellowship of their common faith in Christ, and the common character, ideas, and aims of their new spiritual life. Yet the church is not merely a voluntary association, dependent for its existence on the will of man. It is of divine origin, because it is the spontaneous outgrowth of the "life" that is in Christ, penetrating human history through the Holy Spirit; it exists by divine authority, because it has the reason of its existence in God's redeeming energy working always among men; it is lifted above the creations of human will, and is perpetuated and imperishable in the indwelling of the Holy Spirit and his continued life-giving and renovating agency in the world.

The church, as an organization thus constituted, necessarily made its appearance so soon as Christianity began to prevail. And the principles thus organized in the churches necessarily tended to pass over into the constitution of the state.

Allusion has been already made to the intense individualism of Christianity. This is embodied in the church. The individual is the unit of the organization. This was contrary to the conception of society universally prevalent when the first Christian churches were established. The heathen conception of society emphasizes the race, rather than the individual. It begins with the race, and proceeds downwards to the individual; it begins with institutions, and proceeds downwards to the men who live under and for them. In heathen society the individual is lost in the mass; the individuals exist as the planets did when dissolved and lost in the nebulous matter diffused through space; not, as now, in the solar system, moving in their individuality harmoniously under law. It was an epoch when, in society thus constituted, the apostolic church appeared, an institution embodying the Christian idea of the worth and rights of man — an association of individuals of every caste, rank, and race, "born, not of blood, nor of the will of the flesh, nor of the will of man, but of God." In the church the king and his subject, the master and his slave, the nobleman and the peasant, stand on a level, having equal rights in its privileges, equal vote in the management of its affairs, and equal eligibility to its offices. Such an institution could not flourish, retaining its purity, in such a state of society, without coming into conflict with it, diffusing new ideas, and gradually infusing its own principles into the constitution of the state and the usages of society.

Such has been the historical fact. In the very beginning of the propagation of Christianity we find Peter and John arraigned before the Sanhedrim declaring the rights of conscience, and announcing the principle which has ever since underlain the martyrdoms and conflicts for liberty of conscience and the rights of man against oppression. Even amid Roman imperialism, the churches retained their primitive constitution for a time. After being corrupted and consolidated by taking into itself the imperial idea, the church long retained features of its original constitution in the election of bishops, in holding its offices open to men of every degree, in its steady and successful opposition to slavery, in affording through all the reign of violence an asylum for the oppressed, in its action through the Middle Ages in the interest of human rights against the tyranny of the secular rulers, and in its attitude as an adjudicator of wrongs by an appeal to justice and law in antagonism to the brute force and bloody lawlessness of the feudal barons. People willingly appealed to tribunals that recognized law and the authority of God against lords who decided everything by the sword; and in this way the growing hierarchy was encouraged in its usurpations of authority. Even in the theological writings of the Middle Ages are found distinct traces of the modern doctrine of the rights of the people against oppressive rulers.[1]

[1] "A man is bound to obey secular rulers only so far as justice requires.

After the Reformation, the same principle reasserted itself. The church was organized as an association of persons, and with the recognition of personal rights. The principle passed from the church into the state. Geneva became "the seed-plot of liberty." Subsequently the Puritan churches more completely transferred the principle of their own organization into the Puritan state.

Thus the principle of the organization of the church, as an association of persons united in the fellowship of a common life, common interests and ends, and a common law, went out into human thinking, and became a power in civilization, loosing the bond of race and force with which society had been bound by Satan, bowed down and nowise able to lift up itself during all the centuries. The state is no longer a race united by common descent, and holding down subject races by force; but it is a people, of whatever locality, united by common interests under law; and the jurisprudence of Christendom assumes that government, whatever its form, rests ultimately on the consent of the people. Even the doctrine of the "social contract," elaborated by the Jesuit Suarez, taught by Locke, Sidney, and Rousseau, and terribly declared in the first French Revolution, is a recognition and distorted expression of this truth.

Perhaps it may not be going too far to say that the constitution of the church as an association of *regenerate* persons has furnished an important principle of political and social progress. It is in antagonism to the heathen conception, which regards the man as subordinate to his institutions, and which looks primarily to a change of institutions for the improvement of the man. The same is the error of modern "socialism." In opposition to this error, the church embodies the principle, which all experience veri-

Therefore, if the rulers have not the right to rule, but are usurpers, or if rulers require what is unjust, their subjects are not bound to obey them, unless perhaps, in exceptional cases to avoid scandal or danger." In confirmation he quotes Augustine (*De Civitate Dei*, Lib. iv. Cap. 4). "Aside from justice, what are kingly governments but great robberies." — *Thomas Aquinas, Summa Theologiae*, Second Division of Part ii. Quest. 104, Art. 6.

fies, that the only real progress of society consists in the actual improvement of the individuals composing society. A strong and virtuous people insure a strong and just govern ment.

The second maxim: "Where the church is, there is the Spirit," gives the contrary conclusions. The child is re-regenerated in baptism by the *opus operatum* of the church in its behalf. It is thus born into the church, and thenceforward governed by enforced authority. If afterwards the baptized person deviates from the faith, or disobeys the commands of the church, he is subject to inquisitorial torments and death. Thus the old principle of despotism becomes the principle of the church itself; and the power which was working to redeem the world becomes imprisoned in an iron arm that smites and kills.

III. The Church as an Organization is Subordinate to the Life.

1. The organization is the outgrowth of the life.

Man, by virtue of his rationality, is an organizer. As God expresses his thoughts in worlds and systems, man expresses his thoughts in cities, states, institutions. It is man who forms his institutions, not the institutions which form the man. So Christian faith and love create Christian institutions. The new Christian life displaces the old, and creates all things new. The church, as an organization, is the outgrowth of the life. It may be said to be the organization of the life, as the mustard-plant is the organization of the life of the mustard-seed.

2. The organization exists for the ends or purposes of the life.

The conception is of spiritual persons united in fellowship by their oneness with Christ for the purpose of mutual edification and helpfulness in Christian life and work. This principle is determinant of the constitution of a church. It is incompatible with the conception of a church that it should absorb the individual in the society, or by its organization come down on him to suppress or crush his personality. The conception of a church requires that its organization and its organic action emphasize and develop the individual personality. It exists for the very purpose of subserving the spiritual life, growth, and power of its members. It must not be, therefore, an organization so massive as to oppress the life, but so consonant with the life as to help it, as a trellis sustains and helps the vine.

Accordingly the growth, power, and prosperity of a church are proportional to the degree in which it calls out its individual members to spiritual life and activity. If it becomes only a receptacle, taking in and holding its members as dead things, it is thenceforth only a whited sepulchre, full of dead men's bones.

3. The church is not mediatorial. It does not stand between man and God, to bring the divine blessing from heaven by its sacraments and the *opus operatum* of its service.

The subordination of the organization to the life necessarily involves the three characteristics just mentioned, and is a necessary inference from the principle: "Where the Spirit is, there is the church."

From the church this idea of the subordination of organization to the life has penetrated human thought respecting political and social institutions. When Christ came, the iniquity of the world was full. As at that time religious faith was withered, and scepticism had attained its greatest power and widest dominion, so the principle of government by force had reached in the Roman empire its consummation. The Western nations were ruled under military despotism by the will of one man, and held in his hand for his own personal use and enjoyment. The people, educated through many generations under the reign of force, had lost the capacity of refinement of feeling and the enjoyment of the gentle and kindly emotions, which were displaced by ferocity and blood-thirstiness, so that even theatrical spectacles were insipid if not spectacles of blood.

In the midst of this civilization the Christian church appears, like a dewdrop, distilling silent and unseen from the air. It makes no direct assault on existing institutions. Not claiming the sword, which rightfully belongs to the civil ruler, it can only stand in the presence of the great organizations embodying the power of the strongest, and let its presence do its work, educating the world to understand that institutions are the outgrowth of human thought and life, and that they can never be right and salutary till they embody truth, justice, and love, and not selfishness grasping and ruling by force. It introduced Christian charity as a power in civilization. It taught men self-sacrifice in service. The Roman slavery passed away before it. At last the conception embodied in the Christian church when it first stood in the civilization of the Roman empire, like a dewdrop trembling on a leaf, has created a new conception of political and social institutions and a new civilization. Man is no longer regarded as existing for institutions forced upon him; but institutions exist for man, and are the creation of his thought and life. In like manner, the church has educated man to the true method of securing the progress of man and the reorganization of society. It is not by immediately assailing institutions, as if a change of institutions would recreate the man; but by new creating the man, that he may cast away institutions no longer fitting him, and create new.

It has been the great mistake in the education of the race to believe that there is no safety for man except as by external and superior power he is restrained and constrained, and institutions and rules are framed and put on him, into conformity with which his thought and life must grow. But the words of Milton are always true:

> "Who overcomes
> By force, hath overcome but half his foe."

There is no real progress, except as men accept truth on conviction, conform their lives to it in Christian love, and freely embody their Christian thought and love in institutions. This is the truth evermore embodied and expressed in the Christian church. Fearful forebodings agitate some minds, whether republican government will not prove a failure, and men are discussing what will be the political constitution of the future. But all experience is teaching and emphasizing the doctrine of Christianity, that the true order of human advancement is from the individual to the organic, and not the reverse; and that the grand requisite is to educate the people in knowledge and true piety. An ignorant, selfish, irreligious people will fail under any government. An intelligent and Christian people cannot miss a wise and beneficent government.

All this is reversed by the other maxim: "Where the church is, there is the Spirit." It gives us the organization first, the life created by and flowing from it; the organization externally and authoritatively established, and externally and authoritatively imposed on men, cramping, confining, crushing them to its own rigid form; the individual existing for the organization, and to be used for its purposes. It makes the church as an organization the mediator between God and man. The Spirit of God and his redeeming grace are communicated only through it. The sinner cannot come to God, nor God to the sinner, except through it. Thus the church takes up into itself the principles of heathen civilization, which exalts the organization above individuals, and loses them in the homogeneous pulp into which it grinds them. The church becomes a spiritual despotism, which suppresses the liberty wherewith Christ maketh free, dries up the springs of spiritual life, whence the freedom of man must flow, and perverts the authority of God and the sanctions of the world unseen to uphold oppression.

It is a curious fact in the history of the hierarchy that the inextinguishable truths of Christianity find utterance in it, but in perverted and monstrous forms. For example, the hierarchical church denied the doctrine of the divine right of kings and taught that civil rulers derive their right to rule not immediately from God, but mediately. But it did not teach that doctrine in its true and Christian form, that the civil ruler derives his power from God mediately through the people, for whose good he is God's minister; but through the church, which derives its authority immediately from God. For another example, the church insisted on its own independence of the civil ruler; it denied that the spiritual power is subject to the civil, or can rightfully be coerced by the sword; it taught the separation of the church from the state. The world owes the union of church and state, not to the papacy, but to Henry VIII. and the English Reformation. The pope, it is true, became a temporal sovereign. But the function of civil ruler was distinct from the function of the papal supremacy; and in theory his temporal sovereignty was always for the very purpose that the head of the church might be independent of all civil rulers, and the church be always separate from the state and independent of it. At the same time the church asserted its supremacy over the state, and compelled the use of the sword of the magistrate to suppress heresy; it repudiated liberty of conscience, and subjected not the actions only, but the very thoughts of men to spiritual inquisition and despotism. For another example, the church taught that the subjects of a king who was a usurper, or of a legitimate monarch who issued unjust commands, were not bound to obey him; but in such cases it alone, by its divine supremacy, could absolve the subjects from their allegiance. Again, the church opened an asylum for the oppressed, and took their part against the violence of the red-handed baron or king; but it subjected them to itself in a worse tyranny. Thus the imperishable principles of Christianity were asserted in the darkest ages, but in perverted and monstrous forms. The pure milk of the word was changed into the gall of bitterness. The church, the legitimate mother and nurse of human liberty, became the harlot-mother and nurse of monsters. This world-wide organization claimed to be the mediator, not only between God and the individual sinner, but between God and society itself, determining all political and social action and organization.

IV. The Unity of the Churches is the Unity or Fellowship of the Spirit.

1. The church is local or congregational, not national or ecumenical. It is an association of Christians by their own covenant in fellowship in Christ for their mutual edification in the Christian life and co-operation in the Christian work. If the maxim with which I started and the principles already evolved from it are correct, every such association is a Christian church. Whatever larger associations, national or ecumenial, may be formed, they cannot take away the church-character of these local churches.

2. A church has no authority to govern. Government implies authority to enact laws and to enforce obedience to them. In the proper sense of the word, there is no such thing as church-government. The authority of the church is exhausted in giving or withholding fellowship. A church must determine whether it will give fellowship to any person as a Christian or to any association as a church.[1] Beyond this it has no governmental power whatever, neither legislative, judicial, nor executive. It cannot make laws nor enforce obedience.

Accordingly our Saviour gives to the church the power of the keys, but withholds the power of the sword. But the power of the keys, the power of opening and shutting, is simply the power of giving or withholding fellowship. On the other hand, the New Testament explicitly gives to the state the power of the sword, but withholds from it the

[1] Some insist that the determination of fellowship must be left to the conscience of the individual claiming it; and that every person who claims to be a Christian and every association claiming to be a church, must be received to fellowship as such. But the teaching of the New Testament that the responsibility of determining who shall be received to fellowship is imposed on the church, is explicit. See Matt. xviii. 15–18; 1 Cor. v. 4–13; 2 Thess. iii. 6, 14, 15; Titus iii. 10; Rom. xiv. 1–3; xv. 7.

power of the keys. The magistrate "beareth not the sword in vain." The civil government exists to maintain the peace and order of society, to protect the people in their rights, and to enforce justice by penalty. For these ends it is intrusted with the sword. But it is not intrusted with the keys. It has not authority to determine who are entitled to fellowship as Christians, or to enact any law which presupposes that the state has determined that question, or which in its execution necessitates an official discrimination between Christians and unbelievers.

Here, through the Christian church, comes into human history a principle which has become a power in civilization: the separation of church and state. This principle was unknown in heathen civilization, in which was no religious organization analogous to the church, and the civil and religious functions were not entirely separate. In its application it does not mean that in making, adjudicating, and executing laws, government is exempt from obeying the law of God. Government has no right to shut out the light of Christianity, and to go back and take up heathen morality. It means that the sphere of government's action is secular. Whatever the laws or institutions through which it accomplishes its ends, it is absolutely precluded from deciding who are entitled to fellowship as Christians.

On the other hand, the authority of the church is limited to the determination of fellowship, with no power to inflict any penalty on those from whom it withholds its fellowship. The purity of the church is perpetuated from generation to generation by the spiritual life and the indwelling Spirit. Spiritual things are spiritually discerned. Christ trusts to the spiritual mind always in his church to discern that which is spiritual, to unite by its own spiritual affinities with all which is spiritual, and to repel all that is "earthly, sensual, devilish." It is the only possible preservation of spiritual purity. The difference between the spiritual and its opposite can only be spiritually discerned. When the preservation of the purity of the church is intrusted to the sword suppressing heresy, or to the weight of massive organization, or to ecumenical councils and standards of faith by them authoritatively decreed, these coarse and hard agencies do not discriminate between spiritual truth and life and the opposite, but only between outward organizations. If the Spirit always sustains the spiritual life, and the church is the outgrowth of the life, the spiritual church may be trusted in every generation to discern for itself that which is spiritual. It is because the church is spiritual that it is intrusted with the keys, and authorized to open and shut. Christ alone openeth and no man shutteth, and shutteth and no man openeth. The act of the church in opening and shutting is Christ's act, only as Christ is in the church quickening its spiritual discernment. The power of the keys is not given to the church of a particular generation, but to the church in all generations. We must confide in God's indwelling Spirit, and not imagine that we must see to everything, and bind everything fast for all coming time. The church of a former age had not power to settle all questions of fellowship so as to deprive the church of to-day of the power of the keys. The Comforter, "even the Spirit of Truth," is to "abide with you forever."

Because the unity of the church is the unity of the Spirit, and the authority of the church is limited to determining fellowship, the action expended in sustaining the organization and its machinery is reduced to a minimum, and the combined energies of the church have free course in beneficent service.

3. The national or ecumenical unity of the churches is the unity of the Spirit. It has been already said that Christians are spontaneously drawn into fellowship. It is also true that Christ requires them to be in fellowship. This fellowship is to extend through the world, that all Christian churches may work together in saving the world from sin. But this ecumenical union cannot be by an ecumenical organization, but only by fellowship in the Spirit. Any union by an ecumenical organization is incompatible with the fundamental principle of church organization. The

Romish church is constituted as an ecumenical organization. Its entire history has demonstrated that the differences among men are so great that an organization can never become ecumenical. It has also demonstrated that such an organization, so far as it does extend, is necessarily a hierarchy. The same conclusions are necessary, from the nature of the case.

4. The method by which the fellowship of the churches shall be determined is not definitely and authoritatively prescribed in the New Testament.

The primitive churches seem to have determined their fellowship in the natural method by mutual acquaintance in Christian work. This knowledge was extended to remoter regions by apostles and messengers of the churches sent abroad on various errands of Christian work, or by Christians scattered by persecution. This must always be the primitive method, and it is always valid. If a church is not at its organization regularly brought into fellowship with other churches by a council, and yet, subsequently, by its faith and works, demonstrates its Christian character, it gradually acquires the confidence of the churches, and is recognized as a church. All determination of church-fellowship rests ultimately on this grouud — the knowledge of the Christian faith and practice of a church by the Christian churches in its neighborhood.

The next method is that of the Congregational council, growing immediately out of the primitive and natural method, giving formal and official declaration, after investigation, of the fellowship of the churches, and sometimes, also, rendering to a church in circumstances of embarrassment the advice and aid of sister churches. This is supplemented by the Congregational conference, which, assuming the question of fellowship to be already settled, and excluding all investigation of it, is a union of churches, already in acknowledged fellowship with each other, solely for mutual help and co-operation in the Christian life and work. This is a method of determining fellowship capable of uniting all

Christian churches throughout the world in the unity of the Spirit, without impinging on their Christian freedom.

Other methods, more complicated and imposing, may be adopted without contravening the fundamental principle of the ecclesiastical constitution. The Presbyterian church, for example, may be conceived of in this way. Its presbyteries, synods, and general assembly may be conceived of as agencies for ascertaining and declaring the fellowship, and for making effective the union and co-operation of the local churches. But this method is too complicated and cumbersome to become ecumenical; it issues in a continual cleavage into sections, even when it aims only to be national. And the very weight of the machinery perpetually tends to a unity of organization in which the local churches lose their distinct existence.[1]

The Congregational method is to be preferred, because it is most accordant with the primitive simplicity of the communion of the apostolic churches; because it is most consonant with the scriptural idea that the church in every generation is the creation of the living Spirit, and is to preserve its purity by the sensitiveness and discernment of spiritual life; and because it alone is adequate to secure an ecumenical unity of churches, without extinguishing the local church, or repressing individual life and liberty.

5. The Christian church is necessarily catholic. It is in fellowship with all churches in which is the spiritual life. It acknowledges as a Christian church every association of regenerate persons who are united by their own free covenant in Christian fellowship for the purpose of edification and co-operation in the Christian life and work, whatever be the

[1] Accordingly, while the text of the Presbyterian "Form of Government" acknowledges the local church, a note authoritatively explains that "the several congregations of believers taken collectively constitute one church of Christ, called emphatically *the church*"; and that the government of that one church is by the majority of its representatives in Presbytery, Synod, and General Assembly (Chap. xii. and note). And the Confession of Faith (Chap. xxx.), declares that the government of the church is "in the hand of church-officers," to whom, and not to the church, "the keys of the kingdom of heaven are committed."

particular form of their union, and however encumbered with human accretions. As in a crystal, however peculiar its shape, we find by cleavage the primitive form, and by that determine its kind, so into whatever form the church, modified by peculiar circumstances, has grown, if underneath we find the primitive, apostolic church, by that we recognize it as a true church. Thus the Congregational church is essentially ând necessarily undenominational, catholic, and Christian. It cannot acknowledge as a church a national or ecumenical organization, the synod, assembly, convention, or whatever may be the complicated machinery by which local churches seek concentration and more imposing union. It cannot acknowledge its own council or conference as a church. But in any organization, national or ecumenical, in any association of churches, however confederated, it acknowledges the local churches which are thus united. The Congregational is the primitive, apostolical church. It takes into its constitution only the essential elements of the church. Christ did not institute this apostolic church as a denomination, but as the Christian church, to be in fellowship with Christian churches everywhere. It is in its very constitution catholic. All who insist that human accretions on this simple form are essential to the church — who set up their national or ecumenical organization as the church, and refuse fellowship to the church in its simple and primitive form — are guilty of schism.

V. The Continuity of Christ's Kingdom in History is the Continuity of the Spirit and Life, rather than of the Organization.

The tendency in investigating religion is now to the historic method. The rationalism which develops religion from the personal consciousness, and resolves Christianity into philosophy and ethics, is congenial to an age of metaphysical speculation, and belongs to a period and type of thinking which is now passing away. The profoundest thought and scholarship of the day investigate religion historically. But the history of Christianity did not end with the events recorded in the New Testament. The redeeming grace, working in humanity, creates for itself a continuous history. The apologists for Christianity are not to confine themselves to the evidences of the credibility and genuineness of the Bible used by the apologists of the last century. The argument now must take a wider range. It must show Christianity as a power in human history, evolving a system of truth the most satisfactory to human reason as an exposition of the relations of God and man, and effecting a process of renovation of individuals and of society, and a Christianizing of civilization, which, if completed, will realize the highest well-being of man. Christianity, in what it has accomplished, tends to accomplish, and promises to perfect, proves itself divine. When, in some future age, the Christian idea of the kingdom of God shall be realized in society, and it shall be seen, in tracing the history of Christianity, that from the beginning it had promised this result, and tended towards it, then Christianity will have wrought into history a demonstration of its divine origin.

What I now say is, that the continuity of this historical manifestation, so far as it has yet proceeded, is found in the spirit and the life, rather than in the outward organization.

1. The organization is itself an expression of the life. The church, as an organization distinct from the family and the state, is a peculiarity of Christianity. The Greeks, Romans, and Egyptians, the Mahometans, Boodhists, and Brahmins, have a religion, but not a church. The very existence of a church, separated from the world by fellowship in a new and spiritual life, and distinct from the state, is a peculiar and remarkable manifestation of the divine life in humanity. Recall the characteristics of this organization, the new principles embodied in it, the revolution in human institutions wrought by it, and you will see that the organization itself is a wonderful exponent of the divine and renovating life of the Spirit working in humanity.

2. The organization itself has a continuity that is historical. Man organizes his thought and life in institutions. He is liable, therefore, to take up into the church the ideas and spirit of the age in which he lives, and thus to encumber it with accretions of human origin. But the overlaying of the church with these accretions, does not destroy it. The Lord, who knoweth them who are his, has owned every association of devout and spiritual worshippers as a church. Thus the church, even as an organization, has had historical continuity. It was, indeed, at times, a hidden church,— the real churches not even knowing themselves as such,— yet not the less real. When the Romanist asks: "Where was your church before the Reformation?" the answer is ready: "It was wherever those whom the Spirit had renewed were associated in spiritual fellowship; according to the words of Jesus: 'Where two or three are gathered together in my name, there am I in the midst of them.'"

3. But this continuity is through the Spirit, more than through the organization. If the church is constituted according to the maxim, "Where the church is, there is the Spirit," then the divine action in redemption culminated in setting up a massive organization, in which the Spirit is imprisoned, like a bird in a cage, and which is to stand unchanged through all generations; salvation is only in it, and all that is done in it is Christ's doing. Then the history of Christianity is the history of this organization; Christianity is responsible for its corruptions; the history of Christianity becomes the history of intolerance, persecution, corruption, oppression, and opposition to human progress; and history becomes a perpetual refutation of the claim of Christianity to be from God.

We cannot accept this fatal doctrine. The church of today is not one with the apostolic churches by the line of apostolical succession, stretching without a break through the dark ages, like the electric wire beneath the ocean, and transmitting the life of Christ only by the completeness of the tactual connection. The historical continuity of the church, even as an organization, is the continuity of the life, always quickened by the Spirit and organizing itself in the church. The institution is not perpetuated by the tenacity of the organization, cohering as it stretches through the centuries, but by the organizing force of the inward life; as an animal body is not perpetuated by the coherence of its material, which is always passing away, but by the indwelling and ever-organizing vital force.

Therefore Christianity is not responsible for the abuses which have dishonored the history of ecclesiastical organizations.

4. While the church, in its historical continuity as an organization, manifests in history the continuous presence of God's redeeming grace and of his kingdom, that manifestation extends beyond the church in purifying and transforming society. This is like the diffused daylight, filling the atmosphere, which more than the sun's direct rays manifests his light. This manifestation is in the clearer and more complete system of doctrine evolved by the thought and life of the advancing ages; in the broader, clearer, and more spiritual ethics; in the higher tone of the moral life; in political institutions founded on justice and human rights; in the pre-eminence of philanthropy; in the creation of a Christian civilization.

5. The historical continuity is such that the present is always evolved from the past. While the Christian church does not, by an organization taking precedence of the Spirit, impose the past as an unchangeable mould on the present, yet it does not cut the present adrift from the past. While the unity is of the Spirit, yet it is the same Spirit, advancing always the same truth and life, meeting with the same redeeming grace the corruptions and perversions of humanity in the diverse forms in which in different ages they appear, and setting up the same kingdom of righteousness on earth. As in the individual "the child is father of the man," so in the life of the church the present is the offspring of the past.

This may be illustrated in the Romish and the Protestant doctrines of tradition. Tradition, in its primitive form, was held to be the unwritten teachings of Christ and the apostles, preserved from generation to generation, and promulgated by the church. But tradition as the Council of Trent explains it, includes also interpretations of scripture which had been unanimously accepted by the Fathers, and dogmas and rules which had received the sanction of the church; and the whole rests ultimately on the authority of the church. This crude mass the Romish church imposes on the thought and life of the ages, as the gods put Aetna on Enceladus; and every turning and motion of human thought beneath its load produces volcanic disturbance. The Protestant believes in tradition; but it is tradition which acknowledges the written word as its source, and appeals to it as the sufficient rule of faith and practice; which is itself the meaning of the Bible, as it flows down through the ages in the Christian consciousness of the church, as it finds expression in the writings of theologians, in the creeds of councils and churches, in the teachings of parents and pastors, in the renovated Christian life, usages, and institutions of society, and the growth of Christian civilization. Protestantism puts the Bible into every man's hand to read and interpret for himself; but it comes with surer evidence, with richer meaning, with more diversified and far-reaching applications won from the thought and experience of successive generations. If "the meaning of the Bible is the Bible," the Bible itself comes down through the ages like a river of life, purifying, deepening, and broadening its waters as it flows.

6. While the church has historical continuity, it is in every generation as immediately connected with Christ and his Spirit, as was the first church ever planted. So every generation receives the immediate light of the sun. Christianity has to be received by each generation anew. It comes as new to this generation as to that of Christ. Christianity is never consolidated. Like light, heat, electricity, and vital force, it is perpetuated only as it acts, it continues only as it is perpetually renewed, it must be received afresh

by every one who feels its power. It is old, and yet forever new. It can never be antiquated. It is the same to every generation, as the sun climbs the sky every day, and the stars every night, fresh and vigorous as in the earliest days.

7. Hence the church in its very organization is adapted to human progress; it is receptive of it, and it quickens it. It is not a cast-iron organization, refusing all change and crushing all growth, but capable of existing in any condition of society and under any human institutions. It insists on the free circulation of the scriptures, the right of private judgment, liberty of conscience, the equal privilege of all men to have access to God, justification by faith. Hence it trains its members to alertness to discover and receive whatever light may break forth from God's word, to sensibility to whatever influences may come from the Spirit, to keen spiritual discernment, and to a lively sense of personal responsibility to bring their own lives into conformity with God's will, and as much as in them lies to establish his kingdom on the earth. Hence it always has in it the power of revival and reformation, as fire always has in it the power of kindling. And whatever the intellectual and social progress of man, the church is able both to adapt itself to it and to guide and quicken it. Thus it stands in contrast with a hierarchical organization, which becomes by its massiveness incapable of adapting itself to new conditions antagonistic to human progress, and obliged to perpetuate the unchanged past in order to perpetuate its own existence.

# LECTURE VI.

## THE NECESSITY AND CHARACTERISTICS OF THE HUMAN AGENCY IN ADVANCING CHRIST'S KINGDOM.

God's agency in advancing his kingdom is not extra-human. Even his miraculous revelation was made in and through human history. The Eternal Word becomes the Redeemer of men only as he was made flesh and dwelt among us, under human limitations and in the courses of human history, working redemption. The redemptive energy of God, in each dispensation and in all its manifestations, works in and by humanity. Accordingly, in the dispensation of the Spirit, he works in and by humanity, and intrusts the advancement of his kingdom to his people. On them he imposes the responsibility of carrying the gospel to all mankind.

I. The Necessity of Human Agency.

Why is redemption dependent on human effort? Why does not God's love sweep over all human conditions, and extend his kingdom at once through the world?

1. This is only one form of the general question pertaining to the manifestation of the infinite in the finite. As such it transcends the limits of human knowledge. So far as we can conceive, God can manifest or reveal himself only by limiting or circumscribing himself. Every manifestation of the divine perfections, being through the finite, must be limited, incomplete, and progressive. At any given point of time in the manifestation, it must always be conceivable that a more complete manifestation might be made. This is as necessarily true of the manifestation of his infinite love in the redemption of sinners, as of the manifestation of his infinite power in the works of nature. The delay of

Christ's coming is no more an objection against the perfection of God's love, than the delay in the creation of man is an objection against the infinitude of his power. The existence of heathen on the earth to-day is no more an objection against the reality of Christ's reign of grace than it is an objection against God's government of the world that there have been immeasurable periods when the earth was occupied by animals of a low organization, of which an eminent professor used to say, that he did not believe the time ever was when the Almighty reigned over nothing but bull-frogs. The great cosmic agencies act slowly.

Nor is any force added to the objection by the degree of limitation or incompleteness. Wherever the limitation is drawn around the works by which God reveals his glory, it is still a limitation, and the question recurs: "Why not more?" The worm, were it intelligent, would have no right to complain that it is not a quadruped, nor the quadruped that it is not a man, nor the man that he is not an angel, nor the angel that he is not a thousand times greater. Because the divine bounty is inexhaustible, every divine gift suggests the question: "Why not more?"

If this objection is valid, it proves that God cannot reveal himself in finite effects, that is, that God cannot act; in other words, that there is no God. It arises from attempting to scrutinize with the logical understanding the measureless grandeurs which are revealed to faith. Analogous objections would be met by one who should study the starry heavens with a microscope.

2. Dependence on human agency is involved in the historical character of redemption. God's redeeming grace can manifest itself only in human history. But, since it must be in human history, it must advance by human agency, and its advance must be subject to the processes and changes of human history.

3. The same is evident from the nature of redemption. If, indeed, God converts and sanctifies men by sheer almightiness, accumulating souls in his kingdom as one scoops

up sand in a shovel and throws it over a wall, it might reasonably be supposed that he would at once convert and sanctify all. But God's action on man is in harmony with man's mental constitution. "I drew them with cords of a man, with bands of love." Therefore human faithfulness or negligence, human willingness or opposition, are to be taken into the account in determining the progress of Christ's kingdom.

4. This intrusting of the interests of the Redeemer's kingdom to human hearts and hands is itself the most beneficent and effective discipline in training Christians to love like Christ. There would be no training of men to the purity, the strength, and the helpfulness of Christlike love, if God by his miraculous energy should establish his kingdom, and leave his redeemed with folded hands to gaze indolently on his work.

We may draw from this fact a lesson for our own guidance as Christian ministers. Since God reveals himself and carries on his work of redemption in human history, laying hold of humanity and working through its thoughts, processes, and development, the same law governs our action in preaching his truth. It is not enough for a preacher to express his own thought and life. If his thoughts and his methods are foreign to the thought and life of the people, he cannot carry them with him, nor advance them in the divine life. The seed must take root in the hearer's heart. He alone preaches with power who grafts his thought on the thought and life of his hearers, and from and by these advances them to higher thought and life.

## II. Characteristics of the Human Agency in advancing Christ's Kingdom.

The general principle is that already presented as fundamental in the constitution of the church: "Where the Spirit of God is, there is the church." In all our thinking respecting the human agency in the conversion of the world, we must conceive of the agency of God's Spirit as going before it and quickening it. "We are laborers together with God." Man's Christian work, in every part and aspect of it, is accordant with the truth which the whole work of redemption expresses: "We love him, because he first loved us."

1. The first characteristic is spontaneity. Paul was thus actuated: "Whereunto I labor, striving according to his working, which worketh in me mightily." Here is a wonderful accumulation of the strongest Greek words, expressing the intensity of the apostle's action, and the intensity of the Spirit's energy in him quickening the apostle's action: "Whereunto I labor to exhaustion, agonizing, according to his energy energizing in me with might." As if driven by a resistless impulse, he says: "The love of Christ constraineth us"; "Necessity is laid upon me; yea, woe is unto me, if I preach not the gospel."

This zeal is a fire kindled fresh from heaven, enveloping the soul, like the burning bush, ever burning, never consumed. It does not lead its subjects to announce the marvellous work which they are about to do — as if a reformation could be manufactured to order. They do their great deeds in unconsciousness, because their zeal for truth and right, their love to God and man compel. The greatest works in the kingdom of grace, like the majestic movements of the heavens, are marked by stillness, and reveal themselves by their effects. They come up, like the sun, and reveal themselves by their own light.

Luther did not set out to work the Protestant Reformation. In the outset he did not even see the reformation needed. He simply followed the leadings of the Spirit; and before he was aware, behold, the Reformation.

The first settlers of New England exemplify the same truth. It was no expectation of founding an empire, of being enrolled among the benefactors of mankind, "all of them princes to look to," which brought them hither. With hearts yearning for dear old England they came, impelled by the fear of God and the purpose to worship him according to the dictates of their own consciences. When we see the pilgrims hunting, fishing, digging, suffering, we cannot separate their acts from the glory which has followed; we think of them as acting consciously in the presence of posterity and the foresight of the glorious future. But, in fact, they were buried in a wilderness at the ends of the earth; and as to their future, their concern was, that it should not be to perish by savages or by starvation. Theirs was the stern and suffering toil of poverty, disease, and hardship in every form; and the glory which shone into their unglazed cabins was the glory of Calvary and of heaven. And had it been otherwise, — if, instead of this simple and sublime obedience to the Spirit, they had lived in the foresight of their fame, boasting of the greatness of their mission, — they would not have been the Christian heroes that they were, and the pigmies of this self-conscious age would point at them, and cry: "Art thou, also, become weak as we? Art thou become like unto us?"

Thus history teaches that the power of God, working mightily in the human heart, is the spring of all abiding spiritual power; that it is only as men are constrained by the energy of the inward spiritual life that they do great things for God. It is the spirit of Gordon Hall, who was determined to work his passage to Asia, if he could not go otherwise. It is the spirit which impelled Newell and Judson to create an organization to send them out, when no organization had existed. It is the spirit which moved the Macedonian Christians, who, not waiting to be solicited, sought out an agency through which to expend their gifts, "praying us with much entreaty that we would receive the gift, and take upon us the fellowship of the ministering to the saints."

It is remarkable, in Christ's conception of his kingdom, that he expects the abiding presence of God's Spirit, quickening men to spiritual life; he expects that the enthusiasm of devotedness to God and self-sacrificing love to man, and of fidelity to truth and duty, will be undying powers in human history, overpowering selfishness and inspiring men to toil and self-denial for others. On these abiding spiritual forces he throws himself without reserve.

This enthusiasm has shown itself a power in the world in all the progress of Christianity. They miserably mistake who calculate the courses and issues of human action with the recognition only of the forces of selfishness, and overlooking the power of the Spirit and the forces of the spiritual life.

2. A second characteristic is the prominence given to the individual as distinguished from the organization. This follows from what has already been said of the prominence of the individual in the constitution of the church.

Isaac Taylor says: "The influence of individual men seems to have ceased almost to make itself felt. The course of events and the progress of opinion is the tide-wave of a mighty ocean, in relation to which the very mention of individual agency would sound like a mockery." This opinion grows out of naturalism — the doctrine that man is but a necessary development of nature. It can never harmonize with Christianity, which always depends on the faith, love, and enterprise of individuals whose hearts God has touched. And it is not a fact. Let a Paul arise to-day, and he will wield Paul's power. It is as true to-day as it was in Paul's day, as true in America as it was in Palestine, that a soul filled with God's Spirit will be mighty through him. The contrary opinion, born of naturalism, is the antagonist of faith and the destroyer of courage and enterprise. We talk sorrowfully of the Elijahs, who once moved the world. Where are the Elishas, who call on the Lord God of Elijah, and divide the waters? Oh for the power of God's Spirit to turn the hearts of his people from looking fearfully one to another for help, from trusting to outward machinery, — "sacrificing to their net and burning incense to their drag," — and to inspire them with personal zeal and enterprise in Christ's work. Great periods and great men have the imprint of the divine seal, and prove God present on the earth. If we despair of their reappearance, we despair of Christianity. If we suppose that organization and association alone are left us in their place, we suppose that God has abandoned us to our own devices, and that life and growth have given place to mechanism.

It may be objected that we cannot expect every year to be an epoch, and the whole of life to glow with enthusiasm. This is true; yet Christianity accomplishes something like this. It inspires every soul with the faith and love which are the springs of heroism, and ennobles the most commonplace life with consecration, aspiration, and loving service like Christ's.

It may be objected that the office of a settled pastor is widely different from that of a prophet. This is true. God has in every age prophetic spirits — quickened by the Holy Ghost to declare God's wrath against specific sins, and to call his churches to new thoughts and new duties — who cannot be expected to confine themselves to any professional routine. Yet every minister and every Christian is a witness for God, called and qualified to testify for God's truth and righteousness, and to stand against the world, the flesh, and the devil.

Every Christian, therefore, is to act in his individuality. He must "attempt great things, and expect great things." One secret of the success of the apostolic church was this spirit of individual love and responsibility. When scattered by persecution, they went everywhere preaching the word. Like Michael's angels, fighting against Satan,

> "Each on himself relied,
> As only in his arm the moment lay
> Of victory."

Such a spirit is essential to success. Pervaded by it, "how should one chase a thousand, and two put ten thousand to flight." Then the hosts of God's people, in their organized and associated assaults on the kingdom of Satan, would be like the angelic army,

> "Though numbered such
> As each divided legion might have seemed
> A numerous host; in strength each armed hand
> A legion."

Without this fire of heaven in individual hearts, associations will be powerless as burning-glasses which concentrate moonbeams.

3. Christianity opens spheres of action adapted to the peculiar proclivity and capacity of every Christian.

Carlyle exclaims: "Blessed is the man who has found his work." And, since man's blessedness is realized not in receiving, so much as in giving; not in indulgence, but in work, blessed indeed is the man who has found a work in which he is conscious that all his faculties are putting themselves forth in their full activity, and all his tastes and aptitudes are fully met.

Every situation, indeed, will bring its chagrins which must be swallowed in silence, and its drudgery which must be toiled through with patience. The world has no patience with the weakling who fills the air with complaints of the hardness and disagreeableness of his work, and especially no patience with complaining and disconsolate ministers. Learn to burn your own smoke, and not pour it forth to make the atmosphere sooty and choking to all around you.

Man is greater than his profession. He is many-sided, many-handed. If one pursuit is not open to him, he can adapt himself to another. Yet the most effective work is that in which the man can most joyfully engage, and in which is consciously satisfied the radical and irrepressible impulse to put forth all his powers in action, and to push forth on every side to the utmost compass of his being.

This adaptation of the individual to his work Christianity permits. Since the Christian work is so broad, since every sphere of human life is to be purified and consecrated to God, there is scope for the highest Christian service to every variety of talent and in every sphere of life. Christianity has great breadth, compass, and flexibility. Its spirit is one

— the spirit of faith and love; its service is as diversified as human life.

In this respect, the Romish church has shown itself wiser than the Protestant. It has provided a sphere for every kind of talent and for every type of Christian life. When Loyola arose, with his fiery zeal, setting forth new ideas and new measures, the church did not drive him into opposition by suspicion and antagonism, but allowed him to work in his own way; and the society which he formed became the ally of the church. When Wesley, with his purer, but not less fiery zeal, arose in the church of England, he was driven out. A certain narrowness and rigidity, a certain inability to recognize Christianity except in a specific type and fashion, has been a weakness of Protestantism from the beginning, and has broken it into sects, until the right of private judgment seems almost to mean the right of each Christian to impose his own private judgment on the whole church of Christ.

Here we may properly glance at the Christian work of woman. In the lives both of Jesus and of the apostles, woman is presented as specially susceptible of spiritual impressions and capable of giving forth Christian influence. This has become proverbial: "Last at the cross, and first at the sepulchre."

Dante's Beatrice may be taken as a type of woman's position and influence according to the Christian conception — the quickener, guide, and exemplar of man in the spiritual life. In her pure presence, in conscious shame at his own impurity, he says:

> "Down fell mine eyes
> On the clear fount; but, there myself espying,
> Recoiled and sought the greensward, such a weight
> Of shame was on my forehead. With a mein
> Of that stern majesty which doth surround
> A mother's presence to her awe-struck child
> She looked.

And again, at her appearance

> "Suddenly, upon the day appeared
> A day new-risen; as he who had the power
> Had with another sun bedecked the sky.
> Her eyes fast fixed on the eternal spheres,
> Beatrice stood, unmoved; and I, with ken
> Fixed upon her, from upward gaze removed,
> At her aspect such inwardly became
> As Glaucus, when he tasted of the herb
> That made him peer among the ocean gods.
> Words may not tell of that transhuman change."

The Christian desire of purity early deteriorated into the doctrine of the meritoriousness of celibacy and monasticism. This was natural in an age utterly corrupted by heathenism. It may be doubted whether the licentiousness which from the heathen temples began to show itself even in the apostolic churches could have been successfully resisted except by an antagonism as concentrated and one-sided as monasticism. It is not strange, therefore, that in the Christian Fathers we sometimes find expressions of passionate horror at the fascinations of the fair sex.

But the true Christian conception of woman gradually asserted itself. Not to mention the influence of the more directly spiritual teachings of the gospel, the story of Mary the mother of Jesus, the reverence which it created for her, the expression of that reverence in art, taught reverence for woman and for maternity. The truth inherent in the story of Jesus penetrated society even through perversions and errors; as light is light, through whatever medium it may shine.

The principal spheres of action for the majority of women must always be the domestic and the social. In these realms she reigns — "incedit regina." Those whose lives are in these spheres may give personal aid in specific efforts to advance Christ's kingdom. Others may devote themselves entirely to missionary work. Labors of both kinds are commemorated in the New Testament. Joanna, the wife of a high officer under Herod, ministered to Jesus; Dorcas made clothing for the poor; Lydia opened her house to entertain Paul; Priscilla, Phoebe, and other women were laborers with Paul in the gospel. In modern missions have been women who, by the exaltation of their spiritual lives, by beauty and completeness of character, and by activity in the missionary work, have made their names illustrious. Nothing, during this century, has more than the missionary work exemplified the power of woman, the variety of lines in which she can act effectively, the purity, intensity, and compass of her influence, and thus has illustrated and enlarged the sphere of her activity, and ennobled her in the estimation of man.

4. The human agency in advancing Christ's kingdom demands wise forethought in planning the enterprises to be undertaken, and in judiciously adapting means to ends, and in organizing the agencies to be employed. The doctrine that action must be spontaneous under the inspiration of faith and love, does not mean the disuse of human faculties, but the inspiring of them to intense action. Wisdom and inspiration go together; "The spirits of the prophets are subject to the prophets." Forethought is no substitute for zeal; but zeal is misdirected without forethought. It has been said that the piety of theological seminaries is all kept packed ready for exportation. This would be forethought shutting out the inspiration of faith and love — the fire going out, while year after year you heap the wood-pile; the wood itself meantime becoming dozy and slow to burn. On the other hand, zeal is not to bring you to a premature beginning of activity, to the exclusion of diligent preparation. You must not grind and bake your seed-wheat. So it is in all Christian life. Christian spontaneity is not quietism, which excludes the vigorous use of the faculties, and waits, inactive, for the heavenly breeze; nor fanaticism, which, because the breeze is fresh, neglects to plan and direct the voyage. Christianity lays hold of all the faculties, and its inspiration quickens them to keener discernment, more far-reaching sight, and more vigorous exertion.

I shall apply this thought principally to the choice of a profession. The remark used to be common, that every pious young man should assume that he ought to be a minister, unless he could show special reasons to the contrary. The same remark is sometimes made respecting the missionary work. But this is a drag-net, which gathers of every kind. No pursuit is absolutely the most useful. We can only say that a particular individual may be most useful in a particular pursuit. Providence, indeed, shuts us up closely, and gives to each but a limited range of selection. But, so far as a man has range of selection, he ought to be able to give some positive reason for his choice — some special adaptation, some inward proclivity, some leading of God's Spirit and providence, something to kindle enthusiasm, and make every man believe that for him his own life-work is the highest and best. This cannot be less true of the choice of the missionary work than of ordinary pursuits. A man must not drift into the missionary work merely because he cannot show any reason to the contrary, but must choose it with a positive conviction of duty and earnestness of purpose which shall concentrate all his energies on his work. It is the last work to enter with a divided heart.

The object of enthusiasm is not generic, but specific. We are taught that Christians must live to do good. Yet I suspect no enthusiasm was ever kindled by any object so indefinite as doing good. The most you can get out of it is a mild and diffused daylight of goodness, — very mild and diffused, — never the direct sunbeams, much less the burning focus of his rays. It is analogous to teaching children: "You must be good, because it is good to be good." Enthusiasm is always about something in particular — specific persons, specific truths and errors, specific virtues and vices, specific ends to be attained.

It is a distinctively Christian idea that a man's work is a *calling*. In determining what is your calling, your subjective state, your inward conviction, drawing, and interest are important considerations. He must be comparatively inefficient who is obliged to grope his way by the dim light of prudence, with no inward impulse impelling and guiding him. His whole life must be a groping and a stumbling, advancing slowly, pausing often to consider what is the road, mistaking his way, and losing time in retracing his steps. Happy is the man who runs the way of God's commandments, because God has enlarged his heart — his energies concentrated in running towards the goal, not wasted in groping for the way.

Fenelon, giving directions for attaining a higher Christian life, says: "The essential point is only to follow, step by step, the divine grace, with an infinite patience, carefulness, and delicacy. We must limit ourselves to letting God act, and never lay hold of the pure love, except as God by his inward anointing begins to open the heart to that word which is so hard to souls still clinging to self, and so liable to offend them and plunge them into sin. . . . . . The genuine simplicity of pure love confines itself to following the divine grace, without ever undertaking to anticipate it."[1]

This is the wisdom of God, though it is foolishness with men. Christianity safely trusts and follows the grace of God, without undertaking to anticipate it. It will be fatal if, in the management of our missions, this fundamental principle is left out. Missions can succeed only as God calls, qualifies, and impels into the work men and women "whose hearts God has touched." The perfunctory services of the ablest and most scholarly persons will be an inefficient substitute.

But this special anointing or call is not miraculous. It connects itself with, and manifests itself through, the special natural endowments, the circumstances and events of the life, the specialties of training, of acquisitions, and of spiritual experience which have turned the attention to the work, forced the question of duty on the mind, given preparation for the work, or awakened interest in it. God's Spirit always acts in harmony with his providence. The call to the

[1] Explication des Maximes des Saints, Art. iii.

missionary work differs from the call to any other only as it is a greater work. In determining whether one is called to this work, the Christian is not to wait for a resistless *afflatus;* but he is carefully to study the leadings of God's Spirit and providence, and by the use of his reason determine his calling.

And here love itself is the light by which the Christian sees. "He that loveth his brother abideth in the light, and there is no occasion of stumbling in him." Self-devoting love is the safeguard against mistake in deciding questions of duty. If the pure light of love is clouded by the mingling of selfish desires; if the motive of action is interest in literature and intellectual culture, or ambition to shine as an orator, or desire to be established in an elegant and refined home, these desires obscure the mind and vitiate its decisions.

Hence the duty of entering a missionary life usually appears less clear at the outset, to one called to it, than afterwards. A young man must decide the question before his entrance to the ministry, before he has attained that stronger and purer faith and love which afterwards shine like a cloudless day upon his life. We can hardly expect, therefore, that the inward call will present itself in the most pronounced form, constraining him beyond all doubt. But the true missionary after entering his field sees more and more clearly that it is the work to which God had called him. Hence that remarkable characteristic of missionaries, their joy in their work, their reluctance to leave it, their eagernesss to return to it, and the rounded fulness of life which they seem to realize. Every one, therefore, who is called to the missionary work, has reason, with Paul, to thank God, who counted him faithful, putting him into the ministry. If that call comes in connection with the man's natural endowments, his education, all the providential circumstances and shaping of his life, and the peculiar leading of the Spirit, then evidently the man and his life have been shaped for the work, and the only possibility for that man of realizing the harmony, fulness, and blessedness of life, is to follow the Spirit, accept the calling, and do the work. It is idle to let the fear of difficulties and privation bias the decision; for the work to which he is called is the only work in which, for him, blessedness is possible. Here is the significance of the saying: "It is better to be out of the world than out of the path of duty."

The same train of thought applies to the prosecution of missionary work. It cannot be carried on by the impulse of enthusiasm. It demands the highest practical wisdom in planning and administering, the most thoughtful and persistent action in organizing, concentrating and directing the energies of the church.

5. The work of Christian missions and of social renovation, outreaching the scope of the local church, is properly performed through associations of churches or of individuals, such as the spiritual wisdom of Christ's people, taught by the Spirit and providence of God, shall find most effective to meet the exigency of the time and place.

(1.) This is necessary to enable the churches to meet effectively the changes of time and the peculiarities of place. The church is a permanent organization, the same for all countries and for all time. But as Christ's kingdom advances through successive ages and different countries peculiar exigencies arise, demanding work peculiar to the age or people. For this work special and temporary associations are properly organized.

(2.) This is necessary to Christian liberty. It has already been shown that Christianity opens a sphere of action for every Christian to which, by a peculiarity of natural capacity and proclivity, and by the training of God's Spirit and providence, he is specially adapted. On account of these diversities, every Christian cannot be expected to be active in every Christian enterprise. And in the progress of Christ's kingdom Christian action must be directed from time to time into new enterprises, to meet new exigencies as they arise, the importance of which many Chistians will not at once appreciate. If every enterprise to carry the gospel abroad or to accomplish the renovation of society at home must be carried on by the church as such, this establishes new criterions of fellowship, infringes on the liberty of Christians, and "causes divisions and offences" in the church of Christ.

(3.) Voluntary associations for specific Christian enterprises are accordant with the apostolical constitution of the church as a local or congregational church. If missions and all Christian work must be done by the church in its organic capacity, the local church must be lost in an ecumenical organization. On the contrary, missionary associations are accordant with the constitution, the genius, and spirit of the local church. They are agencies which come into being for a specific purpose. When the work is done, when churches are established no longer needing aid, the missionary association disappears, and the new churches go on with the work.

(4.) The voluntary association accords with the prominence given to the individual in the constitution of the church, and with the spontaneity characteristic of Christian action. It implies, always present in the church, the spiritual wisdom and life, which will discern what Christian work the existing time demands, and will plan the agencies and measures best fitted to accomplish it. The other supposition implies that the church in its organic capacity is to devise, plan, and execute all Christian work, and that the agencies exist organized in it, permanent and unchanged through all time. This necessarily implies that Christian work is not individual and spontaneous, but is given out to be done under orders. The result must be not only the absorption of local churches in an ecumenical church, but also, somewhere, a central permanent power through which the church utters its commands, and in obedience to which all Christians act. An ecumenical church cannot be self-governing. In its very conception it implies a hierarchy.

The supposition that the church in its organic capacity is to plan, direct, and execute all the Christian enterprises incident to the conversion of the world and the renovation of society is incompatible with the local constitution of the church, and logically involves both an ecumenical church and a hierarchical government.

(5.) The voluntary association is in accordance with the methods of the apostolic missions. They were pre-eminently spontaneous and individual, committing the continued prosecution of the work to the local church so soon as one was gathered on missionary ground.

(6.) It is in accordance with the common practice of the church ever since the apostles' day. Even the Catholic church never assumed to itself as an organization all Christian enterprises. Its missions and other religious work gave birth to innumerable orders and associations called into being for special work to meet the peculiarities of particular ages — orders of monks and nuns, the Sisters of Charity, the Society of Jesus, the Society for the Propagation of the Faith, and many others, through which the diversified energies of the church found scope for action. It is in accordance with the universal usage of the church that there be Missionary Boards, Bible and Tract Societies, Young Men's Christian Associations, Temperance Societies, and others, giving scope to the diversified energies and interests of Christians, expressing the ideas and meeting the wants of particular localities and times, and disappearing when the specialty which called them forth has passed away.

(7.) This method of administration is recommended by its superior efficiency. This is an inference from what has already been said.

It may be added that the contrary principle, limiting Christian enterprise to what is done through the church as an organization, deprives Christianity of the credit of its indirect influences on society. The church is separated from the state, and ill-adapted to carry on social reform. Enterprises for political and social progress necessarily fall to individuals and voluntary associations, carrying out Christian principles to their remoter applications. But these, not being recognized as legitimate agencies for Christian action, are thrown into antagonism to the churches, practical morality comes to be separated from religion, and the very influences of political and social renovation which Christianity originated are used as weapons of assault on the churches. This antagonism would be in a great degree avoided, and Christianity have the credit of the indirect influence on society which it actually exerts, if it was understood as accordant with the true conception of the church, that, while it remains from age to age the same, Christian enterprise is always to outreach the organic agency of the church, and enterprises and agencies are in every age to spring up around it, carrying out Christian principles to special applications and by special methods adapted to the exigency of the time.

On the contrary, if the church as an organization attempts this work, it insures a civilization, types of which have repeatedly appeared in history, in which the priestly element is dominant, and the civilization lacks the stimulus, the progressiveness, and the varied development which Christianity gives, and becomes stagnant and monotonous.

Further, the freedom and flexibility and individuality involved in this method are elements of power. "A system which raises the individual to the primary place of religious importance, places him nearest to the supernatural energy of God ..... naturally draws to it minds of marked vigor and trains men in self-subsisting habits." It develops the individual. It inspires him. It works towards the realization of the wish "that all the Lord's people were prophets." It shows its power, not in producing a perfect mechanism directed by one engineer, but in multiplying strong and earnest Christians. And it produces unity of action, not by the mechanical unity of organization, but creating a type of man — men and women acting individually, spontaneously, and earnestly, yet by the formative power of common convictions, and common faith and love, made of one type, so that spontaneous working is working in a spontaneous harmony for one result. Puritanism and Methodism each creates its type of man. The religion and education of New England have produced a type of man. Plant New Englanders anywhere on the face of the earth and they spontaneously reproduce New England institutions. Such is the action of Christianity. It creates a type of man. Christians of whatever age or country understand each other, and sympathize in the deepest experience and most cherished aim of life. Their real unity is here, and not in the unity of organization.

Thus the church is efficient, because it is alive in every part, and

> "Vital in every part,
> Cannot but by annihilating die."

When any organization passes away, this deathless and all-pervading energy embodies itself anew and works out its great result. Such was the ancient prophecy: "The Lord will create upon every dwelling-place of Mount Zion and upon her assemblies a cloud and smoke by day and the shining of a flaming fire by night."

# LECTURE VII.

## THE SACRIFICIAL LOVE OF CHRIST THE TYPE AND MEASURE OF CHRISTIAN LOVE.

In nature God does not reveal the natural sciences; but he makes the worlds, and leaves us to observe and interpret his works as we can. So in redemption God does not reveal systems of theology, creeds, and catechisms; but he works redemption, and leaves us to study his action, and interpret the truth which it expresses. Theology results from interpreting the divine action, and systematically expressing to the intellect the divine thought or truth which the divine action reveals. Something necessarily escapes us in this process. Astronomy is the science of the stellar and planetary systems, expressing exactly the facts and their laws; but the glory of the heavens is lost from its formulas and demonstrations. So theological systems lose something of the grandeur and life of redemption. The glory of God in the face of Jesus Christ cannot be transferred to the catechism or creed. Schleiermacher called doctrine, "cooled lava." It is infelicitous to compare the gospel to so destructive an agent; but the illustration is pertinent, inasmuch as lava in cooling remains the same in substance, yet loses its power. A better illustration would be water in the form of ice, cut in regular forms and packed in the ice-house. In the Bible theological truth is always presented in its historical manifestations and practical applications; it is always living water, running in the river of life, and nourishing the trees whose leaves do not wither and which shall not cease from yielding fruit. So it presents even the greatest mysteries of Christian faith. It brings us before the great mysteries of eternity, towering, like mountains so high that the foot of man never trod their summits, shining inaccessible in the sunlight, or hiding their heads in the clouds; but solid, real, massive, with springs gushing from their bosoms, and sending down streams to gladden the earth, and on their sides sunny nooks and sheltered vales, where nestle the loves and hopes of men.

Thus Paul brings us before the mystery of the incarnation: "Let this mind be in you which was also in Christ Jesus, who, being in the form of God, thought it not robbery to be equal with God; but made himself of no reputation, and took upon him the form of a servant, and was made in the likeness of men; and, being found in fashion as a man, he humbled himself, and became obedient unto death, even the death of the cross." This thought of the apostle is the theme of this lecture. I express it thus: The Sacrificial Love of Christ in his Humiliation, Suffering, and Death for Sinners is the Type and Measure of all Christian Love.

I. The Descent of the Son of God in the Incarnation to save Men from Sin is a Type or Exponent of a Constituent Principle of the Universe.

The descent of the Son of God in the incarnation sets forth a principle of all God's action. It is an exponent of the Christian conception of the universe — always the higher descending to the lower to lift it up.

Contrary to this is the theory of development, which conceives of the universe as always the lower unfolding and expanding into the higher. The words of Topsy, "I 'specks I growed," are exalted into a cosmogony, and become the first principle of all science. But development can only unfold that which already is. If man is developed from the brute, he is only a brute developed. If the universe is the development of nature, there is nothing in it that is above nature. The development of the lower is only the elevation and expansion of the lower, not a change of its inferior nature, nor an origination of anything higher in kind. It is the lower, with its necessity, its destitution of intelligence, its soggy materialism, pulsating higher and higher, circling wider and wider, till it fills and characterizes all. It is the Titans piling up the mountains to scale the heavens and dethrone the gods; but, however high they climb and wide they rule, they are still only Titans, earth-born giants.

Christianity presents the contrary conception: "In the beginning God." At one vault the thought reaches the All-Perfect and the Highest. The action of the universe is no longer the lower, lifting and expanding itself with all its imperfection and blind necessity; but always the higher, descending to the lower to lift it up. The development of nature through measureless eras is the result of the presence of mind, expressing its thought, and steadily advancing to realize its ideals.

The same conception is carried out in the relations of man to nature. He is not a part and product of nature merely — an animated sod, but the lord of nature, placed on the earth to subdue and dress and keep it. As God expresses his thoughts in nature in creating and perpetuating it, man expresses his thoughts in nature in using it, and in dressing and keeping the earth. Nature is civilized as man is. When the mind of man takes a step, the earth takes a step with it.

Alike in the relations of God and of man to nature, it is never the lower developing into the higher, lifting and broadening its own imperfections and incapacities; it is always the higher descending to the lower, the perfect going down to the imperfect, the richly endowed to the poorly endowed, to lift up the lower and to endow it with new perfections.

Inorganic matter is never transformed into living vegetation without the agency of a living plant; and vegetable matter is not transformed into the substance of the living animal without the agency of a living animal. The higher raises the lower, and endows it with a new perfection. Organic matter not under the action of a living body at once becomes subject to a process of degradation, and deteriorates into the inorganic. Thus Owen very beautifully represents the microscopic rotifer as a sentry stationed on the outposts of animal life to arrest the organic matter which is slipping down into the inorganic, and to turn it back on an upward course into the higher forms of life.

The same thoughts are applicable in sociology. The right constitution of society is always on the principle of the higher descending to elevate the lower, not on the principle of the lower expanding and exalting itself by development.

But if the constituent principle of the universe is the principle of the constant expansion and exaltation of the lower by development, then nature penetrates and possesses the sphere of the mind, as mineral matter penetrates a dead body and transforms it into a fossil. Mind itself becomes but transformed force, without freedom. Individual freedom, responsibility, and enthusiasm are fossilized in a stony realism. In the conception of society the race must take precedence of the individual. The individual is the necessary development of the race, is lost in it, and exists for it. There is no longer a place for individual freedom and rights. It is worthy of notice that the hypothesis of development, suggested, but not proved, by modern science, if it excludes the idea of God,[1] necessarily leads back to the ancient heathenish conception of society, founded in the domination of the race and the subjugation of the individual. On the contrary, the Christian conception is, that the legitimate organization of society is from and for the individuals composing it, not the individuals from and for the organization.

The same is the conception of the kingdom of God. God is Love, pouring out ever of his fulness: God in Christ seeking and saving men; God in the Holy Spirit touching and renewing their hearts; men richly endowed going down to those in sin to impart spiritual gifts. Always it is more blessed to give than to receive.

[1] If the idea of God is admitted, there may be a theory of development consistent with the Christian conception. For, on that supposition, through whatever stages nature may have advanced, the conception is always of the higher elevating the lower, the wisdom and love of God advancing towards the realization of their ideals.

Thus the action of Christ in the incarnation, going down to save the lost, sets forth the constituent principle of the universe. The movement is not of the lower expanding its sphere and diversifying its manifestations and increasing its power; but it is always of the higher going down to the lower to impart to it new gifts, endow it with new perfections, and to extend the reign and diversify the manifestations of wisdom and love.

II. Love is in its Essential Character Sacrificial, like the Love of Christ. Self-sacrifice for others is the Reverse Side of Love.

The word "love" is popularly used to denote widely dissimilar mental states — a sensuous appetite, a selfish covetousness, the supreme affection of a holy heart: "I love an apple," "I love money," "I love God." This confusion arises from confounding love with desire. But love and desire are widely different. Desire is not even a distinctive characteristic of love. Holy love does not extinguish the natural desires; it develops also spiritual desires; but the desire is not the love, nor the distinctive characteristic of love. Love is distinctively characterized by self-devotement to its object, not by desire for its object. A character which consists distinctively and essentially of desire must be a selfish character. Desire lays hold of its object to get possession of it for the use and enjoyment of self; Love takes of the resources of self, and imparts them to the loved object. Desire devotes its object to self; Love devotes self to the object loved. The movement of Desire returns on self as the centre, like a whirlpool circling abroad only to return on itself, and suck everything into its own vortex; and because this is its movement itself is always empty and restless. The movement of Love is like that of a fountain pouring out its own fulness to bless all that is around it; and because that is its movement itself is always full and peaceful. Love enthrones its object, and makes us serve it; Desire seizes its object, and makes it serve us. Love admires, reveres, and, in its highest form, adores its object; Desire uses it. Wedded Love, devoting to its object the homage of the heart and the service of the hand, is the inspired emblem of holy love; scortatory Desire, ruining the victim it so hotly seeks, is the inspired emblem of sin. We love persons, who may be honored and served, but cannot be owned and used; we desire things, which may be owned and used, but cannot be honored and served. If Desire, uncontrolled by Love, fixes on a person, it makes the person a toy, a tool, a slave, or a victim.

It is not only in popular language that these dissimilar mental states are confounded. An American philosophical writer defines love as identical with desire: "That which we love we desire to have present, to possess and to enjoy it. . . . . . The loving an object and the desiring its enjoyment are identical."[1] What monstrous systems of Christian ethics must result when the teachers degrade that which is the noblest possibility of humanity, the love which is the essence of God's moral perfection, and which is the godlike in human character, into a desire, the definition of which is equally the definition of an epicure's appetite or a miser's greed. It is such love as a wolf has for a lamb — the desire to have it present, to possess and to enjoy it. It is such love as the gambler has for his victim — the desire to have him present, to possess and enjoy him. It is not love; it is selfishness, limbed with its myriad desires, like a rapacious giant with a hundred ravening arms. If your love to God is no more than this, it is selfishness, audacious to seize on God himself, and use him as a familiar to fetch and carry in your service.

Since love is the fulfilling of the law, the law requires sacrificial love, like that of Christ in his humiliation, suffering, and death for men.

III. The Sinfulness which renders Redemption necessary is Essentially the Absence of Sacrificial Love and the Presence of the opposite Character.

Sin is the opposite of love. But the opposite of love is

[1] H. P. Tappan's Review of Edwards on the Will, p. 18.

not hatred. That is comparatively a rare manifestation of sin. The opposite of love is selfishness. Since love is essentially sacrificial, sin is essentially self-asserting. It has four principal phases. It is *self-sufficiency*, the opposite of Christian faith — a practical affirmation of the absurdity that a created being is sufficient for himself, therefore a repudiation by the sinner of his condition as a creature, and an arrogating to self of the Creator's place. It is *self-will*, the opposite of Christian submission and obedience; putting the will of self, instead of the will of God, as the supreme law and the supreme providence of the world. It is *self-seeking*, the opposite of Christian benevolence; substituting desire for love; putting self in God's place, as the end of all endeavor and the recipient of all service. It is *self-righteousness*, the opposite of Christian humility and reverence, the reflex act of sin; putting self in God's place as the object of praise and homage. The redemption of man from sin must break down this spiritual primacy of self. The man is to be redeemed from his selfishness into the spirit of sacrificial love.

IV. The Doctrine that Christ's Sacrificial Love is the Type and Measure of all Christian Love is of the Essence of Christianity, whether as History, Doctrine, or Life.

The substance of Christianity is redemption. Its central fact is the historical sacrifice of the incarnation and the cross. The ground-thought which it expresses is the eternal and immutable excellence of sacrificial love as the divine character, its eternal and immutable supremacy as the divine law. The ideal which it proposes to realize in the redeemed is the same sacrificial love. Christianity, therefore, as a fact, a doctrine, and a life, is a sacrificial religion. The law of self-renunciation is grounded in the essential character of Christianity.

1. Christianity as an historical fact is sacrificial. Christianity is not, primarily, a divine doctrine, but a divine action; it is not a philosophy, but a redemption; not a

proclamation of divinely-authenticated dogmas, but a divine energy supernaturally flowing into the history of man to redeem him from sin. Of this redemptive action the historical sacrifice of the incarnate Word is the central fact. The redemptive energy working in the world all flows in this sacrifice from God's riven side.

Here is the point of divergence of two opposite and irreconcilable conceptions of Christianity — the one, with whatever truths, fundamentally wrong; the other, with whatever errors, fundamentally right. If, according to one system, Christ is a teacher only, Christianity is a philosophy, distinguished from other philosophies only by greater clearness and comprehensiveness. When the deist says that Jesus borrowed the two great commandments from Moses, that Plato inculcated forgiveness of enemies, that Isocrates taught the golden rule, that Confucius and Zoroaster enunciated pure moral precepts, no defence is left but to show that Jesus was a greater philosopher than they; we are compelled to acknowledge that Tindal rightly entitled his sceptical book, "Christianity as Old as the Creation." But if, according to the other system, Jesus is the God-Man, working redemption by sacrifice, then Christianity is not a system of philosophy or ethics, but a divine action, a redemption by God producing a divine life in men. It is made up not of dogmas, but of facts. It is worthy of remark that the principle of the former of these systems logically exalts doctrines and precepts to pre-eminence, insisting chiefly on "the words of the Master," while the contrasted principle of redemption gives pre-eminence to the divine action and the life which it originates.

Christianity being historical, the central fact is the sacrificial love of the incarnate Word, in his humiliation, suffering, and death for man.

2. Christianity as a doctrine is sacrificial. The ground-thought which the historical fact of redemption by sacrifice expresses is the divine excellence of sacrificial love as a character, and its divine authority as a law.

In the first place, it discloses to us that God's character — the supreme moral perfection of the universe — is sacrificial love. How it is so is a mystery. God's love never ascends; it cannot be a faith; and in descending love he cannot literally deny himself. But in God's love, even as it acts serene and blessed amid the grandeurs of eternity, the element of self-devotement appears in this — that God always gives; he never receives. God is not an infinite sensitivity, seeking gratification, nor a nature unfolding, according to its own necessary law, under a stimulus from without. God is a person, self-moved to act; by the energy of his own will freely expressing the ideas of his own wisdom in the action of his love. As, in the mystery of his infinitude, the perfection of moral freedom co-exists with the impossibility of sinning, so his love is an activity eternally self-moved and eternally blessed, at once absolute self-devotement and absolute self-satisfaction; and the blessedness of the Godhead is not received from without, but like the brightness of the sun is the shining of his love as it pours forth from within.

But amid the glories of his eternal love our finite intellects are blinded by excess of light. What his love is we know from the incarnation. It is the sacrificial love of Christ. It is a mystery indeed; but every revelation of God, like the veil before the mercy-seat, hides while it reveals him. The incarnation, pre-eminently the revelation of God, is pre-eminently the mystery which hides him — the mystery of infinite love which brings him near, the Redeemer on the mercy-seat in the midst of men, yet makes us awfully aware of the depths of his incomprehensibleness and the inscrutable solitude of the infinity and eternity which he inhabits.

It would be incompatible with the divine perfection to admit that God suffers. But even in men we find the suffering incident to self-sacrifice absorbed in the "comfort of love," so that Christians glory in tribulation, and take joyfully the spoiling of their goods. If we follow the direction of this thought, we may suppose that in the Perfect One all that is essential in self-sacrifice may exist in the highest degree, and the sorrow incident thereto be absorbed and lost in the fulness and blessedness of the love.

In the second place, the sacrifice of redemption, as expiatory, presents to us sacrificial love as the supreme law of the universe, and asserts and vindicates its authority. God in this sacrifice expresses the eternal authority, the universal application, and the inexorable demand of this law, and the impossibility of ever offering pardon except in its full satisfaction.

In the third place, it is involved in redemption that the sinner is renewed by the Spirit and justified by faith, receiving in his low and sinful condition help from above. Thus even in the remotest application of redemption to the individual, it is always God going down to man to seek the lost, the higher always descending to the lower to lift him up; it is always salvation by grace through faith, and that not of yourselves, it is the gift of God.

3. Christianity as a life is sacrificial. The ideal which it proposes to realize in the character of the redeemed is sacrificial love.

Love has two phases: the receptive and the imparting — the ascending and the descending. These are popularly designated as faith and love; but, using the word "love" in the comprehensive sense in which Christ used it, as the general name of all holiness, these must be considered as two phases of love, corresponding to the apostolic distinction of faith and works.

Love in each of these phases is self-devoting, like that of Christ.

This is true of faith. Faith is in its nature an act of self-surrender and self-devotement. In it the soul accepts its Redeemer and Lord, yielding its whole being to the plastic hand of the Perfect One, to receive the impress of his thought and will. It is trust in him as Saviour; it is complacency in his character, adoration of his perfections, aspiration to be with him and like him, loyalty to his person; but in every manifestation it is an act of self-surrender to the mighty and gracious One who draws the trusting sinner to himself.

The same is the characteristic of love in its other phase — love active in works of beneficence and justice. It is love prompting to self-sacrifice in allegiance to and vindication of truth and right, and in bringing men to allegiance to the same, and saving them from sin through Christ. Christ's sacrificial love is the type of all Christian love; all love is the same in kind: "He laid down his life for us; we ought to lay down our lives for the brethren." It is the measure of all Christian love. As Christ, being divine, stripped himself of the regal splendors of the divine form, and in the abasement of humanity humbled himself to death on the cross; so Christians, being human, must devote — little, indeed, compared with his sacrifice, yet — all that a human heart and life can give. The cross, central in redemption, exerts a twofold influence, centripetal and centrifugal. It draws the sinner to itself to look on the sufferer "made a curse for us." Then it impels him out into the world, moved by the same sacrificial love, to toil and suffer to save others; never escaping the attraction of the cross, but moving around it, like a planet around the sun, bearing its light and warmth through the outer darkness of sin.

The sacrificial character of Christianity is sometimes urged as a reproach; it is even objected that the doctrine of redemption by Christ's sacrifice encourages sin by leading to trust to the righteousness of another. But we have seen that this characteristic is essential in Christianity, whether considered as an historical fact, as a doctrine, or as a life. We accept it as an honor. Instead of encouraging sin, the sacrificial character of Christianity makes the ideal of moral perfection higher, the authority of the law requiring it more sacred, the motive to obedience stronger — I had almost said, infinitely higher, more sacred, and stronger — than is possible when the sacrificial character of Christ's work is denied. In this we see God's love in its most wondrous condescension, and man's love in its most godlike capability.

V. Sacrificial Love like Christ's is explicitly enjoined.

I can only glance at the fulness and earnestness with which it is required. In the Old Testament, while the sacrifices as such prefigured Christ's vicarious death, as offerings, required to be the best of the flocks, the finest of the wheat, they taught that the spirit of sacrifice must animate the worshipper. In the New Testament, the doctrine is omnipresent as daylight in the atmosphere. It is proclaimed as law. It is propounded as the inexorable condition of discipleship. Here it beams in the examples of saints suffering the loss of all things for Christ; there it glares in the rejection of the rich ruler, who loved wealth more than Jesus, or of Demas, who forsook Christ for filthy lucre. Here it smiles in promise: "Your Father, which seeth in secret, shall reward you openly"; there it frowns in denunciation: "Your riches are corrupted, your garments are moth-eaten, your gold and silver are cankered, and the rust of them shall eat your flesh as it were fire." All, in varied language, proclaim the law of sacrificial love: "Bear ye one another's burdens, and so fulfil the law of Christ"—the law which Christ exemplified and vindicated on the cross.

VI. The same Principle is recognized in the Administration of Christ's Kingdom.

He does not establish it by his visible coming, supernaturally destroying his enemies and giving his church a toilless victory. That dream is contrary to the fundamental idea of Christianity and to the entire method of its administration. He commits his kingdom to the fidelity of a toiling and suffering church, under the guidance of the Spirit, and permits it slowly to evolve through conflict and self-denial, through alternations of defeat and triumph. Says Isaac Taylor: "To touch the substantial miseries of degenerate man is to come within the infection of an infinite sorrow." Jesus was subject to that infection; so are all who labor with him. Even the miracle-workers had no permission to work miracles to save themselves from suffering. Able to raise the dead and to control demons for the advancement of Christ's kingdom, their very handkerchiefs conveying healing to others, they themselves were left under the law of doing good by sacrifice, and, as if no miracle-working power slept within them, were obliged to say: "Even unto this present hour we both hunger and thirst, and are naked, and are buffeted, and have no certain dwelling-place." Parents suffer through their love for the wayward son whom they would reclaim. Whoever would save a sinner must love him; and whoever loves a sinner, and would save him, must suffer anguish in his behalf. The love that saves sinners must bear their sins.

VII. This Principle is recognized more obscurely in the Constitution of Society and symbolized even in Nature.

Society is constituted on the principle that no man lives for himself. Even positivism recognizes altruism, or living for others, as the fundamental principle of sociology.

We find symbols of the same law in nature; though we are too ignorant, as yet, to verify it fully there. But, as a child will recognize the father's voice and the tones of his love, even when he speaks in an unknown tongue, we can recognize in nature the tones of our Father's voice, though we cannot fully interpret the words. The dew-drop which sparkles on a summer's morning exhales its whole being while refreshing the leaf on which it hangs. When, in the early spring, the crocus lifts its pure whiteness from beneath the reeking mould, when the iris puts on its sapphire crown, when the rose unfolds its queenly beauty, it is as if each graceful form said: "This is all I have and all I am — this fragile grace and sweetness — I unfold it all for you." The wild berries nestle blushing in the grass, or droop inviting on the vine, as if saying: "This lusciousness is all my wealth; it is for you." The apples, golden and red, glowing amid the green leaves, seem to be thoughtfully whispering God's own words: "A good tree bringeth forth good fruit." The field submits to be sheared of its yearly harvest, mutely waiting the return of blessing at the good pleasure of him that dresseth it, symbolizing the patient faith of him who does good hoping for nothing again, except from the good-pleasure of God, who is not forgetful to reward the patience of faith and the labor of love. On the contrary, the land which bears thorns and thistles, keeping its own harvest to enrich itself, is rejected and nigh unto cursing. The sun walks regally through the heavens, pouring abroad day, and the stars shine all night, seemingly saying: "We are suns; yet even our opulence of glory we give to others; our very nature is to shine."

Do not say that this is fanciful. The creation was cast in the mould of God's love, and each thing bears some impress of the same. Before the solid earth and the ocean were made, before sun or star shone, before chaos formless and waste, God's eternal wisdom and love filled the void. And when he spake and it was done, the creative fiat only spoke into finite form some eternal thought of his wisdom, only crystallized into finite realization some definite purpose of his love. Hence everywhere, on land and sea, on the earth and in the star-thronged skies, are traces of that law of sacrifice which expresses the essential character of love.

It remains to answer an objection, that if Christianity is sacrificial it takes on the gloom of asceticism, and suppresses and mortifies the soul, instead of developing it. The answer is indicated in the experience of Paul, that love to Christ had transformed what had been his gain into loss, and what had been his loss into gain. Love changes the objects of interest and the sources from which the soul can draw happiness. Love to Christ absorbs the element of sorrow from self-renunciation, and transforms it into joy. It effects the transfiguration of the cross.

The principle underlying this is that a man's affections determine the sources of his enjoyment. Happiness is not bottled up in objects — so much happiness in a house and grounds, so much in a horse and equipage, and whoever gets the object gets that definite quantity of enjoyment. Whether one obtains any happiness from an object depends on the state of the heart in reference to it. A man who has no appetite for food can have no enjoyment in eating. The heart must be upon an object before enjoyment can be derived from it. The happiness is an incident to the love, as a smile is the spontaneous expression of the joy that diffuses itself through the soul. For example, a young man has at present no higher interest than to get his earnings and spend them for his own enjoyment. Afterwards we see him, and the love of wife and of children is in his heart; and this new affection has created new objects of interest and sources of joy. And if, afterwards, he acquires a taste for literature or art, or an interest in some moral reformation, or in a political principle, each opens to him a new sphere of enjoyment, desire, and action. Every new and pure affection opens in his life, like a fountain in a desert, creating a new area of beauty and fertility. It is like opening to him a new world in which to expatiate.

A man is shut up by his affections to the objects of those affections as the sources of his happiness. A brute is shut up by its nature to a limited line of enjoyment; a lamb must crop the grass, a tiger raven in blood. A man is not thus shut up by nature. He may find his happiness in sensual enjoyment, as do the brutes, or in the service of love, as do the angels. But when once his heart is fixed on its objects, he is by his affection shut up to those objects for his enjoyment as rigidly as a brute by its nature. If his heart is on the world, he is shut up to that for his enjoyment, as a caterpillar is confined by the threads issuing from its own body to the perishing leaf on which it feeds; as a shell-fish is bound by the fibres issuing from its own being to a rock under the sea, capable of no other action than to stretch its slimy feelers, and bring what it reaches into its own shell, and digest it into its own cold and sluggish life. Herodias had the offer of half the kingdom; but, bound by her revenge, there was nothing in it for her to enjoy but the bloody head of the prophet who had rebuked her. Nero had the world in his hand, as one holds an orange, to suck all its sweetness into his own lips; but all the happiness which all the kingdoms of the world and the glory of them could give him was the horrid joy of sensuality and cruelty.

If one affection is incompatible with another, the enjoyment of the objects of the second affection is impossible until it displace the first. A miser cannot enjoy a benevolent use of money, till his miserliness has been displaced by love. Then he will wonder at himself that ever he could have found enjoyment in the squalidness of his hoarding.

These are illustrations of the principle on which Paul says that his gain had become loss through the love of Christ. Religion is not merely prudence, shrewdly, but reluctantly, sacrificing present joy for future gain, toiling through the gymnastics of so much Bible-reading and prayer every day, getting down nauseous doses of religion — carefully counting the drops, lest you take too much — to avert impending death. It is love, displacing the selfish affections which have ruled the heart, opening a new world of interest in which to act and enjoy, wide as the welfare of man and great and glorious as the kingdom of Christ. Religion is no longer an outward law, under whose lash the soul creeps reluctant through its daily stint of service, but an inward affection, drawing the Christian in the way in which he rejoices to go: "I delight to do thy will, O God." His gain has become loss, and his loss gain. His hold on the objects of sinful desire is loosened, and he leaves them as filth, while he turns to new and nobler objects. The energies of his being are no longer cramped and crooked in impotence for good; but he presses on the life of faith and love, walking and leaping and praising God.

It appears, then, that Christian self-renunciation is primarily and essentially the self-surrender to Christ in coming to him and accepting him. It is only the reverse side of love. It is a mistake to suppose that it is only relinquishing certain pleasures, giving some money in charity, or drudging through certain repulsive duties. It is immeasurably more than this; it is giving your heart; it is giving yourself. Love is the essence of self-denial: "Though I bestow all my goods to feed the poor, and though I give my body to be burned, and have not love, it profiteth me nothing."

Also, as to the method of self-denial, it is accomplished, not by a dead lift, but by the spontaneous and vital energy of love; as a man drops the plays of childhood, not by a conscious and painful struggle, but because he has outgrown them.

There is, then, no force in the objection that Christianity by the severity of its self-denial extinguishes the joyousness of life, and suppresses and crushes the soul, instead of developing it. It incapacitates the soul for the enjoyments of sin, but capacitates it for the blessedness of love. It enlarges and ennobles it to realize in the life of love its highest possibilities. As one who has been a drunkard sacrifices the pleasures of intemperance, but gains the higher and nobler joys of temperance; as one who has been a slave loses the capacity of being contented in slavery, but gains the higher happiness of freedom, the love of Christ sacrifices the joys of sin, but gains the blessedness of the righteous. The snow-birds of winter are gone; but the summer songsters are tuneful on every spray as it bursts into leaf and blossom beneath the returning sun. All religious services, once repulsive, prayer and praise, formerly frozen words rattling like hail around the wintry heart, works of beneficence, once chafing to the selfish soul, — all are transfigured into joy.

It will be objected, however, that after love to Christ has made religious duty pleasant, we must still forego, in Christ's service, the gratification of innocent desires, and give up comforts, property, or even life, and that these sacrifices must be painful. Certainly, suffering in these cases is inseparable from human nature; yet even this suffering seems capable of being absorbed in love, lost in the superior blessedness of the Christian life. Missionaries seem usually happier in their work than men ordinarily are. None, apparently, make more of life, or get more solid blessedness out of it. Paul gloried in tribulation. His contemporaries took joyfully the spoiling of their goods. No books were ever written under trials more appalling than those which attended the writing of the Epistles in the New Testament; yet no literature breathes a more joyous spirit than these. Martyrs have been joyful at the stake. Love to a person makes it easy to toil for him. Enthusiasm in a cause makes it easy to suffer for the cause. So love to Christ and enthusiasm for his kingdom make toil easy and burdens light.

Self-denial of this kind is, however, no peculiarity of the service of Christ. Whatever a man would achieve, he must concentrate his energies on his work, and that concentration involves self-denial. If a man would succeed as a merchant, a farmer, or a scholar, he must forego ease, deny himself many gratifications, and concentrate his powers on his work. Self-denial is a condition of achievement and success in every human action, as well as in the religious life. Sin itself requires it. Burglars in prosecuting their business practise more self-denial than honest men. The ancient Romans regarded as the essence of virtue this manliness which concentrates the energies on an object, scorns luxury and indulgence, braves difficulty and danger, and endures self-denial in attaining it. Jesus presents the old Roman *virtus* as a condition of religious action, but not as the essence of a religious life. He requires a more profound self-renunciation, involved essentially in love, and blessed in the blessedness of love.

It follows that they who enter deepest into the spirit of Christian self-renunciation are least aware of sacrificing anything for Christ. The more intense the love, the less account they make of the service rendered to the beloved. The reason why men of business are not aware that they deny themselves is, that they are so intent on their object that they make no account of toil and privation to attain it. The raging of appetite makes unheeded the sacrifice of reputation, property, and health in gratifying it; the fierceness of revenge makes it sweet to risk life to satisfy it; the greed of avarice makes the miser glory in his rags. Love to Christ and enthusiasm for his kingdom produce the same oblivion of sacrifices made for him. Great deeds of Christian love are done in unconsciousness. This is what our Saviour requires in the command: "Let not thy left hand know what thy right hand doeth." It does not require you to keep your good deeds secret from others, but from yourselves. Be so full of love that you will take no note of the sacrifices to which love inspires you.

Here we see the difference between asceticism and Christian self-renunciation. Asceticism is a suppression of the soul's affection; Christian self-renunciation is the introduction of a new affection displacing the old. The former is a negation of the soul's life; the latter, the development of a new and higher life. The former produces a constrained performance of duties, a restraint of desires which do not cease to burn, a sad resignation to necessary evils; the latter produces a new affection which makes duty coincide with the heart's love, quenches contrary desires, and quickens to positive joy in the accomplishment of God's will. The former by perpetual constraint makes a *free* life impossible; the latter ultimately insures real freedom, in which obedience to God is unhindered by opposition from within the soul, the impulses of the heart are in harmony with the principles of the reason, and law loses itself in the quicker and coincident impulses of love. The former by its self-mortification, makes a *full* life impossible, and goodness becomes a mere holding back from sin; the latter, opening a new love, develops life in its utmost fulness, gushing in inexhaustible springs of thought, energy, and joy. The former is founded on the error that suffering and self-mortification are in themselves acceptable to God; the latter, on the truth that God is served in the full development of his creatures in life, energy, and joy. The former, therefore, inflicting suffering on self to gain the favor of God, is, in reality, a self-righteousness, a form of self-sufficiency, and not self-renunciation.

In the divine words sadness and joy are mingled: "He that goeth forth and weepeth, bearing precious seed, shall doubtless come again with rejoicing, bringing his sheaves." Why, with this promise of sheaves gathered with joy, the vision of tears watering the seed sown? Are deeds of beneficence fecundated only when steeped in tears? To explain it, we need not resort to the hypothesis that no God governs the world, or, if any, the God of the iron foot, who crushes loving souls beneath his bloody tread as recklessly as he splits the oaks with his thunder-bolts, or scatters the rose-leaves with his winds. Our doctrine discloses a more profound philosophy. God exercises his children in self-denial that they may become strong in Christian love. He is educating them by sacrificial toil to possess a Christlike character and glory, and to be capable of Christlike achievements. The law which calls you to self-sacrifice is severe, not exempting life if its sacrifice is needed; it is inexorable, but it is not arbitrary. Only in it can the essential character of Christianity find expression; only by it can you realize the highest possibilities of your being.

Have your souls faltered before the mystery that under the government of God it costs sorrow and sacrifice to do good? Do you complain of the hard requirement? But were it abated, it would only be so much abated from the divine excellence of Christianity, so much abated from the godlike character to which you are called, and from the divine beauty and power of love. It would unsettle the two great commandments, detract from the meaning of the great words of revelation: "God is Love," eviscerate redemption of its significance, change the character of Christ's kingdom, dim the glory and vitiate the blessedness of heaven, and let darkness in on the eternal day.

# LECTURE VIII.

## THE CHRISTIAN LAW OF SERVICE.

The Christian law of service is proclaimed by the Saviour: "Whosoever will be great among you, let him be your minister; and whosoever will be chief among you, let him be your servant; even as the Son of Man came not to be ministered unto, but to minister, and to give his life a ransom for many." To the ambitious request of the mother of James and John for the highest places in his kingdom for her sons, he had replied by propounding the Christian law of service, and enforcing it with these most touching words, in which he presents his own life of sacrifice and service as the type of all Christian life. This law presents itself in two aspects: Greatness for Service; Greatness by Service.

Greatness *for* service. — Greatness does not entitle its possessor to compel the service of others, while he lives in idleness, sustained by their compelled ministrations; but it binds its possessor to render service to others. Greatness in wealth, learning, talent, position, or power of any kind, is bound to a commensurate greatness of service.

Greatness *by* service. — Service, always degrading from the selfish and heathen point of view, is itself the true greatness, and is ennobled as such by Christianity. The most complete development of the individual and his greatest consideration in society to be attained by service; no artificial ranks in Christ's kingdom, exalting men merely by position — no pygmies on Alps; but greatness by service — an aristocracy of merit. The man who best serves society is to be the man of most weight in society — a king of men by divine right.

In considering this principle as the Christian law of service, we are primarily concerned with its first aspect: Greatness for Service.

I. The Significance of the Law.

1. The *principle* involved: Greatness carries in it the obligation to service.

Jesus refers to the contrary principle of heathen civilization: "Ye know that the princes of the Gentiles exercise dominion over them, and they that are great exercise authority upon them." This principle is, that superior power of any kind is to be used in compelling the services of inferiors; the weak must serve the strong. The position of honor is found in living idly and luxuriously on the enforced service of others. Hence despotism, wars of conquest, race-hatred and domination, slavery, the degradation of woman, characterize heathen civilization. Jesus says: "It shall not be so among you." The contrary principle must characterize the kingdom of Christ. Thus he calls our attention to the fact that in this declaration he not only propounds the Christian law of service as a law for the individual, but in it propounds the germinant principle of a new civilization. In Christian civilization the strong are to serve the weak; the nobility and blessedness of life are to be found in energetic and self-sacrificing work in rendering that service. Christianity recognizes superiority as imposing obligation to serve, and emblazons for every Christian the motto of nobility: "*Noblesse oblige.*"

This principle is set forth in the humiliation and sacrifice of Christ, the type and measure of all Christian love. It is the great law, which he exemplified, of the higher descending to the lower to lift it up; of the perfect seeking the imperfect, the richly-endowed seeking the poorly-endowed, bearing to them the gifts which they lack. It is always the shepherd going to the mountains to seek the lost sheep.

2. The *measure* of the service required is the ability to render it.

In transactions between parties having equal ability to render service, the services must be reciprocal, and the service rendered must be an equivalent for the service received. This may be called the law of reciprocity. This is the law of business exchanges. Every honest transaction in business secures an equivalent advantage to each of the parties. This implies, also, that so far as any one has the power of self-help he has no claim on the unrequited service of others.

But the world abounds in wretchedness which can neither help itself nor make compensation for the help of others, and which appeals for relief to those who are able to render it. Here we have the law of unrequited or gratuitous service — the strong must serve the weak. Human need creates a lien on the ability to relieve it: "I am debtor both to the Greeks and to the barbarians, both to the wise and to the unwise; so, as much as in me is, I am ready to preach the gospel to you that are at Rome also." Every man is debtor, *as much as in him is*, to use his superior power, of whatever kind, in uncompensated service to those who need. And the greater the power to serve, the greater the proportion of this kind of service that is due — pre-eminent ability, pre-eminent service; greatness, great service. Here we reach the Christian principle of stewardship — that men hold property and all means of influence not for selfish ends, but in trust for the advancement of Christ's kingdom and the promotion of the best interests of man.

3. The *applications* of the law are both to the choice and prosecution of business and to the use of its gains.

I shall consider first, and chiefly, the application of the law to the choice and prosecution of business. A man's business ought to be such that the whole action of his life in its prosecution be doing good, even when he is so absorbed in its cares and processes that he does not think of doing good.

The law of Christian benevolence is ordinarily treated as if it were applicable only to the use of the gains of business.

But, if so, then we do good only occasionally and with deliberate purpose; the only scope for Christian beneficence is outside of the business, while within it all is necessarily worldly and selfish; and it is only so far as one can give away something that he can be benevolent. If a mechanic spends nine tenths of his earnings in supporting his family, and gives away one tenth, then of every ten strokes of his hammer nine are for self, and only one for God — but a dribbling of his life for doing good. But a man's business is the main work of his life. When his life ends, the great bulk of what he has done for God and man is what he has done *in* his business, not what he has done outside of it. If that business in its prosecution affords no scope for Christian largeness of heart, if it is essentially a mephitic swamp in which every breath inhales miasma, we may well cry in despair: "Who, then, can be saved?" Then it is not surprising that men should reproach God for requiring them to serve him, while compelling them to spend life in business which consists essentially in serving themselves. Business must itself be such that every stroke in its prosecution shall be a Christian serviee to man — so much business done, so much service to humanity rendered. Business, therefore, should be chosen and prosecuted reverently and in Christian consecration; for it is the life-work. If chosen and prosecuted only for gain, it is chosen and prosecuted in covetousness, and not in Christian love.

And yet the common opinion is, that business is to be chosen and prosecuted only to make money. This opinion has so firm a hold that the majority of men would probably be surprised at the suggestion that a man should engage in business for any other end. Even good men think that Christian benevolence is to be exercised only in the giving of their gains, not in the prosecution of their business. The only exception is the business of a Christian minister, which all admit should be prosecuted not to get gain, but to render service. It is necessary, therefore, to show that every legitimate business is in its very prosecution a service to humanity, and ought to be chosen and prosecuted in Christian love for the purpose of rendering the service, not in covetousness for the purpose of gain. This principle is as applicable to every business as it is to that of the Christian minister.

(1) Exchanges under the law of reciprocity give scope to Christian service. You say: "If I have any of my time or earnings to spare from my business, I am willing to show Christian charity to the needy. But business is business, and must be conducted on business principles, and with it Christian charity has nothing to do." But what are business principles? The fundamental one is the law of reciprocity: "The service rendered must be equivalent to the service received." The fact that, in a business transaction, for the service rendered an equivalent is received does not take away its character as a service, nor preclude Christian love as a motive in the transaction. Every Christian is bound in love to see that in every transaction of business he renders a service equivalent to that received. When in any exchange it is the aim of one party to secure all the advantage to himself, that intent is of the essence of all oppression; for it is using a superiority of some kind to compel the service of another without rendering an equivalent. It is of the essence of all dishonesty; for it is getting possession of another's property without rendering an equivalent. The highwayman does the same, with only the difference that he is rougher in his method of making the transfer. Thus the law of reciprocity exalts every business transaction into a Christian service, and requires every man in every transaction to be as intent on the service which he renders to another as on the equivalent service which he receives. In every transaction is scope for Christian greatness of soul; and the man of business is entitled to adopt the princely motto: "Ich dien," "I serve."

Political economy, the science of business exchanges, which is founded solely on enlightened self-interest, coincides with Christian ethics in this respect. Its fundamental principle is, that every legitimate exchange is the exchange of equivalent services; it is coming to accept the word "service" as best expressing whatever is exchanged.

(2) Legitimate business is in its prosecution a service, because it is productive, and supplies human wants. The farmer raises food for man and beast, and material for clothing. The mechanic and manufacturer fit the raw material for use. The merchant transports products, and makes them accessible to those who want them. The peoples of the world serve each other by their productive labor — the Asiatic serves the European, and the European serves the Asiatic. Over all the world men are industriously serving each other, producing what meets human wants. Thus viewed, the creation and circulation of products through the world, beneficent as the circulation of air and water, rises to the sublime. The circulation of the products of all countries, passing in white-sailed ships over the ocean, millions of wealth always in motion from mart to mart, a circulation so noiseless that the products of the other hemisphere flow daily through the streets unnoticed as the wind, and so equable and complete that you have only to step across the street and the product of any country is stored ready for your hand, and the table is daily spread with the products of every quarter of the globe — this circulation, all-pervading as the flow of blood in the body, binds all nations in the unity of a common interest and life.

Here, again, political economy concurs with Christianity. Whatever advantages in productive industry any person may have over others, it is for his interest that others should have corresponding advantages over him, and should be prospered in their industry; for thereby both the demand for his own products and the supplies for his own wants are increased. For the same reason, every nation is interested in the industrial and commercial prosperity of other nations. The old doctrine that a nation is benefited by crippling other nations is seen to be fallacious.

Thus political economy coincides with the gospel in teaching that we are members one of another, and if one member suffers all the members suffer with it. It coincides with Christian ethics in the law that business should be prosecuted as a service to others, and not merely to get gain for self.

An inference is, that the only legitimate business for a Christian man is one which by its very prosecution renders service to society. Dramsellers, gamblers, lottery-dealers, counterfeiters, adulterators of food and medicine work every day, and the product of every day's work and of the diligence of the life-time is the multiplication of human woes. Persons engaged in business serviceable to society are entitled to gains accruing from a rise of prices, because this is incidental to a legitimate business and a compensation for incidental losses from a similar cause. But speculators, who by combination force an advance, produce no value, and render no equivalent service for their gains. They only force money from the possession of others into their own. This, therefore, is analogous to gambling, and is not a legitimate business according to the Christian law of service.

(3) A man renders service in the prosecution of his business so far as he is able to improve its methods and results. The farmer who "manures his land with brains" not only increases his own gains, but improves the art of farming, increases the productiveness of the earth, multiplies and cheapens products, and puts an addition to the comforts of life within the reach of a larger number of human beings. Every mechanical invention produces similar results.

The result is, that industry, subduing nature, developing its resources, and using its powers, and multiplying and cheapening its products, is steadily advancing human welfare; the purchasing power of labor, measured not by its money-wages, but by its power to purchase the comforts of life, increases; and, in like manner, the value of raw material, measured by its power to purchase manufactured products, increases. Thus cottagers have now comforts and luxuries which two hundred years ago the wealthiest could not buy.

The industrial movement of modern times is a distinctive

characteristic of Christian civilization. Human thought and energy is directed to the study of nature, the mastery and use of its powers, and the development of its resources for the service of man. Industrial enterprise opens a sphere for the largest knowledge, the highest talent, and the greatest energy. Thus it gives scope in this peaceful service of man to the power which in ancient times found scope only in war and selfish ambition.

(4) Every man serves society in his business so far as he ennobles it by strict integrity and a high sense of honor, by a large benevolence, and all the beauty of a Christian character. What honor, for example, has been given to manufacturing by Lawrence and Williston, to mechanical pursuits by Safford and Washburn, and to mercantile life by Budgett and Thornton. Thus the man of business is to silence the sneer that a mercantile people are necessarily mercenary; that mechanics and meanness are inseparable; that earning a living deadens noble sentiments; that men must live at leisure on the labors of others in order to realize the nobility of life.

(5) Every man's general influence in society, outside of his business, is affected by his character in his business. Light must be embodied in some sun or star or candle or burning coal, or it cannot shine. A man's business is the body of his light. If he is not a Christian in his business, he can shed no light beyond it; there is not even a candle or glowing coal to radiate it.

The second application of the Christian law of service is to the use of the gains of business.

It is unnecessary to dwell on this application; because it is the one usually urged, and urged so exclusively that the churches have fallen into the one-sided opinion that Christian benevolence consists principally in giving money. It is necessary only to say that in the use of his gains a Christian will be governed by the law of service. If he would escape covetousness, he must give habitually, in proportion to his income, and with a willing heart. The same principle applies to the use of power and influence of every kind acquired in business.

II. Reasons for the Christian Law of Service.

1. The first is that urged by our Saviour himself: "The Son of Man came not to be ministered unto, but to minister, and to give his life a ransom for many." I sometimes think these the most touching and eloquent of our Saviour's words. As the brightness of the Father's glory, he discloses the love of God appearing under human limitations in service and sacrifice. As the ideal man, he reveals in service and sacrifice the image of God perfected in human character.

2. The best instincts and the moral intuitions of the human soul accord with this law.

If any accident happens, and the better impulses of the heart are roused, men run to help the weak and the suffering. The strong man who calls for help is thrust aside with scorn. It is not greatness and strength which establish a claim for service; it is weakness, helplessness, suffering.

The babe comes into the house, and by its very helplessness commands the service of all. It rules the heart by its weakness. See it waking from its day-nap, the coverlid just drawn off, described as only one who was at once a mother and a poet could describe it:

"There he lies upon his back,
The yearling creature; warm and moist with life
To the bottom of his dimples, to the ends
Of the lovely tumbled curls about his face.
. . . . . Both his cheeks
Were hot and scarlet as the first live rose;
. . . . . The pretty baby mouth
Shut close, as if for dreaming that it sucked;
The little naked feet drawn up, the way
Of nestled birdlings. Everything so soft
And tender — to the little holdfast hands,
Which, closing on a finger into sleep,
Had kept the mould of it. . . . . .
The light upon his eyelids pricked them wide,
And, staring out at us with all their blue.

As half perplexed between the angelhood
He had been away to visit in his sleep
And our most mortal presence, gradually
He saw his mother's face, accepting it,
In change for heaven itself, with such a smile
As might have well been learnt there; never moved,
But smiled on, in a drowse of ecstasy;
So happy (half with her and half with heaven)
He could not have the trouble to be stirred,
But smiled and lay there. Like a rose, I said.
As red and still, indeed, as any rose,
That blows in all the silence of its leaves,
Content, in blowing, to fulfil its life."[1]

Infantile beauty, with power to command willing and loving service. But when the yearling has grown to be a great, strong boy, then, if he demands the service rendered to the babe, he is only laughed at. Thus the unperverted instincts and moral sentiments of human nature assent to the principle that the weak are entitled to the service of the strong. Whoever is growing rich and great with the belief that he is entitled to use his strength to compel the service of others, and to live only to be ministered unto, is in the family of God a sort of overgrown baby, like a stout, selfish boy, who uses the strength of youth to compel from all the family the service due only to the babe.

3. The third reason is found in the second aspect of the law — Greatness by Service.

By service a man attains his own highest intrinsic greatness; by service he also attains the greatest weight and influence in society.

It is commonly objected that the argument from Christian love is an appeal to sentimentality, which cannot be expected to have much influence on practical men. This very objection is an expression of the hard and cold realism of the age, which measures value only by its power to satisfy material wants, which reckons success to be the acquisition of wealth by whatever means, and which makes the crowd stare in admiration at the diamonds, the equipage, and all

[1] Mrs. Browning's Aurora Leigh, Book vi.

the gaudy ostentation of swindlers, thieves, and whoremongers, and calls that success in life.

Certainly, enlightened self-interest accords with the Christian law. But I do not appeal to it here. For what is needed is not merely a more enlightened self-interest, but the spirit of Christian love — the spirit which animated the life of Jesus our Lord — a spirit not of the world, but above it. What is needed is a new and Christian ideal of what constitutes success in life, displacing the low ideal of success by getting rich. And this our Saviour sets before us in this thought, greatness by service.

The giver is always the superior of the receiver. He that confers a favor is, so far as that particular is concerned, the superior of him who receives it. He that renders a service is, in that particular, superior to him to whom the service is rendered. The common opinion, that he who serves is the inferior, belongs to the civilization attending the reign of force, when service was rendered on compulsion. Christianity reverses this doctrine. He who needs and receives service is, in that particular, the inferior and the dependent. The condition of modern society is forcing this obvious, but forgotten fact on the attention.

The character expressed and developed in loving service is the highest and noblest type of character. Jesus reveals the divine in the human, and the human in its ideal perfection. That ideal is found in his life of service; he came not to be ministered unto, but to minister. This Man of Sorrows, in "the form of a servant," is the perfect Man, in whom humanity, long smitten with spiritual death, and producing only degenerate beings, at last, touched by the divine, comes forth in absolute perfection. The first tempter promised: "Ye shall be as gods," and the promise was to be realized through self-indulgence and gratification: "She took, and did eat." It has been the mistake of the world, from that day until now, to expect to become as gods by getting and being ministered unto. The gospel gives us the same promise: "Ye shall be partakers of the divine nature"; but it is by being, like Christ, a servant. The conception of the highest blessedness by being ministered unto is the conception of an everlasting babyhood, an everlasting need and enjoyment of the pap-spoon. The conception of greatness by ministering is the conception of manly strength and power to serve, of resources given without impoverishment. So we assent to the words of Jesus, seeing therein our highest dignity: "It is enough for the disciple that he be as his Master, and the servant as his Lord."

Christian service brings out all the energies into action, and is constantly developing the man to greatness. It is often said that among missionaries is an extraordinary number of distinguished persons. The reason cannot be that they are of a higher order of natural ability, but is rather that their work trains them to greatness. Also, by identifying them with the greatest of human enterprises, it lifts them to notice, and concentres on them the interest of all Christians. No men so act beneath the gaze of all the world. When Mr. Snow went to Micronesia, it seemed like burying him in the obscurest corner of the world. But this faithful missionary to that handful of savages has created an interest and extended an influence throughout Christendom. He is a greater and nobler man, more widely known and influential than he could have been in any parish at home. If Paul had remained a Pharisee, he would have been a prominent man of his city, and at his death would have been forgotten. But Paul the Christian becomes the most influential man in the Roman empire, and perpetuates his influence through all ages. If Luther had remained a monk, he would have been a student, inclined to despondency, having no aim higher than to keep his own conscience in peace. But Luther the Christian is a man of burning enthusiasm, dauntless courage, heroic enterprise, broad, hearty humor—the reformer of Europe. William of Orange, at the age of twenty-seven, was a Romanist, a favorite at the court, spending his immense revenues in magnificence and luxury. But William became a Protestant, and spent his subsequent life, with almost superhuman energy, and against innumerable difficulties, in establishing the liberty of his country and defending the faith against the powerful and bigoted monarch of Spain. All history demonstrates that greatness is by service.

Great responsibilities develop greatness. A sea-captain may be ordinarily a commonplace man; but when his ship is in danger his responsibility ennobles him; his form seems to swell to grander proportions; his attitude becomes majestic; his eye kindles; his voice deepens; his mind acts with preternatural energy. Analogous to this transitory influence of a great crisis is the constant influence of Christianity, quickening and ennobling the whole life with the consciousness of a great trust, a grand responsibility, and an urgent service.

The greatest energy in the service of self fails to develop a character so noble, a power so grand, and an influence so wide and lasting. Contrast Paul and Napoleon — both conquerors; the one by force, the other by truth and love; the one for self-aggrandizement, the other for the welfare of man. Contrast them in the imprisonment in which their lives were ended, when, isolated from all factitious splendor and support, you see the men themselves; Napoleon, though surrounded by the comforts of life, querulous, morose, weak, not self-poised and self-sustained — like a rank vine grovelling on the ground when its prop is gone; Paul, imprisoned rigorously, yet how grand his bearing, how self-poised and self-sustained, how peaceful and triumphant.

It is a condition of abiding influence that the life be identified with truth, which lives forever. The life expended on selfish ends is transient as the selfish objects it seeks, and narrow in its scope as the interest of self. Contrast the influence of Paul and Nero, of Luther and Charles V. — when they lived, the Christian seemingly so insignificant in comparison with the emperor; but in the subsequent ages the emperor fading into insignificance, the Christian brightening with increasing glory.

Thus, whether we consider intrinsic nobleness, or the duration and scope of influence, it appears that greatness is by service. The man of greatness in the church is the man who greatly serves the church. These are bishops by divine right, pre-eminent by pre-eminent service, pre-eminent as Paul was, "in labors more abundant, in stripes above measure, in prisons more frequent, in deaths oft." Such are the men by God's own anointing great in the kingdom of heaven. Such is the true *ἀνὰξ ἀνδρῶν*, whom no revolution can dethrone.

The same thought is true of society. Society can attain its best condition only as it is governed by the law of love. The ambition which by force compels the service of inferiors which characterized ancient civilization, the greed of gain which characterizes modern civilization, must give place to the law of service before a Christian civilization can pervade the world. Obedience to this law is indispensable to produce the popular virtue and national character essential to self-government and Christian civilization.

Consider the different characters which the greed of gain and obedience to the Christian law of service respectively indicate and develop. If industry is merely for gain, it will be accepted as a drudgery, and shirked when practicable. The brightest dream of success will be realized in the acquisition of means to live luxuriously with exemption from work. But if industry is regarded as Christian service, the true man will covet the opportunity to work. Idleness will be counted a disgrace. No one's education is complete till he learns not to shrink from work as a drudgery, but to rejoice in it as a service.

If business is regarded as a service, the aim of the workman will be to do all work thoroughly, as for God. The mechanic will congratulate himself, when his day's work is done, not merely that he has received his earnings, but also that his work has been well done, and will render good service. The manufacturer will congratulate himself, not merely that he has made a profit on his contract, but also that he has given employment to many hands, and paid them the full worth of their labor, and has turned out an article well made, which will do good service. The merchant will congratulate himself, not merely that he has made large and profitable sales, but that he has given his customers a full equivalent for their money, taking advantage of no man's ignorance, carelessness, or necessity. Thus work in every department develops a noble and generous character, inflexible in integrity, intent on rendering service to men.

But if work is only for gain, the only joy in the work done is in the gain acquired. The day-laborer works unfaithfully, and is idle, if not watched. The mechanic slights his work, and turns out articles that will not wear. The manufacturer grinds his operatives to the lowest wages which their necessity or his opportunity permits, and produces articles of inferior material and make. The trader adulterates or misrepresents his goods. The man no longer regards his employer, his workman, or his customer as a fellow-man to be served, but as a victim to be plundered, a goose to be plucked; and he plucks him as near to the life as he dares. Then he boasts how much he has made *out of him* — of the sharpness with which he cut his neighbor's property out of him without rendering an equivalent.

Work thus prosecuted strengthens the greed of gain. The man becomes rapacious. His life is a Sahara, sucking into burning sand the sunshine and the rain, but returning no green thing. He becomes unscrupulous, reckless of justice and honor. As Dr. South says, he retails heaven and salvation for pence and half-pence, and seldom sells a commodity but he sells his soul with it, like brown paper, into the bargain. He becomes mean in getting and niggardly in spending. He becomes hard, reckless of the rights and interests of others, incapable of compassion, heeding no appeal to help the wretched; diligent and energetic as an iron steam-engine at work, and as hard and heartless as it. He lives not to benefit society, but to prey upon it — a pirate seizing prizes — a devil seeking whom he may devour.

If such a character pervades society, society is corrupt and its civilization decaying. Society becomes impotent to produce great men ; its consummate flower is the smart man, keen, shrewd, and knowing; it does not produce great men, men of broad views and large hearts, whose names will be powers of beneficence forever.

In ancient civilization, families and races which had won power by the sword compelled the service of the inferiors subjected. It has been the struggle of modern times to break political tyranny, and to secure to individuals their rights. The motto of modern civilization is: "A career open to talents" — every man free to make the most of himself and for himself. But this is demonstrating itself to be but a half-truth. Society constituted on individualism perverts individual liberty into self-assertion — every one grasping all he can for himself, without care for the rights of others. Society says to the individual: "We open to you a career. Make of yourself and for yourself all that you can. But look out for yourself; for every member of society will make everything out of you that he can. But then we are Christian; if you cannot run this gauntlet, — if you break down into utter destitution, — we will send you to the poorhouse, and keep you from starving at the least possible expense to ourselves."

It has become plain to the thoughtful that this principle of individual liberty is inadequate. Under it the old principle of the domination of the strongest still creeps in; the tyranny wrested from government reappears in the social sphere ; the purse is as forceful as the sword. When competition does not pay, the competitors combine to force prices above the natural level; the rich grow richer, and the poor poorer. Inequalities not only increase, but stiffen into castes; it becomes more and more difficult for the inferiors to rise by honest industry to independence. The whole tone of society becomes more and more vulgar and coarse-grained; bent on sordid ends, and seeking them by sordid means.

The masses that have been the less successful in this selfish competition are becoming uneasily conscious of their inferiority. But they fall back into the old error that the strong may compel the service of the weak. They have discovered that ten are stronger than one, and that by combination the many can compel the action of the few. They are lifting their solid mass to take from the individual the open career which by the conflicts of centuries he has won, and to enslave him again to society. They proclaim that rights belong to society, to the individual only duties — that he is the creature and tool of society. They proclaim the old error (exposed by Jesus) that man exists for his institutions. But however excellent the sentiments embodied in institutions, if they are constituted on the error that man exists for his institutions, they only bring back the old oppression in a new form. The re-organization thus proposed by the socialists among the labor-reformers is the old tyranny in a new form, and the worst form in which it has ever appeared. It is the organization of mediocrity, the lifting of inferiority to rule by the power of mere mass; it restrains genius, ability, and industry from gaining more than imbecility, mediocrity, and indolence; it closes the career to talent; it makes human progress impossible.

The evil itself, and the greater evil of these methods of attempting to right it, can be met only by Christianity. Under the Christian law of service individual liberty and rights are respected; a career is open to talent; the strongest stimulus to individual enterprise and development exists; all that has been won by the struggles of modern times is retained. Yet every right is acknowledged to have its correlative duty; the individual is followed in his acquisition by the Christian law of service; he accepts the obligation to choose and prosecute his business, and to use all that he attains by it, to render service to man. Higher ideals of life are created; men live for higher ends, and seek better things. The coarse and vulgarizing influence of the greed of gain abates, and, instead, "sweetness and light" pervade society. The tendency to inequality is arrested, and society advances towards equality, because all are engaged in productive, and therefore legitimate, business, and prosecute it as stewards of God's grace and for the service of man; and equality is ultimately realized, so far as the diversities of talent, and of diligence and skill in the use of talent and opportunity, permit. The evils growing in our civilization can be removed only by obedience to the Christian law of service. The progress of society is possible only so far as the individual members of society become freely conformed to the spirit and law of Christ.[1]

III. It remains to Determine the Dividing Line between Selfishness and Christian Benevolence.

1. Worldly business is not necessarily worldliness. Money is not an evil, but a good, indispensable in every enterprise, Christian or unchristian; and it is every man's duty to strive to acquire it. It is not money, but the love of money, which Paul says is a root of all evil. It is not proof of covetousness that a man is diligent in business, rising early and working late and working hard; nor that he is frugal, and eats the bread of carefulness; nor that his business absorbs his thoughts, his interest, and his energy; nor that he rejoices in success and is grieved at failure; nor that he is successful, and rapidly accumulating property. Because forecast, diligence, concentration, and energy are essential to success in all undertakings. Thoughtlessness, negligence, indolence cannot succeed; and on them Christianity pronounces no blessing. Besides, a man's business is his life-work; and if it is worthy to be his life-work, it is worthy of the concentration on it of his thoughts, his interest, and

[1] The terrible history of Communism in Paris confirms the views here presented. Dr. Maudsley advances the opinion, and maintains it at considerable length, that the existing greed of gain is a cause of insanity, and also is causing a physical degeneracy of the race. — Physiology and Pathology of the Mind, pp. 205, 206.

his energy. A man's business is like a warfare; and he feels an interest like that of a general in planning his campaigns and marshalling his forces, and similar joy in victory and sorrow in defeat. All these are characteristics of efficiency in business, not of covetousness.

Covetousness is not merely, as commonly defined, an excessive desire of acquisition. The difference between covetousness and Christian justice and benevolence is not of degree, but of kind.

Covetousness is the desire of gain for selfish ends, and not for its uses in the service of man. If a man is doing business simply to make money, he is covetous.

When Jesus says: "Take heed and beware of covetousness," he uses a Greek word, which literally means, a grasping for more. And this is a peculiarity of covetousness; it is a desire for more, rather than a desire for much; a desire to be richer, rather than a desire to be rich. A rich man who has riches already and a poor man who never expects to be rich may be equally covetous, grasping for more. This is the wolf in the breast, always ravening and always hungry; the fire in the soul, to which every acquisition is fuel, making it burn more fiercely.

The philosophy of it is this. In the nature of man is a radical and indestructible impulse to put forth his energies in action, to push out in every direction to his utmost capacity. A man's business is the work which he has chosen for life, in which this radical impulse must find sphere and scope. The success of any enterprise gives him joy, because it is a triumph of his skill and energy, and not necessarily because it is an acquisition of gain. But the very acquisition furnishes means for further and larger enterprise, and thus stimulates the impulse to further risk and larger undertakings. So that, however large the acquisitions, the man is still driven to strive for more, with the same forecast, frugality, and energy which have hitherto insured success; and to this the power of habit is added, impelling to continued action in the same direction.

The blame here does not rest on the impulse to enterprise; for that lies at the very root of our natures. Nor does the blame attach to the indestructibleness and insatiableness of the impulse; for these are inherent in it as a radical impulse of nature. The impulse to action, the same grasping for more, appears in Christian beneficence. Success in one Christian work stimulates to effort in another. The soul is insatiable in its zeal to do good. It is driven to new toils and new achievements. Xavier, thinking he served God by his own sufferings, when enduring severe privations and suffering, cried: "More, Lord, more." Paul counted it all joy to take the spoiling of his goods, or whatever suffering was incidental to his missionary enterprises, and was planning a mission to Spain, ever pressing on to enlarge the sphere of his Christian enterprise. A man who in the work of his life does not find his nature crying out for more, and driving him to new work, and does not find in that "fresh fields and pastures new," is enervated; so far his manhood is spent out of him. So profoundly is it true that a man is not to be ministered unto, but to minister; his blessedness is not by being indulged and receiving, but by achievement.

So far as eagerness and insatiableness in the enterprises of business are the result of the natural impulse to action they are not blameworthy. The blameworthiness is that the covetous man spends his energies for himself. He may hoard his gains, or invest them in larger enterprises, or use them to gain office or power, or spend them in ostentation and luxury. But in every case it is for self, using his superiority to insure being ministered unto, not to minister to others. Thus, working only for himself, he is like a steam-engine of a thousand horse power, driven night and day to manufacture fuel to feed its own fires.

2. The law of service is not fulfilled merely by consecrating to benevolence a part, however large, of the income. The business itself and its whole income are consecrated. Christianity teaches stewardship; we are not our own, but bought with a price; we are stewards of the manifold grace of God.

In every action, investment, and expenditure we are to determine how we can best use the powers and possessions which God has intrusted to us for the establishment of his kingdom on earth.

3. The line between benevolence and selfishness is not to be drawn between what one expends on himself and his family and what he gives away. This line is not marked by outward acts. What you expend on yourself and your family need not be expended selfishly. It ought to be expended in Christian consecration and benevolence as really as what is given away.

It may be, and probably is, the use of money by which you most effectively benefit mankind. To take the lowest view possible, it is relieving society from the support of so many persons. The division of society into families is the best possible constitution of society, and insures the most rapid and abundant creation of wealth. It also is the best possible arrangement for the promotion of intelligence, culture, and piety. To create a happy home — one of the many happy homes which make a happy people, to create a well-ordered Christian home — one of the many which make a Christian people, is to render the greatest and best service to society. On the other hand, if in expenditure on yourself and your family you are seeking only your own gratification, only ostentation and display, only to have everything pleasant about you, only to be ministered unto, however lavish you may be, the very lavishness is but the outshining of selfishness.

4. Is a Christian justified in expending money on himself and his family beyond procuring the necessaries of life? And if so, how far may he incur expense for enjoyment and luxury, or for developing and satisfying the taste for beauty and the desires which belong to culture and refinement?

The mass of human misery is so great as to overtop all individual resources. When one thinks of himself as a debtor to all mankind, as much as in him lies, to render them service, the first impression may naturally be that he must literally divest himself of all his goods, and reduce his personal expenses to the measure of bare necessity. This train of thought is met at once by another equally sweeping and obvious — that, if carried out, it puts a stop to civilization, and reduces us to the wigwam and the blanket. In this line of thought, different persons stop at different points. A common stopping-place has been that a Christian ought not to wear jewelry. But the same line of argument would forbid expenditures for pictures or other ornaments in the house, for a flower-garden which might be more lucrative in potatoes, for any dress more costly than the cheapest which is sufficient for warmth and decency. On this principle a parishioner of mine reached a correct conclusion, who, being informed that a savage tribe at a mission-station were beginning to wear shirts, expressed his regret that they should be subjected to the needless expense and trouble. In seeking a principle by which to answer our question, some light may be obtained by considering two marked types of civilization, expressing respectively the life of indulgence and the life of service.

The highest form in which the former of these two types can appear is the civilization of aesthetic culture and luxurious refinement — a luxuriousness that delights appreciatively in wit, literature, and art; a civilization like that of which Burke says "that vice lost half its evil by losing all its grossness" — words more epigrammatic than true. Aesthetic culture is the highest possible form of this type of civilization. The emotion of beauty is non-moral, that is, it precludes selfish desire and the consideration of uses, ends, and duty. It is never didactic, but regards the expression of things. A feast tastefully arranged is beautiful; we say it is too beautiful to be eaten. When appetite comes in, the veil of beauty drops off, and there remains only a mass of victuals. It is this non-ethical character of aesthetic emotion which makes it compatible with a life of indulgence, and aesthetic culture the highest form of that type of civilization.

The best example is the civilization of ancient Greece. "Athenian life was a sunny, unanxious, careless, pagan life; unguided by any high code of duties, unvexed by the dread of the future which should demand the discipline of self-denial; without a thought, or even a comprehension, of that purity to which the Hebrew legislation pointed with unfailing finger, and which made the central mandate in the ethics of Israel. Greek life was a life of the exchange, the academy, the circus, the bath. It was a breezy, open-air life, which guarded the body from disease and the mind from morbidity, which habituated the intelligence to delight in the subtilty of the Socratic dialectics, and which hourly placed before the sculptor consummate models of human beauty. Undisturbed by the fierce promptings of religious zeal, the mind naturally turned with sunny complacency to the worship of that beauty which was written everywhere on sky, on sea, on hillside, and the forms of men and women." To such a civilization the moral earnestness of the Hebrew scriptures would be simply incomprehensible. When preached in the gospel of Christ, it was to the Greek foolishness. The aesthetic mind of the Greek could not receive, much less originate, the idea of a kingdom of heaven on earth, of missions for the conversion of the world, or even for the propagation of moral ideas and reformations, of the indebtedness of every man to render service to mankind, and the consecration of life and all its powers and possessions to that service. All these conceptions were totally foreign to his thought; they could be received only by quickening a new life, which would unfold into a new type of civilization.

The religion possible in such a civilization must be a religion of beauty — either a pagan religion, like that of the Greeks, peopling the heavens and the earth with gods full of passionate, roystering life, and giving to every mountain, tree, and spring its nymph; or else pantheism, concerned with God only as the infinite expressing itself in all that is; never as a Lawgiver, forbidding sin and enjoining duty; much less as a Redeemer, saving men from sin and quickening them to work with him in establishing his reign of righteousness on the earth.

The most striking example of this type of character in modern times is Goethe, intent on personal culture, but hard and cold as polished marble; more interested in a controversy of the French Academy than in the French Revolution and the wars incident to it which were changing the political ideas and destiny of Europe; paying court to the conqueror of his own country so as to awaken the conqueror's contempt — a striking contrast to Fichte, who, when his course of instruction was interrupted by the invasion, dismissed his class with the inspiriting words: "Gentlemen, these lectures will be resumed in a free country."

The doctrine that the highest end of man is personal culture is a form of the error that man's blessedness is found in receiving, and not in giving, in being ministered unto, and not in ministering. It is the highest and most refined form in which the error can appear, and the civilization resulting may have great refinement and elegance; but it is incompatible with the Christian law of service; the civilization which it develops is essentially the development of selfishness, and will inevitably disclose the defects and wrongs which are inseparable from the error of which it is the development.

The other type of civilization is that in which the moral element predominates. Everything is considered in reference to its ends or uses; duty occupies the thoughts; everything is under law and subject to retribution; life is a life of service, not of indulgence. The Hebrew and the Puritan are examples.

According to this type of civilization, blessedness is possible only in the realization of moral ideas. Whoever misses this is a lost man. It considers all human interests only in relation to right and wrong; it enforces duty; it demands rights; it resists injustice and oppression; it seeks to bring the whole world into conformity with moral law; it expects progress; it looks on history as a panorama in which truth and right are contending with error and wrong, and advancing with brightening glory to control the world. Therefore it generates intense earnestness of purpose, contempt for ease, indulgence, and luxury, the consecration of life to the realization of moral ends.

Such a civilization is necessarily propagandist. Missions to establish moral and religious ideas are inconceivable in a civilization of indulgence, whatever its culture and aesthetic refinement; they are essential and inevitable in a civilization in which the moral element predominates. Müller says that Boodhism teaches a purer and more complete morality than any outside of the New Testament; and it is they onl form of heathenism which has been a missionary religion. Mohammedism, borrowing from Christianity a moral element, and especially proclaiming the unity and spirituality of God in antagonism to the idolatry of corrupt Christian churches, was intensely propagandist, though by the sword, rather than by truth and love. The moral element predominated in the earlier history of the Roman republic; and, though the Roman *virtus* is hardly worthy to be called virtue in the light of Christ's teaching, yet, as distinguishing the Roman civilization from the aesthetic refinement of Greece, it made Rome a conqueror, carrying over the Western world the Roman law. Christianity is essentially moral; and it alone commissions preachers to go into all the world and preach the gospel to every creature.

In history this type of civilization has often been one-sided and defective. It spreads a certain gloom over society. Law supreme, universal, inexorable, broken by all; penalty terrible and inevitable, hang glooming and threatening over the world. Beneath its shadow pleasure is an impertinence, the interests of earthly life trivial, secular business an intrusion; worldliness is driven out by "other-worldliness"; the sunny cheerfulness of life fades before the intensity of the sense of duty and responsibility; weariness of life falls on the soul; and asceticism drives men to deserts and monasteries for the mortification of the flesh. The very absoluteness of the truth demands an acceptance complete and unhesitating; the very supremacy of the law demands uncompromising obedience. But the unlimited faith and uncompromiisng obedience of the believer pass into imperiousness in enforcing a like faith and obedience on others. The gay indifference of the aesthetic Greek to the opinions and religions of others gives place to an intense solicitude in the presence of a religion claiming to be the only and universal religion, and of a law of right which is the only and universal law. That solicitude passes into intolerance. Heresy is hunted by inquisitions, conformity is enforced by persecution, and the true faith propagated by crusades. When the progress of Christianity puts an end to these, still zeal for doctrine eats out love to persons; intolerance usurps the place of fidelity; and, in forgetfulness that persons are the proper objects of love, theological hatred, calumny, and proscription in the interest of truth are accepted as expressions of Christian zeal.

Thus this moral type of civilization puts on both a certain moroseness and a certain fierceness. Its iconoclasm comes to be directed against the joyous and beautiful because they are such, and by being such prove themselves earthly and idolatrous. And its missionary zeal becomes intolerance and cruelty.

Christian civilization belongs to that type in which the moral forces predominate. But it brings these moral forces into action in a manner peculiar to itself. It does not put foremost truth and law, but God, the Redeemer of the lost sinner; it does not put foremost zeal for truth and the sense of duty as the inspiration of the new life, but faith in God, the Redeemer of sinners, and love to God who redeems, and to man for whom Christ died. Here, then, in Christianity, is that which saves the moral type of civilization from the gloom, intolerance, and severity which so often have characterized it. The moral life, vitalized by faith and acting in love, is no longer one-sided and defective, but complete, comprehending all that belongs to the blessedness of man.

The Christian life springs from the sense of sin and condemnation. From this the sinner is delivered when he sees God's redeeming love in Christ. In that faith the gloom of the law and of condemnation passes away; the life becomes trustful, hopeful, and joyous; the old Greek joyousness reappears, intensified and made spiritual — not now the joy of forgetfulness of God and his law, but joy which springs up, through faith in God's redeeming love, after acquaintance with God and the law has awakened the moral nature and the sense of sin. The moral type now appears, not in the inquisitor or the crusader or the ascetic, but in the Christ-like man, with all the earnestness of the inquisitor and the crusader and the ascetic, but also like a little child, living a life of simplicity, trustfulness, and joy, and, like Jesus himself, full of tender compassion and self-sacrificing love to sinners. Inspired by this faith and love, the man in whom the moral element predominates is no longer indifferent to secular interests and weary of life, no longer stern and intolerant in the consciousness only of law; but, like Christ, is sensitive to every human interest, taking children in his arms and blessing them, ministering to the sick, comforting the bereaved, helping the fallen in their efforts to rise, joyous at a wedding, teaching the principles of Christian civilization, alive to every interest of man.

The advancement of Christ's kingdom is not linear only, in the conversion of souls, but also diffusive, advancing in completeness and power. Civilization is said to multiply human wants. This is only another way of saying that it multiplies the powers and capacities of the man. To withhold satisfaction to these wants is to undo the development of the man, and to reduce him to his original infantile and savage state. Christianity must show itself the religion of civilization, competent by its vital force in a savage community to quicken progress to civilization, competent in civilization to stimulate, purify, guide, and ennoble it.

Christianity, then, is not to repress the culture, the refinement, the aotivity, and manifold development of man, but to vitalize and Christianize it. And thus it reacts, and accelerates its linear advancement. Christian interest in the progress of humanity, in the highest human culture, in all that pertains to human welfare, is itself a powerful recommendation of Christianity and an important influence in quickening men to a new spiritual life.

With this train of thought the true idea of the beautiful accords. Beauty is perfection — an ideal of the mind, expressed in the concrete. Goodness and truth, therefore, when manifested in finite things, are beautiful. When the expression is of that which transcends our power of conception, the emotion of the beautiful passes into the sublime. Hence the close affinity between the admiration of beauty and the awe of the sublime, and adoration. A moral movement which excludes the beautiful is defective and self-destructive; as if a tree in an effort to multiply its fruit should shake off the glory of leaf and blossom and the golden and blushing beauty of the fruit. Beauty is the bloom of truth and goodness; it is their radiance, their glow, their smile.

Therefore, within the scope of Christianity there is room for expending money, time, and talent on any work essential to the culture, development, and well-being of man. Civilization of the most intensely moral type does not exclude aesthetic culture. Its defectiveness in the Hebrew and the Puritan was the result of the incompleteness, rather than the completeness, of the moral life. It was because morality came in the awfulness of law, rather than in the freedom of Christian faith and love, and even as love, in the Puritan, concentrating attention on the conflict with wrongs and oppressions immediately urgent, so as to leave no time for the completeness of human culture.

But Christian love, when completely manifested, must bloom in beauty. When the gospel has free course, it must be glorified. The limping god of work is the one who wins and marries the goddess of beauty. The moral force which

Christianity has made a power in civilization is essentially an energy of reform and progress. As love to man, it is diffusive, and not restrictive, concerned with the interests of man, not conservative of the privileges of a class. There is, necessarily, a certain severity about it in some of its conditions. Sweeping away the tyranny and debauchery of courts and aristocracies, it cannot well avoid sweeping away with them their elegance, refinement, and aesthetic culture. But as its purifying and renovating force works out its legitimate results, it gradually diffuses through the whole people the refinement and culture once limited to a few. And this accords with prophecy: "The wilderness and the solitary place shall be glad for them, and the desert shall rejoice and blossom as the rose. Instead of the thorn shall come up the fir-tree, and instead of the brier shall come up the myrtle-tree. And I will make the place of my feet glorious."

But, while Christian civilization is to beautify itself with aesthetic culture, no man has a right to live in luxury and self-indulgence, using his powers only for his own enjoyment. Whatever he does, he must do it in Christian service. It is right to break the alabaster box of precious ointment; but it must be broken on the Saviour's feet; and it must be the spontaneous outpouring of Christian love, not a substitute for that love, nor for Christian toil in saving men from sin. Peter, John, and Paul would not have converted the world by breaking alabaster boxes of perfume.

# LECTURE IX.

## CHARACTERISTICS OF THE GROWTH OF CHRIST'S KINGDOM.

THE progress of Christ's kingdom is *extensive*, so far as it gains new converts and Christianizes new peoples; it is *intensive*, so far as it advances the sanctification of its converts, and develops a higher type of piety and a more Christian civilization. Some characteristics of this progress will now be considered.

I. It is Spiritual.

It is spiritual in the sense that it is the work of God's Spirit. God's redeeming love is not merely a bland accessibleness if any choose to seek him — a mild rainbow over his throne, encouraging any who venture to brave the darkness and clouds that are round about him. It is an energy of redeeming grace, the Spirit of holiness, working in human history, enlightening, striving, life-giving, reproving, comforting. The progress of the kingdom is the constant product and manifestation of the ever-present and prevailing energy of the Holy Spirit.

It is spiritual, also, in the sense that it is the progress of spiritual life in men — the life of faith and love that centres on Christ and his cross.

Hence, so far as man's agency is concerned, the progress of the kingdom is by action in faith; and the life of faith is a life of inspiration and enthusiasm, rather than of prudence and calculation. The believer has courage to attempt whatever God has had grace to promise. In the words of Bishop Hall: "Faith is never so glorious as when she hath most opposition, and will not see it. Reason looks ever to the means; faith, to the end; and, instead of consulting how to effect, resolves what shall be effected." The very obstacles become a stimulus to effort: "I will tarry at Ephesus; for a great door and effectual is opened unto me, and *there are many adversaries.*"

II. The Progress of the Kingdom is by the Instrumentality of the Gospel.

It is the historical gospel of redemption through Christ and the Holy Spirit, as distinguished from abstract truth. "I determined not to know anything among you, save Jesus Christ and him crucified." Rationalism treats Christianity, which is a divine action redeeming men from sin, as if it were only a process of thought; as if its whole aim were the analysis and systemization of truth to the intellect. It regards historical Christianity as the lantern, not as the light, and breaks the lantern that the light may shine more clearly. The result is that the light is blown out. The gospel must indeed be apprehended by the intellect. It presupposes the truths of religion and morals which men may know without revelation. Man, as a rational being, must interpret the facts of the gospel, and define their significance to his intellect; must harmonize them with the truths of natural religion, with the principles of reason, and with all knowledge. This produces theology, which is the gospel interpreted, analyzed, and systemized by and for the intellect. But the gospel does not terminate in the intellect, nor exist only as a process of thought. It is addressed to the heart. It is thought transformed into life. And it is only in its historical origin and influence that it is rightly understood. Christianity is like the sun, whose warmth and light are dependent on being held in the earth's atmosphere and reflected from its surface. To rise above the earth's atmosphere in order to get nearer to the sun is to lose his warmth and light. So philosophy, rising above the historical and human to come nearer to God, finds, in the dizzy heights of speculation, darkness and cold.

While, then, it is necessary to man, as a rational being, to define and interpret the gospel to the intellect and translate it into systematic theology, there is inherent in so doing the danger of falling into a rationalistic habit, and regarding Christianity as a philosophy. Especially should there be caution against this danger in theological seminaries, in which the student is necessarily occupied in defining, interpreting, vindicating, and systemizing the gospel to the intellect. There is danger that he come to be interested in the mere intellectual investigation of truth, rather than in Christianity as the power of life to sinners; that a *dilettanteism* of interest in philosophy and literature displace the earnestness of Christian interest in men and Christian zeal to bring sinners to Christ; or, in a different direction, that the spirit of controversy and the eagerness of theological discussion displace Christian love to men and interest in the minister's appropriate work of saving men from sin. There is danger, also, that the student be entangled and held powerless in his own speculations; so many are the questions suggested in defining, interpreting, and systemizing the facts of Christianity, and so severe and protracted the intellectual effort in the process, that they become associated in the student's mind with the facts of the gospel; and the life-giving truths come to his mind not in the freshness, simplicity, and power of the gospel, but as the nucleus of questions and difficulties, of metaphysical distinctions and nice adjustments of thought; and he is entangled and held fast in the bristling *chevaux-de-frise* which his thinking has constructed around every truth of the gospel. There is danger that he be rationalistic, regarding Christianity only as a process of thought, and finding its whole significance in the definition of truth to the intellect. So, also, the history of Christianity must be studied as a history of doctrine. But there is danger in so studying it that the student come to regard the determination of doctrine as the great work which Christianity has accomplished in the past, as the entire significance of its history. In one age it determined the doctrine of the Trinity; in others, successively, the doctrines of sin, of atonement, of justification by faith, until, as an eminent living divine has said, there remains nothing to be determined by the church of the future but the Christian doctrine of the church itself. But the history of the church is not found merely in the history of doctrine, but also in ideals which in Christ have become powers in the world, in confessions and martyrdoms, in missions and charities, in self-denial and heroism, in Christian experience of penitence, faith, and love, in triumphs over death, in the progress of justice, and of Christian customs, laws, and institutions, in reformations and the growth of Christian civilization.

Accordingly, the gospel does not address itself merely to the intellect, and especially not to the observing, analyzing, and classifying faculties, which positive science exclusively addresses. It addresses itself to the faith, to the moral nature, to the spiritual necessities, aspirations, and intuitions. This Paul recognizes in his preaching: "Commending ourselves to every man's conscience in the sight of God." Jesus recognizes it: "If any man will do his will, he shall know of the doctrine." And the intimations of the moral and spiritual nature are as trustworthy as those of our observing and comparing faculties; for they are of the very core of our being; and if they are false, the whole being is vitiated with falsehood. There is, then, a philosophical basis for the answer of an unlettered candidate for the ministry, who, when asked at his examination for ordination: "What proof have you that Christ is divine?" answered, with tears: "Why, bless you, he has saved my soul." And if the keen definition and proof of truth by and to the intellect is separated from the knowledge and evidence of spiritual experience, and we are obliged to choose which of the two is the safer preparation for preaching the gospel, I should not hesitate to choose the latter: "Blessed are they that have not seen, and yet have believed."

It follows that the effectual preaching of the gospel is more than the clear presentation of the truth from the intellect to the intellect. Education is not only the impartation of knowledge and of intellectual discipline; it is also inspiration. And the effective preaching of the gospel is an inspiration to the hearer. But he who inspires another must live and breathe himself. All inspiration is vital. It is from the heart to the heart. The soul itself is the only vehicle which will convey spiritual truth from man to man. Even God, making his love a power in human history, brings it in a human soul. Preaching is not a mere intellectual process; it is not a mere thinking; it is an action — the action of the whole man on his fellowmen. Lecky notices "the extremely small influence of definite argument in determining the opinions either of an individual or of a nation." It is faith, love, service, life, rather than argument, which convey the truth as a power of life to human hearts. Lord Bacon says: "Truth prints goodness." One cannot easily read lead types; an imprint must be taken off. Goodness is the imprint by which truth is read. The power of the primitive church was not merely the power of convincing argument and eloquent speaking; it was rather the power of the Christian life of faith and love.

III. The Progress of Christ's Kingdom is not to be promoted by Force.

Our Saviour says: "All they that take the sword shall perish with the sword." Institutions founded on force shall be overthrown by force. Institutions that are to be permanent must be founded on truth and right. Institutions resting on force must fall before superior force. If Christ's kingdom rested on force, it would be subject to the same law, and in some great convulsion of society would be sure to pass away. But it is founded on truth and love. Force moves in a different sphere from these, and cannot destroy them. Therefore it is a kingdom which cannot be moved. It can decay only when Christ's redeeming love falters, and justice and love die out of the heart of man. The history of the world has been a continuous demonstration of the truth of our Saviour's words down to the overthrow of American slavery. There is no real progress except so far as truth establishes itself in men's convictions, and love rules in their hearts.

The state itself may not use force for the propagation of religion and good morals. Admit in any instance the duty or even the right of government to propagate religious and moral ideas by the sword, and you admit all that is terrible in persecutions and crusades.

IV. The Progress of Christ's Kingdom is without Observation.

The growth of the kingdom is not manifested merely in the organization. Statistical tables of the number of churches, of communicants, and of ministers are but imperfect indications of the extent and power of Christ's kingdom. Its growth is in the inward experience of the soul. Whenever any human soul is quickened to penitence for sin and faith in Christ, it is a growth of the kingdom of God. And in society, every Christian truth which establishes itself in human thought and begins to control the life, every removal of an unchristian custom, every elevation of human sentiment, every transformation of an institution into accordance with Christianity is an advance of Christ's kingdom. Thus the progress is in its nature without observation. Souls are born into the new life; Christian ideas take their place in human thought; and men, intent on their worldly schemes, take no note of them; just as the workman, plodding homewards his weary way, takes no note of the stars which come out, one by one, and take their place in the evening sky. The kingdom is in the world, transforming the world into itself, as the mustard-seed is in the soil, transforming it into its own substance, and organizing it into the silently growing life and beauty of the plant. Thus pass years, of the results of which the statistician can make but a meagre report; but when they are gone we are surprised at the extent and power of the advance of Christian thought.

V. The Progress of the Kingdom is Providential.

God does not leave his truth to go out alone to its conflict with error; he goes before it in his providence. Indeed, it is not merely that his providential working in history is parallel with his work of redemption; it is rather that his work of redemption is his work in human history, and what we call his providential action in history is only incidental thereto.

God goes before and with Christian workers now, in his providence, as he used to go before and with his people in miracles. The Christian may work in obscurity; but God notes his work with loving interest. He may be opposed by men; but he is a laborer together with God. A providence silent and unseen works with him while he works, and for him while he sleeps; corrects what he does imperfectly, and completes what he leaves unfinished, and so gives to feeble beginnings a strange success, to obscure endeavors a world-wide emblazoning, and on counsels of faith and love which had seemed foolish and rash brings out at last the stamp of a wisdom beyond the age; and schemes at which contemporaries had sneered, posterity honors as evincing insight and inspiration from on high. It is common for Christian workers to find the way strangely prepared before them through obstacles seemingly insurmountable, as to the Israelites through the Red Sea. Even the beast of whom it was said: "The Lord hath need of him," had its way strewn with garments and palm-leaves. Where there is God's work to be done, there is God to do it. A little church in Scotland, harassed by persecution and ready to despair, wrote to Rutherford for advice whether they should give up. He answered: "So long as there is any of the Lord's lost money in your town, he won't put out the candle."

God's providential action is a perpetual proof of his continued redemptive action. Even miracles are scarcely so decisive proofs of his presence, or so lasting in their influence. Elijah brought fire from heaven, and consumed the priests of Baal; but the fire had scarcely ceased to burn when the idolatry was resumed, and Elijah fled in despair to Horeb. Luther did not bring fire from heaven; but the Protestant Reformation as really demonstrated the divine presence, and its influence has continued to this day. Moses opened the Red Sea to the Israelites. No miracle-working rod was stretched over the ocean when the Pilgrims came to Plymouth; but the presence of God with them working in the interest of his kingdom is scarcely less evident than at the Red Sea.

Equally significant God's providence in removing seemingly immovable obstacles. American slavery vanished like a cloud in the presence of the very generation who were declaring its removal impracticable. The temporal power of the Pope scarcely arrested attention when it passed away. The great men of the world do still, as a prophet declared of an Assyrian king, accomplish God's plans, though they intend it not: "He meaneth not so, neither doth his heart think so; but it is in his heart to destroy and cut off nations not a few"; but he is "the rod of mine anger and the staff in the hand of my indignation."

God's hand is revealed not merely in great epochs, but also in the quiet advancement of his kingdom. This is exemplified in the growth of what is called the spirit of the age; so that the leaders in any great historical movement seem not so much the authors of the movement, as the mouth-piece to utter the common thought, and the hand to execute the common purpose of the age. All history shows that the great epochs of history are not instantaneous in their origin. Though their coming is sudden and startling, yet it is the result of growth — the opening of a flower which for a century has been maturing — the bursting from its chrysalis of the winged Psyche which in all its transformations has been silently preparing its birth of beauty. Every great change attempted for which God's providence has not wrought a preparation will be but a new patch on an old garment. The silent preparation for the great epochs which burst on the astonished world is as decisive a proof of God's presence in history as the epoch itself; as the growth of the bud reveals God's power not less than its opening into blossom.

Another example is the growth of interests, customs, and institutions incidentally favorable to the growth of the kingdom. When the first American missionaries went to India, the British power seemed the greatest obstacle. But it has exerted influences essential to the missionary work which it was entirely impossible for the missionaries to exert. It is said that Constantine embraced Christianity for reasons of state polity; but how had it come to pass that it was politic for him so to do? It is said that Luther could not have succeeded without the aid of the German princes; but how came it to pass that the German princes found it expedient to aid him? As the lictors with axes and staves went before the Roman consul to open a way for him, and to enforce his commands, God in his providence compels princes and all secular agencies to open the way for Christian truth. It has been said that the Puritans came to New England not for religious interests, but to engage in fisheries. Suppose the allegation to be true, what then? Then God in his providence disclosed valuable fisheries in the interest of his kingdom to bring to New England a Christian, Protestant, and republican civilization; "the earth helped the woman"; providence worked with redemption. Then these Puritans, while intent in all simplicity on getting an honest livelihood by fishing, were so full of Christian truth and life as to send out incidentally, as sparks fly from hot iron simply because it is hot, the education, political liberty, and religion of New England. It would enhance our estimate of their piety and intelligence, if they were so full of spiritual light and life that these were but the unpremeditated and spontaneous results of their living and working for secular ends, and so the salvation of the world was a second time connected with fishing; just as it would enhance our estimate of the fulness of miraculous power in Peter to know that his shadow would heal the sick on whom it fell, when he without thought of exerting that power was going to the baker's to buy his daily bread, as really as when he purposely determined to work a miracle.

It has been said that modern progress is due to the fact that science, since Bacon, has been directed to practical ends, and thus has multiplied inventions; that the sentiment of brotherhood and opposition to war is due to commerce, steamships, and telegraphs; that the opposition to slavery and the honor given to labor are due to the industrial movement which is so remarkable a characteristic of modern civilization. But the question recurs: How has it come to pass that Christian civilization has produced a Bacon, stimulated invention, created an industrial movement, and in every line of action concentrated thought on human welfare; while heathen civilization has never produced such results, or shown any tendency to produce them? Was it not the fresh figs which commerce brought from Carthage which fired the Romans to destroy that city? Why does commerce in Christian civilization create the sentiment of brotherhood, and discourage war, when it had no such influence, and even a contrary influence, in ancient times? The answer must acknowledge Christianity as the cause, and not the effect. These facts disclose God's providence working with redemption, and bringing secular interests, customs, institutions, and agencies to aid in the advancement of his kingdom.

The fact of God's providential action in subserviency to redemption teaches two practical lessons. One is that when God's Spirit rouses a people to any Christian work, it is a reasonable presumption that in his providence he will open the way for them to do it. When his Spirit say: "Go forwards," his providence will divide the sea. The history of any signal enterprise of the church is found to be full of signal interpositions of providence. The history of missions, of God's church in America, of Christianity everywhere, is a continued verification of God's providential action in the interest of his kingdom. The same is remarkable in the lives of individuals eminent in piety. The attempt has been made to explain the frequency of providential interpositions in the lives of such men by saying that they who look for providences will not fail to find them. A sufficient explanation is found in the harmony between God's Spirit and his providence. When God by his Spirit rouses a man to work, by his providence he opens the way for him. He that will work for God will be permitted to work with God.

The other practical lesson is, to concentrate missionary labor on fields where God is providentially preparing the way for it. We must not waste our energies toiling all the night and taking nothing, but must let down the net on the right side of the ship. He that believeth will not make haste to outrun the providence of God, nor will he dare to lag behind it.

VI. The progress of Christ's Kingdom is by epochs.

There is a certain rhythmical movement attendant on the exertion of physical force. When force is at its greatest tension, the quivering or vibration is apparent to the sense. Something analogous appears in the exertion of spiritual power, pulsating in waves through the life of humanity. Even revelation has its epochs. There are epochs of miracles — one more, at least, yet to appear in connection with the second coming of the Lord. There are epochs of prophetic inspiration. The same is true of all spiritual life. The Christian reverts to memorable epochs in his own experience — conversion; subsequent to conversion, epochs when he has risen to higher planes of thought and action. A church grows by revivals. The advance of Christ's kingdom in the world and the progress of Christian civilization is by epochs memorable in history.

This accords with the Saviour's analogy — first the blade, then the ear, after that the full corn in the ear. The growth of grain is continuous; but it is also by epochs — the blade, the ear, the full corn. In maize, for example, is first the blade, then the stalk marked by its successive joints, the tasselling and silking, the setting of the corn, its ripening, and the opening of the husk from the full ear.

1. The epochs are not themselves the growth of the kingdom, but are the results of the growth by which it is signalized. The grain grows continuously. The successive epochs of the blade, the ear, the full corn, are not the growth, but the result and manifestation of growth. They are the new forms in which the advancing life must manifest itself. They are the crises which mark the growth. So the continuous vital growth of a Christian or a church will manifest itself in new and higher forms of Christian life, and thus will create epochs. Epochs, therefore, are crises incidental to growth; but they are not the growth, nor is the growth confined to them.

2. An epoch is not necessarily by violence. When an apple-tree bursts into blossom, and covers itself with sweetness and beauty, that is an epoch in its growth. When this beauty passes away, and the fruit sets, that is an epoch; in this case attended with the falling of the blossom, cast off because its work is done. But these epochs are peaceful, because all the organic forces in the tree are subject to its life and in harmony with each other, and the crises of its growth come peacefully, as the natural expression of the life. So in the kingdom of God, if the spiritual life is full and unobstructed, its epochs come quietly, as the blooming and fruiting of a tree. The old falls away because its work is done, and peacefully gives place to the new. The change is not less, the epoch not less glorious, because it is peaceful. Revolutions and convulsions are not essential, nor desirable, in the great epochs of human progress. And in the individual, the spiritual life may blossom into the glory of a higher Christian experience, or, dropping the blossom, may concentrate itself on perfecting the fruit, without an attendant spiritual convulsion driving to the verge of despair. In general, the more completely the spiritual life possesses the soul, the more peaceful will be its successive epochs of growth; and the more completely Christian ideas rule society, the more peaceful will be the successive epochs of advancing Christian civilization.

3. Christ's kingdom is not responsible for the violence and revolution which are incidental to the epochs in its progress, and are occasioned by the opposition of the kingdom of darkness.

The kingdom of darkness is always in antagonism to the kingdom of light. It is founded and perpetuated in selfishness, and therefore powerful interests become enlisted in perpetuating its abuses, and in resisting the progress of the truth. Hence any epoch in the progress of Christ's kingdom is liable to encounter violent and bloody opposition, and the advancement of Christ's kingdom may be in the midst of revolution and convulsion. In reference to this our Saviour said: "I came not to send peace, but a sword." But the responsibility for the evil rests not on the progress of Christ's kingdom, but on the opposition to its progress and the selfish endeavor forcibly to perpetuate error and wrong. Vigorous maintenance of Christian truth and right, and opposition to prevailing error and wickedness provoke opposition; and the opposition is intensified, for the time being, as the vigor of Christian action increases; but truth and righteousness and love are not responsible for the opposition which they occasion.

It must be added, however, that if Christian fidelity is constant and uniform, as well as vigorous, there will be less danger that the opposition culminate in violence; for it will not have opportunity to gain strength and enlist the interests of society in its behalf. Negro slavery, for example, might easily have been excluded from the American colonies in the outset, if Christians had been clear-sighted to discern its evil, and decided in opposing it. Lack of spiritual discernment, unfaithfulness, and spiritual declension make Christians remiss in exposing and resisting evil, and thus the liability to violence and convulsion in the epochs of Christian progress is increased. The wicked are God's sword to punish the community which connives at their wickedness, or is negligent of Christianizing the people. Every ignorant person whom the community has neglected to educate, every drunkard who poisons the air with his breath, every debauchee who corrupts the young, is a sword in the hand of the Almighty to punish the remissness which has taken no pains to train them aright. Every blasphemer who hardens the young in irreverence, every worldling who stupefies men's nobler sentiments and accustoms them to honor successful sordidness, every knave who blurs the sharp line between right and wrong and makes fraud familiar and respectable, every oppressor who gilds tyranny with prosperity and deadens the sensibility to human rights, every pretender who reconciles men to shams and weakens the sturdiness of sincerity and truthfulness, is a sword in the hands of God to punish men for remissness in Christian duty. The iniquity by toleration acquires strength, enlists powerful interests in its perpetuation, and renders certain and terrible the convulsion and violence attendant on putting it away.

The charge is often made that the Protestant Reformation carried the revolution in its bosom, and is responsible for the revolutionary and disorganizing tendencies of recent times; while it is claimed that the Romish church is the steadfast conservator of government, order, and tranquility. It may be admitted that Protestantism, coming necessarily in the form of a protest against error and wrong, assumed an antagonistic attitude, and has been the occasion of revolution and convulsion. Yet the responsibility does not attach to Protestantism, but, according to the principle just now explained, to the Romish church, which allowed error, superstition, and oppression to usurp the place of truth, piety, and justice. "It must needs be that offences come; but woe to that man by whom the offence cometh." The woe is not on the truth, nor on its preachers, but on him who by his alliance with error and wrong makes the preaching of the truth an offence. It is not Elijah, but Ahab, who "troubleth Israel." In fact, since the Protestant Reformation, it is the most distinctively Catholic countries which have been characterized by political discontent, by abortive revolutions, and by the insurrection of socialists and the enemies of social organization and order, while the people have made little progress toward well-ordered liberty; and it is the most distinctively Protestant nations which have been characterized by steady progress and comparative freedom from domestic revolution and disturbance.

4. The violence incident to an epoch in the growth of Christ's kingdom is an evil. Because our own government was founded in a revolution, we are in danger of associating a revolution with glory, of thinking that the overturn of what has been established is in itself progress to something better, and so of falling into that insatiableness of reform which, like Saturn, perpetually devours its own children; or, as Izaak Walton puts it, whets the knife till there is no steel left in it. But the American Revolution scarcely was a revolution in the proper sense of the term. It perpetuated the principles and, with little change, the form of government to which the colonies had been accustomed; it only separated them from a distant nation; it only accelerated an epoch which was coming as the inevitable result of growth; only shaking the tree to hasten the fall of the ripened fruit. The benefits accruing are not the result of the revolution, but come, in spite of the evils of revolutionary violence, because the change effected was the natural result of healthy growth. The immense majority of revolutions attempted by violence have been failures, and have hindered, rather than helped, the progress of society.

5. The epochs in the growth of Christ's kingdom are often not recognized as such at the time of their coming.

They who are not in sympathy with Christ fail to recognize them, because they have not spiritual discernment, and "cannot see the kingdom of God." So the Jews did not know the Messiah for whom they were eagerly looking, and their fathers before them did not know God's prophets. And even good men may fail to recognize such an epoch, because it is attended with confusion, conflict, and distress. Hence, in such an epoch, the noblest sentiments will be ridiculed as fanaticism; the principles of justice, when propounded as the principles of constitutional law and social organization and order, will be flouted, and they who are the prophets of righteousness abused as disturbers of the peace and order of society. In every such epoch are persons of the type of those who said of the apostles: "These men are full of new wine."

For the same reason such epochs are attended with discouragement and reaction. The Israelites, amid the hardships of their journey to the promised land, clamored to be led back to Egypt. It is a type of the reaction attending the epochs of human progress. Men see only the difficulties of the crisis, and long for the ease and quiet of the former life. The glory of such a period is fully seen only after it is past. It does not shine till the observer is far enough removed to see it in its wholeness. Then it shines like the moon, full-orbed in silver light, with only the dimmest intimation of its dismal ravines and horrid mountains. We then think all the actors in it to be heroes, and wish we could have shared in a work so great, and witnessed events so glorious.

6. In the epochs of the growth of Christ's kingdom the progress is usually further than the agents in them had originally intended. This is true of epochs in political and social progress. The American Revolution began with no intention of achieving independence; our civil war began with no intention of freeing the slaves; the Italian war began with no intention of giving unity to Italy. The same is true of the progress of Christ's kingdom. The Protestant Reformation began with no intention of separating from Rome; Wesley began with no wish to leave the church of England; American missions began with no expectation of becoming so extensive as they now are; even the apostles began to preach Christ with no very clearly defined purpose of separating from Judaism. God is bolder than man. His grace and providence are at work in human progress. Therefore the people find themselves borne on by a power beyond man's will, a wisdom outreaching man's counsel, a

boldness beyond man's daring. It is wonderful to see how, in such a time, the mere progress of events solves problems which had seemed insoluble, removes difficulties which had seemed insuperable, and makes safe and easy measures which had seemed perilous or impracticable.

7. Epochs necessitate new ideas and a new policy. The gospel is always the same; but what is wise in policy and practicable in statesmanship changes with the changing time. "The wisdom of winter is the folly of spring." It is not strange that in great epochs the old lingers after the new has come, like blocks of ice lingering on the river's bank after it has been broken up in the spring, and melting but slowly into the running stream. Sympathy with Christ and his kingdom is necessary in order to understand an epoch, to know the ideas, and wisely to determine the policy fitted to the changed conditions.

Here is the difference between the preacher of righteousness, the reformer or prophet, and the statesman. The former is a prophet rebuking sin, holding up the ideal of moral perfection, and warning against the displeasure of God. He preaches Christ's kingdom and righteousness to elevate the people and to prepare them for institutions embodying the highest moral purity. But the maxim of the statesman is always the words of Hesiod, with a new application: "Fools, who do not know how much better half is than the whole."[1] The statesman does not attempt to carry through measures and laws, and to create institutions realizing an ideal perfection. He seeks the practicable, rather than the ideal, approximating to the ideal as rapidly as the actual advancement of society admits. He knows that the attempt to embody in institutions an ideal of perfection far in advance of the actual character of the people would probably result in a reaction, undoing much of the progress already attained. The half is better than the whole. God himself has

[1] Νήπιοι· ὀυδὲ ἴσασιν ὅσῳ πλέον ἥμισυ παντός,
'Ουδ' ὅσον ἐν μαλάχῃ τε καὶ ἀσφοδέλῳ μεγ' ὄνειαρ.
Ἔργα καὶ Ἡμέραι, 40, 41.

sanctioned the principle that political institutions and laws are to be modified on account of the hardness of men's hearts.

Hence it is the Christian, in sympathy with God's truth, who sees the kingdom of God, and understands the epochs of its growth when they come. In the quiet times before the epoch comes, the Christian may be at fault. Intent on his moral ideals, and impatient of the seeming slowness of God's movements, he may unwisely insist on the immediate expression of all truth in institutions and laws, putting new wine into old bottles, and sewing a new patch on an old garment. But when the epoch has come, possessing the hearts of men with its new ideas, and demanding a new policy, then it is the Christian who sees clearly; while the man accustomed to the statesman's habit of thought is confounded, and, unable to see the significance of the new as it penetrates the old, babbles.

VII. The Progress of the Kingdom is Cumulative.

So our Saviour predicted: "He will show him greater works than these, that ye may marvel." Christianity has always undeveloped resources; its progress is a perpetual surprisal. Examples in our own day are the inception and growth of foreign missions, the results of home missionary work at the West, the termination of American slavery, and of the temporal power of the Pope. Every great advance of Christian truth is a surprisal even to those who had labored for it. It reveals undeveloped resources. Men marvel at the presence and energy of a power whose existence had been unknown or forgotten. The same is true of local revivals. Men acknowledge the presence and work of God; they marvel at the divine power in the Christian life.

The divine grace which advances Christ's kingdom is an inexhaustible fulness of power, which while old is always new, and every manifestation appears in the freshness of its divine nature. And the energy of faith and love which it calls forth in men is an energy which has never been put fully to the test, and continually surprises by its character and results. Thus Christianity never grows old. It is like fire, always the same, if it exists at all. It comes to every generation as fresh and young as at the beginning, as the sun and the stars go up the sky as bright and glorious as in the day of their creation. It is this undecaying freshness of divine grace and human faith and love which gives to Christianity in every generation the power of astonishing the world by its new developments. And there is to-day a power in faith and love which Christians as yet imperfectly appreciate, which, if fully exercised, would do greater things in advancing Christ's kingdom than the world has ever witnessed. The greatest earthly power is the power of a human being thoroughly in earnest. And when that earnestness is sustained by faith and love, its power is immeasurable. The work accomplished by every Christian thoroughly in earnest, from Paul's day until now, has been a perpetual surprisal; before him and his achievements all men marvel.

This power is therefore cumulative; it is always able to produce greater and better effects.

The progress of the kingdom is cumulative, also, from the increase of numbers. Every convert becomes a new spiritual power for the world's conversion.

It is cumulative, also, from the Christian growth of individuals. The power of each one grows in intensity, is freed from conflicting elements, and reaches out in new directions, and finds wider scope for itself in resisting evil and bringing men to Christ.

Christian ideas, also, become incorporated into society, form public sentiment, determine customs, laws, and institutions, and thus create for themselves an organic force. Then the customary ongoings of life and civilization help the progress of Christ's kingdom. The currents of popular thought, political agitations, inventions, manufactures, commerce, contribute to its advance. Influences are incorporated into society which work with the Christian while he works, and work for him while he sleeps.

By this cumulative progress Christianity is working out in human history a demonstration of its divine origin and power. And when it shall have prevailed through the world, the demonstration will be complete. Humanity itself will have become a living epistle, known and read of all men — a word of God, declaring Christ the living Word — a second incarnation of the divine in humanity, demonstrating the reality of the incarnation in Jesus Christ.

Precisely here is the great want of this age — a demonstration of Christianity by its life-giving power. The Tartars worshipped their own scimetars — the mightiest and best helpers they knew. Civilized men will worship the steam-engine, if it prove itself mightiest and best. They must see a power, proving itself divine by its superior beneficence, using the steam-engine itself for high and beneficent ends.

Infidelity itself now unwittingly testifies to the power and truth of Christianity. It has become pious and philanthropic, and claims acceptance on the ground that it does more Christian work than Christianity itself. "The magicians of Egypt did so with their enchantments." When the apostles cast out devils, Simon Magus insists on doing the same. The gospel must silence modern infidelity, not merely by proving that the philanthropy which characterizes modern civilization is the gift of Christianity, but also by showing a benevolence purer, more self-sacrificing, and universal; motives to beneficence more energizing and persistent; philanthropy more wise, comprehensive, and efficient; a character more complete, and a power more divine in the renovation of men. It stands before modern infidelity, as Paul did before the seven sons of Sceva, and must prove its power to cast out devils by doing it, leaving to the pretenders the shame of hearing the devils answer: "Jesus I know, and Paul I know; but who are ye?" Its challenge must always be, like that of Jesus himself: "The works that I do bear witness of me; though ye believe not me, believe the works." The world accepts the challenge: "What dost thou work? Show us the desert blooming beneath thy tread, the dead in sin living at thy touch, the powers of hell fleeing before thy voice." Faithful Christian workers, mighty in faith and love, are the best evidences of Christianity. We are not to prove that it is from God merely by its great works in the past. We are not to be obliged to point to the primitive church as the most beautiful exhibition and the sufficient proof of the power of the gospel, but to create now an age of Christian purity and power. "The fathers did eat manna in the wilderness"; we thank God for that. "But they are dead"; God now is giving us the living bread, that we may eat thereof, and not die.

# LECTURE X.

## THE PROGRESS OF CHRIST'S KINGDOM IN ITS RELATION TO CIVILIZATION.

We are now to consider the progress of Christ's kingdom in its relation to civilization. While it modifies civilization and makes it Christian, it is itself modified by civilization.

### I. Civilization is not a Product of Christianity, but has an Independent Existence.

What is civilization? Man is endowed with a radical impulse to put forth every power in action. This appears in the child as the play-impulse; in the man, it is trained to work. Play is action for the pleasure of the action itself; work is action, not for the pleasure of action, but for an ulterior end. The child lives in the present, with scarcely a reference to the future, following its impulses with little reference to consequences, and acting for the present pleasure of the action. His action is play. In maturity the man acts with reference to the future, foregoing present pleasure for future interests, and concentrating his energies in work, not for the present pleasure of the work, but for the value of the end to be attained. A great part of education consists in training the pupil to concentrate his energies on the attainment of ulterior ends; it is subjecting impulse to reason, transforming play into work. The difference between the savage and the civilized is analogous to that between the child and the well-trained man. The savage acts from impulse, for the pleasure of the action, or, otherwise, only to satisfy some imperative instinct or craving; he lives in the present; his action is the impulsive, unpersevering, changeful action of a child. Civilization begins in forecast. It is distinguished from barbarism by the habit of acting with reference to ulterior interests as distinguished from present impulse; by the subjection of impulse to reason; by concentration in planned and forecasting work, instead of dissipation in play, or impulsive exertion under the urgency of a present want. This is the source of the strengthening and development of man's power, the enlargement of his acquisitions, and of his control over the resources and powers of nature, the multiplication of his wants, and therein the development of the man himself, making him many-sided and capable of more varied activities, and of more varied and more refined enjoyment. The twaddle of the new education, that because a child acts joyfully from the play-impulse, therefore education must give to all study the zest of play, would emasculate education, taking out of it that which constitutes its essence as education, and out of civilization that which is its essential distinction from the savage state. Civilization is a thing of degrees; it begins whenever forecast begins to get the supremacy over imperative impulse, and play gives place to persistent work for ulterior ends.

Christianity is not necessary to create civilization. If preached to a barbarous people, it finds the capacity of civilization, and develops it; but other agencies, without Christianity, might have developed it. Usually some form of civilization has existed before Christianity is brought to a people. Christianity at the outset found itself confronted with the Hebrew, the Greek, and the Roman civilization. It is remarkable that the apostles instituted no missions to barbarians. The first and prominent fields of their missions were the cities, whence Christianity spread more slowly into the country. The word "pagan," or "villager," gradually came to denote an idolater. So, usually, Christianity comes to nations already civilized. It finds society already constituted, with opinions, usages, government, civilization, religion.

II. Christianity imparts to Civilization and makes effective in it the Spiritual Forces necessary to its Purity, Completeness, and Perpetuity.

Comte and Buckle teach that human progress arises wholly from material conditions and intellectual development. This is not true, even if human progress is used as meaning only the progress of civilization, which is but a part of human progress. For prudence itself, or acting with reference to ends, which is the essential characteristic of civilization, belongs to the sphere of moral action. There is, however, some truth in the position, so far as mere civilization is concerned, if civilization is regarded as consisting merely in the development of power and of intellectual keenness and strength; for this development is possible under the direction of selfishness, as really as under the direction of love.

But civilization does not of itself constitute man's highest welfare. Developed under the impulse and guidance of selfishness, it contains the leaven of its own fermentation and corruption. As the development of power, it establishes the dominion of force, and civilization carries with it wars of conquest, tyranny, caste, and slavery. If, as it was in Greece, it is more distinctively the development of intellect, culminating in literary and aesthetic culture, still it carries in it the same principle of the right of the strongest, and presently decays into luxury and effeminacy; as the refinement of Greece degenerated into Corinthian debauchery. Or, if the civilization turns to industrial enterprise, wealth accumulates with the few, and the many are in hopeless poverty. Or, if such a civilization, partially Christianized, begins to open a career for all, the greed of gain takes possession of the community; worldliness creeps like a glacier over society; meanness, venality, and rapacity characterize the people; and "wealth accumulates, and men decay."

To secure man's highest well-being in a healthy and permanent civilization, something more is needed than the increase of power and intelligence. There must be also moral and spiritual quickening and development. "Man shall not live by bread alone, but by every word that proceedeth out of the mouth of God." Otherwise civilization is materialistic in its tendencies, and brings to man only what is possible to him as the highest of the brutes, nothing of what is possible to him as the child of God.

Natural religion never supplies this defect. In every condition of society will be found religions, all of them capsules containing some seeds of truth. But natural religion has not been able to supply the defect in civilization, and its force has usually been weakened by civilization. The ethnic religions have usually their greatest purity and power in the earlier periods of the national life. The earlier Romans were religious, and their religiousness was an important influence in the growth of the republic. The religiousness decayed as the national greatness advanced.

Christianity introduces into existing civilization, and in it makes effective and permanent, the moral and spiritual influences which lift man from the earthly, the sensual, and the devilish, and quicken him to act in reference to the moral and spiritual realities and possibilities of his being.

Human nature realizes its perfection only through Christianity. Though Christianity is supernatural, it is not foreign to humanity, and does not aim to superadd to humanity any accretion foreign or contrary to it. It is just that divine action which is necessary to bring man out from an abnormal condition, and to effect the complete development and perfection of humanity. Man in his normal condition, if he had never fallen, would realize his perfection only by faith in God and in communion with him. Dependence and faith are inseparable from man's condition as a created being, and their necessity is not a result merely of his abnormal condition as a sinner. The union with God by the indwelling Spirit belongs to man's normal condition. Man was made to be a worker with God, and to act under divine influences. Redemption restores him, through Christ and the Holy Spirit, to this normal union with God, so that the divine life unfolds its character in him, as the life of the vine unfolds its character in the branches and their fruit. The real freedom of man is the freedom wherewith Christ maketh free. Christianity, therefore, is necessary to the development and perfection of humanity, and the establishment of Christ's kingdom is essential to the development and perfection of human society.

Therefore, in every unchristianized condition, humanity must show its consciousness of incompleteness, and a yearning and striving, or at least a groping and fumbling, after the divine life and redemption which Christ alone brings. This is so marked in history as to give speciousness to the doctrine that Christianity is merely the more complete development of natural religion.

Christianity, therefore, is not only a power of spiritual regeneration to the individual, but, because it is so, is also the power which restores human nature to its completeness and society to its best condition. The transformation of human society into the kingdom of God creates the highest and best civilization.

This influence of Christianity in civilization makes it possible to realize a civilization which shall be permanent. Unchristian civilizations have either perished by their own corruption, or, as the Chinese, have become stationary, capable only, like Swift's *Struldbrugs*, of mumbling from generation to generation the ideas of a remote past. It is often said, as if it were an indisputable maxim, that states must have their youth, manhood, old age, and dissolution. Says a brilliant writer: "Each civilization rests on an idea or group of ideas. But these ideas are forms of thought, and thought by its own nature is constant change. Universal principles develop themselves to fresh and special results, and facts familiar or strange give rise to new general principles. Thus ideas change no less than outward relations; and a civilization which has grouped itself about an idea is but the shell of a germinant seed. The seed will germinate, and the shell must be broken and destroyed. The task of the historian, often a sad one, is to show how in each civilization lies the sentence of its own death."[1]

If, indeed, there are no unchanging principles, laws, and ideals, — if principles themselves are but forms, changing with the changing exigencies of thought, — then principles are as transitory as their outward manifestations; and a civilization which shall be permanent is in the nature of things impossible. But there are principles of truth, laws of character and action, and ideals of perfection which are unchanging and eternal. If these can be realized in civilization, there is no reason in the nature of things why the civilization should not be lasting.

Civilization in itself does not contain the elements necessary to perpetuity. If no supernatural influence comes down on humanity, we may expect that what has been will be, and that the principles of truth, justice, and love will never find complete expression in any civilization. But just this supernatural and redemptive agency comes into humanity through Christ. Christianity, therefore, has the word of promise inherent in it; it is no longer to be admitted that what always has been will be, but always the promise: "I will show you greater things." Christ makes effective in civilization the principles of truth, the law of love, the ideals of perfection which are unchanging and eternal. He consecrates all growth of physical and intellectual power, all discoveries and inventions, all philosophy and statesmanship, all poetry, painting, sculpture, and music, all thinking and acting, to God in the service of man for the realization of truth, love, and beauty in human life. Such a civilization has in it the elements of perpetuity. Such a state is not destined to decrepitude and death. There will still be new discoveries and inventions; the modes and fashions of life, customs, laws, and institutions may change; yet they are all but the exuberant outgrowth of the same life; the essential character and power of the civilization will abide unchanged.

It is sometimes objected that if Jesus were at once so

[1] Prof. C. C. Everett, Science of Thought, p. 44.

good and so great as Christianity represents, he would have revealed modern discoveries and inventions, and thus have spared mankind the dreariness of the dark ages, and given at once to the world the blessings of modern civilization. But by the very act of doing so he would have taught that these are the essentials to the redemption of the world and the highest well-being of man — that the Son of God came into the world to give to man "all the modern conveniences." Thus he would have intensified worldliness, and sanctioned a materialistic civilization. On the contrary, Christ asserted the pre-eminence of the spiritual, and brought into humanity that divine grace which in every civilization rouses man to the spiritual realities, relations, and possibilities of his being, and makes effectual those spiritual principles, laws, and ideals without which the most advanced civilization is selfish and self-destroying.

III. Christianity, by the Spiritual Forces which it introduces and makes effective, gradually creates a Christian Civilization.

It has been said that genius does not establish a school, but kindles an influence. The method of Christianity in Christianizing civilization is the same. It kindles an influence which creates the new beneath the old, and so pushes the old off. Its method is not the mechanical change of organization, but the inward process of life. Christ and the apostles made no direct assault on the existing forms of government, nor on slavery. But they taught principles, and required of individuals a life of faith and love, which, as they prevailed in society, would necessarily overthrow those institutions. By this leavening action, by this development of life, Christianity gradually removed the ancient Roman slavery; afterwards removed the mediaeval or feudal serfdom; and now is causing negro slavery to pass away.

IV. The Progress of Christ's Kingdom in Successive Ages will be modified by the Existing Civilization.

The truths of Christianity and the redeeming grace of

God are always the same. But they must work in and through humanity, and the results by which they declare themselves must be realized in and through humanity. Therefore the manifestations of the effects of God's grace acting in any age or nation, the forms in which Christian truth and life appear, the opinions, customs, laws, and institutions in which they embody themselves, must be determined by the existing condition of society and state of civilization. The type is the same, but its forms of manifestation vary; as the vertebrate type is the same through successive geological eras, but its forms diversified. We need not be surprised, therefore, if in the progress of Christianity, as of animal life, the type should appear in defective or even seemingly monstrous forms, or should be found in temporary alliance with weakness, error, or wrong.

1. Christianity, being the religion for all time, and the power that is to act through all ages in renovating and perfecting society through redemption, necessarily has meanings and applications which can be disclosed only by the progress of Christ's kingdom through the ages.

An objection is urged against the Bible that the advance of science and civilization necessitates new interpretations and evokes new meanings. But this must be so, if it is the revelation of God. Christ compares his words to seeds; they are germinating words. We must see more in them when grown than we saw in them as seeds. The acorn contains the oak; but we cannot understand what the acorn contains until we see the oak. The oak is the only adequate exposition of the acorn; and it takes as long to make the exposition as it takes the oak to grow. The kingdom of God, as it grows silently through the ages, is the only adequate exposition of Christ's germinating words. Its growth necessitates new interpretations, and reveals new meanings. From the nature of things, so long as humanity is imperfect, and civilization imperfectly Christian, there must be an inadequate apprehension of the meaning and application of Christian truth; and so long as Christ's kingdom is advancing, new meanings and applications of the truth must be disclosed.

Therefore the significance of Christian grace and truth in its application to society cannot be immediately understood. No uninspired thinker of the apostolical churches could have delineated the peculiarities of civilization which Christianity has already produced. Such a civilization, even if described to him, would have been comparatively unintelligible. It was only by the actual experience of Christian life and the actual conflict with the kingdom of darkness that the full significance of the principles hidden in the gospel, the varied applications which they require, and the consequent changes in the social condition, could be learned. Living in a civilization saturated with the vices of heathenism, the Christian must soon have become aware of a sharp antagonism to the world, and to its opinions, laws, and institutions. Thus, at the very outset, we find the apostles before the council exclaiming: "We ought to obey God rather than men" — a declaration containing the principles of individual rights, and liberty of conscience, and the supremacy of God's law above man's, which are the seed-thoughts of modern political progress. At every step the Christian was thus applying Christian truth and gaining the knowledge of its far-reaching and profound significance. And only by the progress of the church through the ages, the actual experience of the Christian life in removing the old and creating the new, could its meaning and application be discovered.

2. Man is prepared to appreciate and receive new meanings and applications of Christianity only when, in the progress of Christ's kingdom, the exigency to which they are pertinent has arisen, and man has been brought, in the providence of God, to a position in which he can see their necessity and value, and has been educated to a capacity to appreciate them. No age can appreciate new meanings and applications of truth, however clearly declared, much in advance of that stage of culture which, under God's education of the race, it has already attained. The first prophets of a coming

epoch are always rejected. A child must understand the fundamental rules of arithmetic before the more advanced rules are intelligible; and there must be an analogous progressiveness in the education of the race.

Even discoveries in science and inventions in art are rejected when communicated to a generation not sufficiently advanced to need, nor sufficiently educated to understand them. They perish like seeds which rot because sown too early in the spring. History is full of instances. It is common, after a great discovery or invention has been made, for some curious explorer of history to find the same announced in some forgotten writing of a former generation.

Here we strike that remarkable fact known as "the spirit of the age." Before a great epoch all minds seem moved simultaneously with the same thought, as the leaves of the forest rustle together at the first breath of the coming wind. The man who speaks the effective word seems rather to express than to create the thought of the time. This "spirit of the age" seems to outreach and control individual influence, as an ocean current bears onward a ship, however the crew may trim her sails or hold her helm. It is not a blind process of nature in which the personality of individuals is lost. But in the progress of Christ's kingdom a people are in contact with the same truths and subject to the same influences; they receive in God's providence the same education, and reach the consciousness of a common want, and, as a class under the same teaching, are all simultaneously prepared for the next lesson. The agency of individuals is not excluded. Even the teachings of rejected prophets, the persecution and martyrdom of "reformers before the reformation" have been important influences in educating men to receive those once rejected truths.

So long as humanity is imperfect, and God in redemption is advancing his kingdom, there must be an inadequate apprehension and application of Christian truth, and a progressive discovery of new meanings and applications.

In addition, then, to the reason already given why Jesus

should not have taught the modern discoveries, we now see another — that if he had revealed them, they would not have been appreciated or received. For the wonders wrought by his science and inventions he would have been likely to be pronounced a magician, while his discoveries and inventions would have been forgotten. Or, if he had at once set himself to abolish slavery and tyranny, and to reorganize the state, he would have been put to death as a disturber of the peace, and his doctrines forgotten as the dreams of a fanatic. It is one of the remarkable characteristics of Jesus, by which he is raised above all other men, that he was immeasurably in advance of his age, and yet infused his thought and life into it; that he was in advance of all ages, yet his thought enters as a power of life into every age, and every age finds in him its ideal and its inspiration. His teaching is never without significance and power because it will be pertinent to the future, nor antiquated because it was pertinent to the past.

3. In every age and people the Christian life will be modified in its manifestations by the existing civilization.

God's grace in Christ and by the Holy Spirit will not immediately impart a knowledge of chemistry and astronomy, nor of the power-loom, steam-engine, and telegraph. No more will it immediately change existing laws and institutions, nor even all opinions and customs into conformity with itself. The redeeming grace will be accepted in faith and penitence, and faith will work by love, and purify the heart, and overcome the world; but the manifestations of the new life will be modified by the civilization of the time. The Jew will still be a Jew, and the Greek a Greek, after they have become one in Christ; and their respective culture and type of character and usages, and even many of their prejudices, will long survive. The Hawaiian becomes a Christian, but not an Anglo-Saxon; the Greenlander becomes a Christian, but he cannot escape the influences of his Arctic climate. Not yet are the narrowness, jealousy, and antagonism of race extinguished, though in the beginning Paul proclaimed the unchanging principle: "There is neither Greek nor Jew, circumcision nor uncircumcision, barbarian, Scythian, bond nor free; but Christ is all and in all." The modern industrial movement is an outgrowth of Christianity in civilization; but it gives scope to the selfishness and greed of gain of an imperfectly christianized people. Christianity is the same; but Christians, though one in Christ, are as various as the varying nations and conditions of men.

This law holds through the times of God's supernatural revelation, not less than now. Supernatural revelation and the power of miracles did not lift a man out of his own age and country. It is distinctive of Jesus, that, though he was an ancient, an Asiatic, and a Jew, his life and words never suggest an outlandish man — a man of another age or time, — but only a *man*, in sympathy in all things with ourselves; and that this has been the same to persons of every generation, country, and condition. In every other scriptural character the peculiarities of race, country, and time are prominent. Samson would not pass for a very good Christian now; but in his day he was signalized as a man who acted from faith in God. The type was in him, appearing in what is to us a strange and monstrous form, like a megatherium of a geological period, a paleontological manifestation of the very type which now appears in man. David was an oriental despot; and some of what we call the crimes, but what were then regarded as the rights, of a monarch appear in his history. Yet in the essence of his character he was a man of faith in God and obedience to him; maintaining the knowledge and worship of the true God against idolatry, and profoundly penitent for his sin, when by the teaching of a prophet he was made to see as a crime what, according to the current sentiment of the day, he at first had not thought of as other than the exercise of a monarch's right. The same principle is exemplified in Christ's disciples, expecting that Jesus would be a temporal king, planning almost to the hour of his death ambitious schemes of pre-eminence under his reign, and receiving Christ's own rebuke; "O fools, and slow of heart to believe." In God's education of the race each lesson must be learned by protracted discipline; and each must be learned before the next can be understood and mastered.

4. Hence Christianity sometimes comes temporarily into alliance with imperfection and error, and gives to them a life and perpetuity which otherwise they could not have had. There is an important truth in the common remark, that error and wrong perpetuate themselves by the truth, or partial truth, which they contain. Aspects and sides of truth find their affirmation temporarily in connection with error and wrong; and false theories and wrong practices are made current by the truth or half-truth which they emphasize, rather than by the error which accompanies.

The Christian church gradually absorbed the idea of government belonging to imperial Rome, and became a hierarchy. In the dark ages attending and following the dissolution of the empire and the barbarian invasions, when lawless and unlettered barons plundered at will, when in the secular government club law was supreme, and violence filled the earth, the people turned gladly to ecclesiastical tribunals and priestly protection, where the appeal was always to law and justice, rather than to the sword; they welcomed the growing power of the church appealing to the unseen and eternal, as a refuge from the violence and lawlessness of the secular powers. The ancient Catholic church was the advocate and helper of the people against the tyranny of secular rulers; the vindicator of the reign of law and justice deriving authority from God, against the reign of force; the refuge and helper of the oppressed against the oppressor. In the greatest power of the hierarchy, it asserted and vindicated the truth that the church is not dependent on the state, and asserted the reign of justice and law against the reign of arbitrary will and superior force. Its claim to depose kings and to absolve subjects from their allegiance was the assertion that kings are subject to a law above their own wills; that their authority rests not on might, but on right; and that, if they abuse their power by injustice and oppression, they forfeit their right to the obedience of their subjects. These truths were carried in the bosom of the Catholic church, though manifested in perverted forms, as they must have been to accord with the idea of the church as a hierarchy. Thus they temporarily aided in building up that spiritual despotism which became the wonder of the world.

Asceticism, as it appears in crowds of filthy and begging friars, is disgusting; yet at first it was probably a very natural reaction of the Christian mind against the corruption tainting all heathen society. The vestiges of Roman life preserved in the museums of Italy and remaining in Pompeii reveal how powerfully a pure-minded Christian must have been impelled to separate himself from society so corrupted from the core to the rind. Asceticism would be a natural result of that antagonism to the world and to all that was in the world which was necessary in such a state of society. As civilization becomes penetrated with Christian ideas, and the customs and institutions of the world come into accordance with Christian purity, truthfulness, justice, and mercy, antagonism to the outward manners and customs of the world becomes less sharp and defined. In our civilization, therefore, it is difficult to appreciate the state of society which, in the earlier centuries of the Christian era, made asceticism a natural, though a perverted, expression of genuine Christian feeling.

So, also, the Crusades were an abnormal manifestation of the missionary spirit, accordant with the spirit and institutions of the times.

Even intolerance and persecution were a one-sided and perverse manifestation of zeal for truth. And the gloom which overhung the Middle Ages, the fear of devils and witches, the terror awakened even by Christ as the Judge of sinners, were results of truth contemplated only on its terrible side.

5. Christian truth is often suffocated in the perverted form

in which it is temporarily manifested, and utterly overwhelmed by the error with which it is associated, so that the whole manifestation becomes a corruption, needing to be put away.

### V. Christianity, even while subject to Modification by the Civilization and Spirit of the Age, Creates a Higher Civilization and a Purer and more Christian Spirit.

By the very action of Christian truth and life through the forms of an existing civilization, the old becomes inadequate, and new customs, sentiments, laws, and institutions are demanded. Christianity, by acting in the old medium, makes it useless. It has worn the garment out, and, patching it no longer, throws it away for a new one. By working in the old form, it has created the necessity for a new; then, the fulness of time having come, it comes out of the old, turns against it, and thrusts it away.

But men, mistaking the form for the life that had worked in it, insist on the form after it is no longer needed; and continue to patch the garment after it has become too rotten to be worn. This is the source of corruption. It is not that Christianity is corrupted; but the old forms, through which in an earlier period Christianity had naturally manifested itself, are perpetuated as essential after Christianity can no longer act through them. Christianity, in whatever form of civilization circumscribed, is a power of life, like the germ within the seed, bursting the seed-envelop and leaving it to decay. Hence Christianity in one age may be found protesting against the very forms and institutions through which, when civilization was less advanced, it had exerted its life-giving energy. Christianity is not subject to the civilization and spirit of an age; but, while temporarily acting through them, it creates a new civilization and spirit of the age, before which the old must pass away.

It is the error of Rome that it adheres to the form, instead of to the life; that it adheres to the form after the life is gone; that it opposes the life itself in the new and higher forms in which it appears. The true Christianity, on the contrary, protests against the form after the life is gone, and adheres to the life in its new manifestations. This is the true and Christian Protestantism. Rome is as really protestant; but the protest is against the old truth and life when the form is new. The protestantism of Rome is the loudest protestantism now extant; but it is protestant against Christ's truth. Romanism sits patching the old garment; and the last patch put on was the dogma of infallibility, which declares that the garment never was patched, and never needed it. Hence Rome sits in impotent and scolding protest against all Christian progress.

I may remark, in passing, that it is not necessary to determine precisely how far new thoughts, methods, and agencies are the direct result of Christian influences, and how far the result of civilization only. The revival of letters may have been, and probably was, the result of Christian influences quickening the human mind; or it may have been the natural outgrowth of the progress of human thought. But the essential point is that Christianity was in the civilization of that day, laid hold of the new powers and influences developed in the revival of letters, and made the revival of letters issue in the Protestant Reformation. The hierarchy protested against the study of Greek as endangering the church; but Christianity gladly laid hold of it, and consecrated it to Christ.

Christianity is not only in general a power of progress; it is also a power of revival and reformation. If it is ever hidden, it is fire beneath the ashes, with all its power of burning when it is raked out. No other religion carries in it this power. Other religions manifest themselves in connection with the civilization of their times; but they have no power to quicken and advance the civilization; the civilization remains stationary, and the religion moulders in its old forms. Let any higher civilization from without come in contact with it, it crumbles and passes away. Once decayed, it is impossible to revive it. No power could revive the worship of Jupiter and Venus. The divine origin and power of Christianity, the presence in it evermore of God's grace are declared by the contrast,—always quickening progress in civilization; always outgrowing the forms of the civilization into which it enters; always a power of renovation and revival when its forms have become effete and are ready to pass away.

VI. In the Progress of Christ's Kingdom the Present is always the Outgrowth of the Past.

The new is not a new creation, but is a development of the old. The progress has the continuity of a vital growth. We have seen that Christianity is perfect, and cannot be transcended; not so the measure of its apprehension on the part of mankind, nor of its appropriation in the consciousness of the church. This has the character of a growth. Hence the new has a unity with the old; the truth, spirit, and life pass out from one temporary form of manifestation into another. And the change, when it comes, is the natural result of the growth: first, the blade, then the ear, after that the full corn in the ear.

It is often objected against Protestantism that it is unhistorical. But the objection is of no force, since Protestantism drops only the old forms, which, having lived their time, were already waxing old and ready to pass away, or even were already corrupted, and accepts the new manifestations of the truth and life. In fact, Protestantism is the true historical development of the church. It is in it that the spirit and life have found their genuine outgrowth. All the wealth of piety and thought of the ancient Catholic church belongs also to Protestantism, which is the genuine outgrowth of that piety and thought, and the legitimate offspring of that Catholic church.

On the other hand, the Romish church is, in reality, unhistorical, since it has retained the effete forms, and allowed the unfolding and growing life to pass away from it.

The right of private judgment does not imply that every

man is to cut adrift from the past, and by his own meager intellect think out a system of truth for himself. That would be as absurd as if in secular life each man should strip himself of the knowledge and civilization acquired in the past, and begin, *in puris naturalibus*, as a barbarian, to study nature and acquire the arts of civilization. The right of private judgment is the right of judging in the light of the past. Some truths we may assume as settled by the thought and life of the past. Man is not always learning, and never coming to the knowledge of the truth. We rightly reject the Romish doctrine of tradition. The tradition of that church is not merely the clearer and fuller unfolding of the meaning of the Bible by the Christian experience and thought of the church, resting ultimately for its authority on God's word; but it includes the dicta of the church, resting on the infallibility of the church, and superadded to the Bible as of co-ordinate authority with it. Protestantism has its tradition; but it is simply the fuller exposition of the Bible, gained by the experience and thought of successive generations, and the application of the Bible to the new and changing conditions of man. Protestant tradition is the truth which flows from the fountain of God's word, and rolls down through the centuries, widening and deepening as it rolls — the stream which Ezekiel saw issuing as a little rill from the threshold of the sanctuary, and swelling as it flows into a great river. Protestant tradition is the Bible itself as it has flowed into human thought and life.

Because the kingdom of Christ is perpetually unfolding out of the past, the unchanging grace of God ever manifested under new conditions, the old truth and life appearing in new manifestations, the history of redemption is necessarily typical, that is, an epoch is the type of a succeeding epoch. A prominent actor in one epoch will be the type of a prominent actor in another epoch. In every epoch there is seen

> " The baby figure of the giant mass
> Of things to come at large."

Thus we have a philosophical basis for the theological doctrine that events and persons in the Old Testament are typical of events and persons in the New Testament.

VII. The Progress of Christ's Kingdom tends to produce a Homogeneous Civilization throughout the World.

The broad differences of civilizations must gradually disappear; the insignia of an outlandish man become less marked; thought and products be more fully and rapidly interchanged; interests will become more identified, and wars impossible; and the world will become a family of fraternal states.

It remains to apply these principles to determine what is the duty of the modern missionary in respect to teaching civilization.

If Christianity is taught to a people by preachers having the same civilization with themselves, then the full significance and scope of its principles will be gradually discovered, and Christianity will manifest itself in varying forms, and sometimes in alliance with error. But it is different when the missionary goes from a people having a superior and Christian civilization to a people of inferior and unchristian civilization, or still barbarous. In the civilization with which the missionary is familiar, the principles of Christianity have been carried out to many of their remote applications, and the results of ages of thinking and acting under the light of Christianity are embodied. Thus a new element is introduced into the problem. Shall he preach only the grand facts and broad principles of the gospel, leaving the people slowly to discover for themselves their remoter applications? Or, shall he also teach the detailed applications of Christian truth to the customs and institutions of society as already known to him, and teach therewith the industrial arts of the higher civilization?

1. He must not preach civilization antecedent to the gospel, and as a preparation for it. The preceding course of thought has demonstrated that a people is incapable of

having new institutions and a new civilization fitted upon it as a tailor fits a coat. It is the people who must be fitted to the civilization. Give to a savage a sewing-machine, or a power-loom, and the gift is useless. The man must be educated up to the machine, or he cannot use it, nor, indeed, have any occasion to use it. The same is true of political institutions. They do not create or mould the life, but are the outgrowth of the life. It is as useless to force free institutions on a people not educated for them as to tie artificial flowers on a rose-bush in the winter. The right of self-government in the hands of Paris communists is a curse to them and the world. Christianity is itself the most effective agency in awakening the savage to progress towards civilization, by stimulating the habit of acting for ulterior ends, and subjecting impulse to the control of reason; and in purifying and renovating heathen civilization by introducing and making effective spiritual truth and a regard to spiritual reality.

Besides, all that is distinctively Christian in civilization is the result of Christianity. To insist that the apostles ought to have taught the civilization of modern Christendom in Jerusalem, Greece, and Rome, before teaching Christianity, or that modern missionaries ought to teach American civilization in China before teaching Christianity, is to put the effect before the cause. Christian civilization can be produced only by Christianity. Christianity must first be preached, in order that Christian civilization may be possible. The only real progress of society is the progress of the men and women who compose society. Society advances only as the men and women composing it advance in knowledge and culture, in wisdom, in self-control, in purity, truthfulness, and justice, in Christian faith and love.

This position is confirmed by the fact, constantly recurring in history, that the contact of civilization with barbarism or an inferior civilization, unaccompanied by Christianizing influences, is injurious to the inferior.

2. In reference to the personal character and duty of converts, the missionary is not to withhold Christian truth

and its application out of deference to the errors inherent in the civilization of those to whom he preaches. It is one thing to admit that Christian truth taught to a people, by teachers participating in their civilization, will be slowly and gradually apprehended and applied; and quite another thing to say that Christian teachers, having the clear knowledge of Christianity belonging to the highest civilization, are to accommodate their teachings to the prejudices and customs of heathenism; for example, to admit members to the church while practising polygamy and observing the rules of caste. This is of the type of pious frauds, and of the adoption by Christians of heathen usages and festivals under Christian names, which early corrupted Christianity in the attempt to propagate it. The justification of it involves a false interpretation of the parables of the new patch and the new wine; as if they meant that a patch must be found for the old garment as rotten as it, and for the worn-out bottles wine as weak as they. They mean the life must be invigorated, or a new life created capable of receiving the new institution. It is the statesman's business to adapt laws and institutions to the existing condition of society, just as the physician adapts medicine and food to the weakness of the patient. But the missionary is in the position of a prophet; it is his business to proclaim the truth which will create a new life. He is not to attempt the immediate subversion of existing institutions; but he is to declare Christian truth as the law of personal Christian action. Otherwise, the people cannot be educated in Christian truth, and prepared for Christian civilization. The missionary and his disciples may suffer persecution, and even martyrdom, for their fidelity; but these, if they must come, are themselves powerful agencies in educating the world in Christian ideas.

3. The missionary will introduce the arts of civilization incidentally, as he has opportunity and the people are prepared for them. These are educating influences which will help him in his Christian work. And in this respect he will be aided by the intercommunication of thought and of commercial products among the nations.

# LECTURE XI.

## THE SCRIPTURAL DOCTRINE OF THE TRIUMPH OF CHRIST'S KINGDOM DISTINGUISHED FROM MILLENARIANISM.

The kingdom of Christ is destined to triumph. It will be universal in extent: "The earth shall be full of the knowledge of the Lord, as the waters cover the sea." A higher type of Christian life will be common: "The light of the moon shall be as the light of the sun, and the light of the sun shall be sevenfold." Civilization will be Christian, and society transfigured into a kingdom of "righteousness and peace and joy in the Holy Ghost," under the spiritual reign of Christ: "In his days shall the righteous flourish, and abundance of peace so long as the moon endureth." The entire conception of the kingdom is nugatory, if it does not include its triumph.

I propose to consider the Scriptural Doctrine of the Triumph of Christ's Kingdom, in Contrast with Millenarianism.

There is no disagreement on the following points: The final triumph of the kingdom; Christ's second advent; the completion of redemption and the delivery of the kingdom to the Father; the resurrection and general judgment; the eternal, heavenly blessedness of the redeemed going on in ways and methods not revealed to human comprehension.

The millenarian error is essentially this: The dispensation of the Spirit under which we live is not intended to secure the gradual extension and ultimate triumph of the kingdom; the preaching of the gospel to every creature is not intended to convert the world, but to be a witness to all nations; the dispensation of the Spirit, therefore, will fail to effect the triumph of the kingdom, but is intended only as a preparation for it; the kingdom is to come hereafter and suddenly, at Christ's second advent. When the gospel shall have been preached as a witness to all nations, and the failure of the dispensation of the Spirit shall have become apparent, Christ will come in the clouds, will destroy by natural and supernatural judgments the anti-Christian powers, "except a residue certain, but indefinite"; "will raise from the dead the elect of past ages," "take to a place of security all the elect then living," and change or transfigure them in a moment, in the twinkling of an eye; will miraculously subvert and transform the present state of things, purify the earth by the fires of his judgments, deliver it from the curse of sin, and restore it to a paradisiacal state — new heavens and a new earth. "On the restored and purified earth a new social, civil, and ecclesiastical organization shall be set up among the generations of men then ensuing, who will be all converted by the continual presence and power of the Holy Ghost, so as was unknown in the preceding ages." Over this renovated society Christ will reign in person, and "sit as king upon his holy hill of Zion," assisted by the risen saints, who shall preside with him over "the successive generations and inhabitants of the repeopled earth." "After this millennial age — the great theme of prophecy — the seventh decade — the Sabbath of time" — Satan will be loosed for a season to deceive the nations; will gather the nations which are in the four quarters of the earth to battle; God will then send fire out of heaven to devour the hostile forces that shall compass the camp of the saints and the beloved city; will raise the rest of the dead, and award the sentence of the final judgment.[1]

In opposition to this, the scriptural doctrine is: Christ sets up his kingdom at his first coming. After his ascension, he reigns in heaven over his kingdom on earth, and administers its government, and advances it to its triumph through the Holy Spirit; the dispensation of the Spirit is the last; in it, by the efforts of Christ's redeemed going into all the world

[1] President Nathan Lord's Essay on the Millennium, p. 35–39.

and preaching the gospel to every creature, the kingdom of heaven — being spiritual and coming not with observation — will gradually grow like a seed, and extend like leaven, till at last it will pervade the world with its life, and "the earth shall be full of the knowledge of the Lord." This happy condition will be of long continuance. Whether this period will be followed or not by an apostasy, in the fulness of time Christ will come in the clouds; the dead will be raised, and the living changed; the earthly work of redemption will be completed, and the kingdom presented to the Father; the final judgment will be pronounced, and the righteous shall go away into everlasting life. In connection with this will be a grand epoch in the physical world, represented by the earth being burned up and the elements melting in fervent heat, preparatory to a new cycle of the divine manifestations, which the glorified in heaven will see, but which it is not permitted us to understand.

Among millenarians there are many differences as to details, and not a few extravagances.[1] But the more judicious millenarians are not to be held responsible for peculiarities and extravagances of opinion which they do not accept.

## I. The Literalism insisted on by Millenarians is a False and Impossible System of Interpretation.

The argument is, that prophecies so explicit as that of the first resurrection (Rev. xx.), the establishment and exaltation of the mountain of the house of the Lord (Micah iv. 1, 2), the standing of the Lord's feet on the Mount of Olives, and the cleavage of the mount, and its removal, half to the north and half to the south (Zech. xiv. 4), must be literal; and that, if they are interpreted as figurative, or as symbolical of events in the progress of Christ's kingdom under the dispensation of the Spirit, every prophecy and promise of the

[1] "The king is a perfect human being, the Son of man and the Son of God; now possessed of flesh and bones, but not of blood, because that he shed for the race of Adam." — Prophetic Expositions, by Josiah Litch, Vol. i. pp. 17, 18. Mr. Litch was a follower of Wm. Miller, whose millenarianism differed in several particulars from that which is described above.

Bible may be explained away and divested of its literal and obvious meaning.

This is a plausible way of putting it, and probably is more effective with the popular mind than any other argument; especially when accompanied by an appeal to the importance of adhering to the literal historical sense of the Bible, in opposition to rationalistic interpretations. My limits forbid a complete answer to this argument, which would require an extended exposition of the principles regulating the interpretation of figurative language and of symbols, and of their application to the figures and symbols of the Bible. I will confine myself to two remarks.

In the first place, this reasoning leads to conclusions so extravagant as to prove that there is a fallacy in it. David N. Lord, lately editor of the "Theological and Literary Journal," and a most able advocate of millenarianism, insists that the eighteenth Psalm describes a literal deliverance of David, not elswhere historically recorded, and wrought with all the sublime visible and miraculous manifestations there set forth. The argument would be, if these are not literal, how can we prove from any words of scripture that God ever made any visible manifestation of himself to men?[1] The same reasoning would require us to interpret as literal history the familiar hymn beginning:

> "Once on the raging seas I rode;
> The storm was loud, the night was dark."

By similar reasoning Mr. Lord is driven to the conclusion that the carnivorous animals mentioned in Isaiah (xi. 6–9) will be transformed into graminivorous animals and continue to exist in the millennial period.[2] Some millenarians are led by similar reasoning to maintain that the prophecies teach not only the literal restoration of the Jews to Palestine, but also the revival of circumcision, sacrifices, and the temple-worship.[3] The same principles of interpretation must carry

[1] Treatise on Figurative Language, by D. N. Lord, pp. 191, 192.

[2] Theological and Literary Journal, Vol. i. pp. 386–390, and Vol. iii. p. 601.

[3] Theological and Literary Journal, Vol. ii. pp. 262, 266, 457, 472.

us still further. Ezekiel prophecies that in the future triumph of Israel, David shall be their king forever.[1] Literalism requires that it shall be David in his own person who is to reign over the renovated earth forever. In truth this method of interpretation is precisely that of the Jews in interpreting the prophecies of the Messiah's first coming. If it is the right method, the Jews were right in expecting Elijah to come in his own person, and not merely one coming in Elijah's spirit and power; and in expecting the Messiah to set up a temporal kingdom and be a mighty conqueror, according to the predictions in Psalms ii. and cx. Since events have proved that this is a wrong method of interpreting the prophecies of Christ's first coming, it must be equally wrong in interpreting the prophecies of his second advent.

President Lord insists that the millenarian doctrine is necessary from the historical character of redemption; that to deny it is to abandon this simple historical character and to substitute for it speculation and rationalism.[2] But this position is not well taken. The doctrine that Christ's second advent will follow the millennial triumph of the church emphasizes the historical character of Christianity and distinguishes it from rationalism as really as does the doctrine of his premillennial advent. The difference pertains to the question: What are the future events predicted and the order of their occurrence; not at all to the question whether Christianity is a philosophy or an historical redemption. President Lord here uses an argument *ad invidiam* which his character and standing would not have led us to expect.

My second remark, respecting the principles of interpretation which we are considering, is, that their incorrectness is exposed by reducing them to a precise and definite statement. This Mr. D. N. Lord has attempted to do. The third principle of figurative language which he lays down is: "The figurative terms are always predicates, or are employed in affirming something of some other agent or object."[3] It is

[1] Ezek. xxxiv. 23, 24, and xxxvii. 23, 24.
[2] Essay, p. 42.
[3] Theological and Literary Journal, Vol. i. p. 354.

not easy to apply this principle to such expressions as these: "When the cat is away the mice play"; "Ho, every one that thirsteth, come ye to the waters." Mr. Lord calls a figure of this kind a *Hypocatastasis*; although he insists that "in that figure, as well as in the metaphor, the trope lies wholly in the predicate, not in the subject to which it is applied."[1] But though he does call this figure a Hypocatastasis, and insist that the trope is in the predicate, yet it is true that such a figure may run through an entire sentence or series of sentences, and, so far as the sentence or sentences are concerned, with all the appearance of literalness. And the admission that such figures abound in the Bible is the admission of all that is demanded to justify the interpretation of figurative language in the Bible in harmony with the doctrine, that Christ's kingdom is to be extended through the world under the dispensation of the Spirit and before the second coming of our Lord.

Mr. Lord enumerates four hundred and fifteen symbols, which, he says, is the whole number in the scriptures. From an examination of these and their interpretations, he educes "the laws of symbolic representation." The first is, "that the symbol and that which it symbolizes are of different species or orders, and that the relation of the representative to that which it represents is the relation of analogy." Yet he is obliged to admit this sweeping exception: "When the symbol is of such a nature, or is used in such a condition or relation that there is no analogical agent or object which can represent it, it is then used as its own representative, or the representative of one or more of its own kind." Among the many symbols belonging under this exception, he includes the souls of the martyrs, in Rev. xx., and acknowledges that this vision itself is symbolical.[2]

It is evident, then, that the argument which we have been considering is a popular appeal, rather than an argument. It legitimately leads to conclusions that are extravagant;

[1] Theological and Literary Journal, Vol. iii. p. 601.

[2] Ibid. Vol. i. pp. 182, 214, 237, and Vol. iii. pp. 669, 670.

and when we attempt to give it definite statement, and to educe the law or principle of interpretation which it involves, it breaks down entirely. Therefore, the doctrine that Christ reigns in heaven over his kingdom on earth, that he administers and advances it through the Holy Spirit, that its triumph will be completed under the dispensation of the Spirit and antecedent to Christ's second advent, is a doctrine which violates no valid law of interpretation. In advocating it, we cannot be stopped at the outset by the objection that we are forsaking the literal, historical meaning of the Bible for abstractions and fancies. The Bible abounds in imagery and symbols. We approach it recognizing this fact. We determine whether any passage is literal, figurative, or symbolical from the passage itself and its connection, and in like manner we interpret the figures and symbols which we find.

II. Millenarianism is Inconsistent with the Doctrine of the Bible as to the Time, Object, and Concomitants of Christ's Second Coming.

1. Christ's second advent is at the completion of his kingdom on earth, and not at its beginning or establishment.

The dispensation of the Spirit is habitually spoken of as the last, the last time, the completion of the ages (*συντελεία τῶν αιώνων*, Heb. ix. 26). These texts cannot be explained as denoting the end of a dispensation; for they were applied to the dispensation of the Spirit at its beginning in Christ's first coming. Joel, in the passage quoted by Peter on the day of Pentecost, was comparing one dispensation with another; and so Peter applies it.

The kingdom is to be complete at Christ's second coming, and as such to be delivered to the Father (1 Cor. xv. 24). Whatever difficulties attend this text, it certainly means that the mediatorial work on earth is finished, the number of the redeemed completed and presented to the Father. And it is certain, from the context, that this delivery of the completed kingdom to the Father is connected with Christ's second advent and the resurrection of the righteous.

Christ's second coming is habitually called the end, and presented as the terminus of all gospel invitation and all Christian endeavor to save men from sin (1 Cor. xv. 24; Matt. xiii. 37–49; xxiv. 31; xxv. 1–13; Luke xix. 13).

2. Christ's second coming is declared to be to judgment, in marked contrast with his first coming, which is declared to be to salvation (John iii. 16, 17; xii. 47, contrasted with Matt. xxv. 31; 2 Thess. i. 6–10).

3. Millenarianism is irreconcilable with the assertions of the Bible as to the events which will accompany Christ's second coming.

Christ's second coming is to be attended with the resurrection of all the saints who have previously died, and the change of the living saints from corruptible to incorruptible and from mortal to immortality.

It is accompanied, also, by the resurrection of the wicked. The prediction of Daniel (xii. 2) is interpreted by millenarians as a prediction of Christ's second advent; yet it expressly foretells the resurrection both of the righteous and the wicked. Our Saviour predicts the resurrection of the righteous and the wicked (John v. 28, 29). Their resurrection is evidently simultaneous, hearing together the voice of the Son of Man; and the dead hearing the voice of the son of Man and raised thereby is a form of expression which elsewhere indicates the second coming of Christ.

The second advent is accompanied by the conflagration of the earth, and the saints are caught up away from the earth to meet the Lord in the air. This is entirely incompatible with the continued occupation of the earth by the human race, and the personal reign of Christ at Jerusalem (2 Pet. iii. 7–13; 1 Thess. iv. 16, 17). Millenarians resort to various expedients of interpretation to evade this insuperable difficulty, in which they depart very far from the literalism on which they insist in other cases.

Another concomitant of Christ's second coming is the general judgment and the separation of the righteous and the wicked to their final and eternal state (Matt. xvi. 27;

xiii. 37–43; xxv. 31–45; 2 Thess. i. 6–10; 2 Tim. iv. 1). The assertion is explicit that the judgment here mentioned is to be at the second coming of the Lord. Millenarians are obliged to interpret these and similar passages as referring to the destruction of the wicked who will be alive on the earth at Christ's second coming. These sublime predictions of the judgment of the wicked mean, therefore, only that a part of the ungodly in the generation living when Christ shall come will be put to a violent death. Universalists do not more violently wrest passages of this sort from their obvious meaning. While thus interpreting passages inconsistent with their own theory, millenarians cannot consistently enforce their literalism on their opponents.

Millenarians assert the continued existence and propagation of the human race under Christ's millennial reign. The Theological and Literary Review asserts that there will be three classes of men — the risen and glorified saints, who will reign with Christ; the saints living at Christ's coming, who by their change will be made immortal, but will not receive the spiritual and glorified body; and the remnant of the wicked who escape destruction at the second coming, and who, being converted, will continue the human race in its natural life from generation to generation. This class President Lord calls "a residue certain but indefinite," who will repeople the earth. All of the foregoing biblical representations are utterly incompatible with the continued existence and propagation of the human race in its natural life after the second advent.

It remains to glance at Rev. xx., which is claimed as teaching a first resurrection and a pre-millennial coming of Christ.

The vision here described is a vision of the *souls* of certain martyrs, who lived and reigned with Christ a thousand years, Observe what this vision is not. It is not of a resurrection, but distinctively of the *souls* of martyrs. This is subsequently called the first resurrection. It is not of all the saints, but only of those martyrs who had been beheaded, or, if the several verbs each has a different subject, only of those who had been beheaded and those who had been faithful to Christ under the persecutions and deceitful arts of the beast — whatever particular period that may denote. It is not a vision of Christ's second advent, which is not mentioned, and which necessarily connects itself with the events subsequent to the thousand years, and represented at the close of this chapter and in the next. It is not a vision of Christ's personal reign on earth. It is not said that the thrones seen and the martyrs reigning were on earth; but consistency with the antecedent and subsequent representations of the book requires that the scene of the vision be in heaven. It is not a vision of the destruction of the wicked living on earth; but it is preceded by a vision of the binding of Satan, and the consequent deliverance of the nations from his temptations and deceits, which indicates their conversion rather than their destruction. In view of the use made of this vision as putting millenarianism beyond all question, it is remarkable to notice what is *not* in it. It is extraordinary reasoning that, because John saw the souls of some of the martyrs living and reigning with Christ in heaven, therefore Christ's advent will be pre-millennial, he will at his coming put the majority of the wicked to a violent death, raise the dead saints and transfigure the living, and reign in person in Jerusalem for a thousand years.

If, therefore, you are constrained to admit that the vision implies a literal resurrection of some of the martyrs in connection with the coming triumph of Christ's kingdom, that carries with it no necessity of admitting millenarianism. Such a resurrection would be analogous to the resurrection of some of the saints when Christ rose, and would be consistent with the triumph of Christ's kingdom before his coming and under the dispensation of the Spirit. This admission, however, the right interpretation of the vision does not require.

The vision presents a symbol of the final triumph of Christ's kingdom and the long continuance of its universal sway.

This interpretation is necessary to harmonize this with the whole Apocalypse. To suppose this vision to be of literal historical events would be to give it an entirely exceptional interpretation. Especially this interpretation harmonizes with the vision of the souls of the martyrs in chap. vi. 9–11. There they are seen under the altar, crying: "How long, O Lord, holy and true, dost thou not judge and avenge our blood on them that dwell on the earth"? And they are comforted, and bidden to wait a season. There are presented to us the depression and conflict of Christ's church. In chap. xx. the souls of the martyrs are seen again, not beneath the altar, but reigning with Christ. As the former vision symbolized the church under oppression and persecution, this necessarily symbolizes the church in its prosperity and triumph; and there is nothing whatever in it which intimates that its triumph is to be realized any otherwise than under the dispensation of the Spirit, through the faithful efforts of Christians carrying the gospel to all mankind, and applying its principles to the conduct, usages, laws, and institutions of human life.

III. Millenarianism is Inconsistent with the Scriptural Doctrine of the Nature and Growth of Christ's Kingdom.

1. Christ, at his first coming, came as a King, set up his kingdom, and began his mediatorial reign.

The Jewish prophets predicted the Messiah as a King, coming to establish a kingdom of righteousness and peace, and to extend his reign throughout the world. These are uniformly prophecies of his first coming, the prophecies which created the Jewish expectation of the Messiah, and which Christians believe to have been fulfilled in Jesus. If the Messiah was foretold at all, he was foretold as a King who was to set up a kingdom to endure as long as the sun and moon endure.

Jesus began his preaching by declaring: "The kingdom of heaven is at hand." He announced himself as Messianic King; his kingdom was the constant subject of his preaching. He expressly teaches that his kingdom is not of this world, but is spiritual; that at his ascension all power is to be given him in heaven and on earth; that he is to sit at the right hand of the Majesty on high, and reign there as Messianic King, continuing his agency on earth through the Spirit whom he should send. He avowed himself a King to Pilate, and as claiming to be such he was crucified. He is acknowledged as King in the Acts and the Epistles. His common appellation is κύριος, or "Lord," a name applied at the time to the Roman emperor. Peter says explicitly: "Let all the house of Israel know assuredly that God hath made that same Jesus whom ye have crucified both Lord and Christ. . . . . . Him hath God exalted to be a Prince and a Saviour." In the Epistle to the Hebrews we have this explicit declaration: "This man, after he had offered one sacrifice for sins, forever sat down on the right hand of God, from henceforth expecting until his enemies be made his footstool." This certainly intimates that there is to be no other mediatorial reign, and that under his reign in heaven he expects the triumph of his kingdom.

Both the Old Testament and the New teach that the mediatorial reign begins in connection with Christ's first coming, and particularly his ascension and the outpouring of the Spirit, and not with his second. So Jesus says: "There be some of them that stand here who shall not taste of death till they have seen the kingdom of God come with power."

2. The New Testament, in treating of the growth of Christ's kingdom, emphasizes his humiliation and death, his ascension and intercession, and his sending the Spirit: "I, if I be lifted up from the earth, will draw all men unto me"; "Lo, I am with you alway, even unto the end of the world." Jesus also bids his disciples rejoice that he goes away, because it is the appointed condition of the descent of the Holy Spirit; thus implying that his administering his kingdom by the Holy Spirit is better than his personal presence on earth.

3. The kingdom is not of this world, is within the soul, is

spiritual and invisible; its progress is gradual, and its coming is without observation. It is "righteousness and peace and joy in the Holy Ghost." It is the leaven working unseen within the flour. It is the mustard-seed growing into a tree. Even Daniel's prophecy of the stone smiting the image on the feet, though cited by millenarians to prove that the coming of the kingdom is sudden, miraculous, and public, proves the contrary. It is explicitly said: "*In the days of these kings* shall the God of heaven set up a kingdom which shall never be destroyed." An event yet future cannot be said to happen *in the days of these kings.* And the stone, which represents Christ's kingdom, was at first so small that it could smite the image *on the feet*, and after the image had fallen the stone grew into a mountain and filled the whole earth.

It should be added that in the very discourse in which Jesus declares that his kingdom cometh not with observation, but is invisible and internal, he distinguishes it from his second coming, which, he declares, shall be sudden, public, and startling as the lightning.

4. The triumph of the kingdom is dependent on human agency.

The whole scriptural representation is that redemption goes on in human history, and the advance of Christ's kingdom is by human agency. Millenarianism makes the human element and agency to be only docetic, not a reality. The kingdom is not established by man working together with God, but miraculously, by the Son of God himself. After thousands of years seemingly working in and through and by humanity, he at last breaks free from all human relations and from all the continuity of history, and establishes the kingdom by a miraculous stroke of Almightiness.

5. The kingdom depends for its advancement, under God's Spirit, on truth and love, and not on force.

The genius and spirit of Christianity take men off from the reign of force, and establish the reign of ideas, of truth, and love. But millenarianism strips Christianity of this its essential glory, confesses that the world cannot be saved by truth and love under the dispensation of the Spirit, and falls back on force as that by which alone the kingdom of God can triumph, and on which it ultimately rests. When millenarians are charged with teaching that Christianity is a failure, they reply that, while they do not expect the conversion of the world under the dispensation of the Spirit, they do expect the triumph of Christ's kingdom at his second coming. But I charge them with teaching the failure of Christianity in a sense far more profound. They acknowledge the failure of truth and love by the power of the Spirit to save the world from sin. They acknowledge that the triumph of Christ's kingdom must depend at last on force. Faith in the triumph of ideas and the reign of truth and love by the convincing of men's intellects and the renovation of their wills through the Holy Spirit passes away. The world will be subdued by Almighty power, never converted by redeeming love.

6. The kingdom, as supposed to be realized under Christ's personal reign, would not be a realization of the highest ideal of Christianity.

On the one hand, it presents a semi-sensuous paradise. It does not concentrate the Christian's efforts on attaining an overcoming faith, a divine love and purity, as constituting blessedness or true well-being under whatever circumstances; it rather leads to waiting and longing for an adjustment of outward circumstances to make life blessed. It does not set the Christian's heart on toiling and, if necessary, suffering to deliver men from error and sin, as constituting their misery; it rather leads them to wait supinely for the coming of the Saviour to rid them of their enemies by his destroying sword. It tends, therefore, to ascetic disgust with life, and separation from the world, instead of a compassionate and Christlike interest in the world to save men from misery and sin. Thus it unconsciously runs into that false philosophy which places blessedness in indulgence and gratification, to the abandonment of the Christian and only true philosophy that man's blessedness consists in his character and action, rather than in his circumstances and possessions; in what he is, rather than in what he has; in working and serving and achieving, rather than in receiving and being indulged. "All that is in the world ..... passeth away; but he that *doeth* the will of God abideth forever."

On the other hand, the conception of the personal reign supposes the introduction into the natural life of men of the elements of the heavenly state, and a consequent state of things in which the interests and affairs of man's natural life seem insignificant and out of place.

Thus the personal reign, anticipated as the issue of all Christian endeavor, vitiates the Christian character and life in the present dispensation.

IV. Millenarianism gives no satisfactory Theodicy, or Vindication of the Ways of God with Man.

It affords no tolerable explanation of the delay in the coming and triumph of Christ's kingdom, nor of all the processes and agencies during the long ages preceding it. The true doctrine is, that redemption must of necessity enter into humanity, act through human agencies, and realize its results through the courses and the continuity of human history. It follows that God's redeeming love may fail of bringing man at once to him; that the growth of his kingdom must be modified by the human element connected with it; and thus that only in the fulness of time and through innumerable trials and difficulties can the kingdom possess the earth.

But if, after all, the kingdom is not to be established in this way, if all God's working in and by humanity and in the courses of history is to be a failure, and the Messiah is at last to throw himself clear from all the human elements and historical courses through which he has worked so long, and to set up his kingdom by sheer Almightiness, no reason can be given why that might not have been accomplished four thousand years ago as well as now. Redemption ceases to be a true and satisfactory philosophy of human history;

it becomes something outside of it and above it, and is consummated at last in a violent disruption of all the continuity of that history. And every explanation of the slow progress of Christ's kingdom founded on the fact that it is advanced in humanity and by human agency ceases to be available.

V. The Practical Influence of Millenarianism is Evil.

It takes away the most powerful motives to Christian endeavor, and tends to an incomplete type of Christian life.

It is the glory of Christianity that it first and alone has spoken the word of promise and of hope to man, and predicted for mankind in the progress of Christ's kingdom a future on the earth ever better than the past. Under the stimulus of this promise civilization has become progressive, and progressive in justice and love to man. Under this stimulus Christians have learned to have faith in truth and right and love, and in God's present and redeeming grace. In this faith and hope they are valiant for the truth; believing that, however opposed, it will through the influence of God's Spirit establish itself, and find expression in the lives of individuals and in the customs, laws, and institutions of society.

Millenarianism "keeps the word of promise to our ear, and breaks it to our hope." It dissociates the triumph of Christ's kingdom in the future from its antecedent progress and from the endeavors of Christians to advance it. The triumph comes at last miraculously, magically, by the stroke of almightiness, with no dependence on previous fidelity to truth and right and God; by occasion, indeed, of the persistence and prevalence of sin, not of the persistence and prevailing power of Christ's saints.

Modern progress is humanitarian. Christian civilization is characterized by regard for man, by the recognition of his individual personality, which can never be absorbed and lost either in race or organization; of his greatness and the sacredness of his rights; of the principle that institutions exist for man, not man for his institutions; of the brotherhood of all nations; of the obligation to turn human endeavor in every line of thought and action to the promotion of human welfare. It will be characterized by the recognition of the Christian law of service restraining the self-assertion and rapacious self-seeking of individualism, and leading men to live not for themselves, but for others. In our modern apologetics we insist that the world owes these ideas to Christ. But the millenarian system has no place for these ideas. Christianity, as that system presents it, does not aim to renovate society by truth and love. It aims in the present dispensation only to save a few elected ones from the pains of eternal death, while it looks to the total overthrow of the existing state of society and the re-creation of the earth itself preparatory to the miraculous establishment of a preternatural kingdom, having no dependence whatever on the present progress of Christian civilization or the Christian culture of men. It therefore repudiates the promise and hope of human progress, and declares them delusions of philosophy and rationalism, and no part or incident of Christianity. It therefore must regard Christianity, in its very conception, alien from all efforts to put an end to slavery and tyranny and to reform social abuses, and thus it gives its support to an argument which is at this day prolific of scepticism, that Christianity is not in sympathy with human progress. It must insist that the one business of Christianity is to convert souls — to save a few, if possible, from eternal death amid the hopeless errors, sins, and sufferings of the present state. President Lord, for example, declares that one of "the appalling practical consequences" of the current belief is that "Christian men and ministers of the gospel ..... are wasting much of their energies upon delusive schemes of educating, reforming and reorganizing society, with a view to its supposed development into a perfect state." [1]

The Christian, it is indeed admitted, is required to work for Christ; for the command is: "Occupy till I come." But he is to work with the deadening consciousness that his efforts will fail to make the world better. President Lord

[1] Essay, pp. 46, 47.

says: "It is historically and certainly evident that hitherto every tribe, nation and race of men on the earth — a few righteous men alone excepted, — have successively declined into greater wickedness, and that at this present time Christianity is spreading in the world in no proportion to the increase of the wicked population of the globe and the spread of atheistic, pantheistic, or polytheistic belief. . . . . . The rapid development of our present worldly civilization is more and more alienating society from God, and making it more difficult for his servants to preserve themselves in the simplicity of their faith."[1] So it is to be until Christ shall come. Under the dead weight of this certainty Christians are to fulfil the command: "Occupy till I come." They are to toil and suffer, knowing that all their efforts avail nothing to establish the kingdom of righteousness and peace on earth.

In the light of the Christian promise rightly understood, we accept Christian work as a privilege, because in it we are workers together with God to save sinners from their sins, to multiply the number of Christian workers, to hasten the deliverance of the world from its sin and misery, and to advance the Christianizing of civilization and the progress and universal prevalence of Christ's kingdom. Work thus becomes a part of the Christian's education. It trains him to love all men as Christ did, to be valiant for the truth, and to be strong in faith and hope; it develops a broad and intense interest in humanity and in all that affects human welfare, and creates a large-hearted, genial, and healthful Christian manhood. Millenarianism, teaching the inevitable failure of all efforts to reform and renovate society, deadens the interest in human affairs, trains the Christian to disgust with life and a desire to flee from the world in order to save himself from its dangers, and to nurse his own spiritual emotions in retirement rather than to interest in toil for the world's renovation. It trains him to a longing to die in order to escape from the toil and conflicts of the Christian — a saintliness which is ungenial, ghastly, and remote from all the interests of human life.

[1] Essay, p. 27.

# LECTURE XII.

## THE PROGRESS OF CHRIST'S KINGDOM IN ITS RELATION TO THE SPIRIT OF THE PRESENT AGE.

THE present age is scientific, and disinclined to acknowledge the supernatural. It is rationalistic, rather than believing; self-sufficient in the pride of virtue, rather than humble in the sense of sin; philanthropic, rather than spiritual; utilitarian and realistic, rather than sensitive to sentiment and enthusiasm. I propose to consider the progress of Christ's kingdom in relation to the characteristics of this age.

I premise that Christianity comes to every generation as new as to the first generation to which it came. When the mother tells the story of Jesus to her child, the wondrous story is as new to that child as to those to whom it was told in the days of Paul. It comes anew to every generation and to every man, a message fresh from heaven, and every one must consider it and receive or reject it for himself.

I premise, also, that Christianity remains unchanged. It is always God's love redeeming men from sin through the humiliation, death, resurrection, ascension, and continued reign and intercession of Christ, and the abiding presence and work of the Holy Spirit. As such, by the lapse of ages it never grows old. It rises on generation after generation, as day after day the morning rises in dewy freshness on the awakening world, and as night after night the evening reveals the unchanging glory of the starry sky. In these respects, one generation has no advantage over another.

Each generation has peculiarities which present peculiar obstacles to the gospel. We have no reason to believe that the peculiarities of this age are more formidable obstacles than those of other ages. A careful study of the age of Luther or of Paul would exemplify this.

The general principle underlying the discussion is this: Christianity can prevail in any age, only as it meets the thought and life of that age. It must meet and satisfy the *thinking* of men respecting the problems of human life and destiny, and give repose to their intellects. It must meet the *life* of men, and give light, peace, wisdom, and strength for the work, the suffering, and the wants of the time. To have met and satisfied the thought and life of a previous age avails nothing to meeting and satisfying the thought and life of this generation. The manna which came down from heaven yesterday will nourish no soul to-day. Christianity must meet, help, and save men in the conditions and necessities of the age in which they are.

Two thoughts are involved in this general principle. The first is: It is *Christianity* which is to meet the thought and life of the age, not something substituted for Christianity. The second is: Christianity *must meet the thought and life of the age.* In the first, we have that which is permanent in Christianity; in the second, that which is transient.

The first of these thoughts is important, as meeting an existing danger. Whatever the thought and life of the age which Christianity is to meet, it is not by preaching progress, reform, and civilization that the work is to be done, but by preaching Christianity in its application to these. The "New Timothy" is not a sensationalist preaching to the times, but also preaching the times; he is a Christian preaching to the times, but preaching Christ and him crucified. This is the permanent in Christianity—"Jesus Christ, the same yesterday, to-day, and forever." Through the confusion of the time, and all its diversified action and interest, always resounds the grand message of sin and redemption, as at the sea-side, through all the coming and going, the clatter and confusion of frivolity, passion, and business, resounds always the solemn roar of the ocean.

If this thought is allowed to lose its prominence, and the

permanent in Christianity is forgotten, the very attempt to apply Christianity to the times becomes fruitful in error and corruption. Men, in their eagerness to preach to the times, present what is of man and his conditions to save men, till they substitute the ethics and wit of the popular lecture for the gospel of Christ. Or they mistake the transient for the permanent, and insist that the peculiar prominence necessarily given to a particular Christian truth in one age, must be maintained in the next; that the peculiar application of Christianity needed in one age, and perhaps the very errors which incidentally accompanied it, must be carried over to another age when no such application is needed; and that the philosophies and speculations of one age be inculcated as permanent truth in the next; and so the church is compelled to stand dozing and ruminant on the thought and life of the past.

Reform and progress are always by going back to Christ, taking the treasures of wisdom and knowledge hidden in him, and applying them fresh to the existing life. So he commands: "Take my yoke upon you, and learn of me." We study the preceding ages only as helps to a better knowledge of Christ, and to a wiser and fuller application of his gospel to the exigencies of our time.

The second thought involved in the principle is as really important. Christianity must *meet the thinking and life of each age.* Christianity must be known experimentally. We must take Christ's yoke, in order to learn of him. We must be willing to do his will, in order to know the doctrine. Every one must both receive the truth as it is in Jesus, and not as it has been in other men, and receive it in his own experience and its adaptation to his own wants, and not in the experience of others and its adaptation to their wants. The food which one has eaten is necessarily excrementitious to another. The conditions and wants of different individuals and successive generations are varying and transient, and the applications of Christian truths to varying and transient conditions are varying and transient, though the truth remains unchanged. In order to preserve the doctrinal purity of Christianity in the thinking of any age, and its power in the life, it must meet the thinking and life of that age. Christianity must bring the same unchanging Christian truth; but it must bring it not as Athanasius thought it for his day, nor as Augustine thought it for his day, nor as Thomas à Kempis, Calvin, and Edwards thought it respectively for theirs, but in the channels and methods of modern thought, and touching the topics on which modern thought is occupied. The Christian life produced is not the life of the ancient hermits and monks, nor of Calvin at Geneva, nor of the Puritans of the seventeenth century, nor of the Methodists of the eighteenth. It is the life of this age transfigured by Christian faith and love.

I proceed to consider the application of this principle to the thinking and life of this age. Time will permit, however, to consider only some of the characteristics of the age, and how Christianity is to meet them.

I. The Alleged Deficiency of this Age in Religious Susceptibility.

1. There are two types of thought on religious subjects. Paul selects the Jew and the Greek as their respective representatives: "The Jews require a sign, and the Greeks seek after wisdom."

In the type of mind of which the Jew is the representative, the intuitive or faith faculty predominates over the logical, and the mind is awed in the presence of the unseen, the incomprehensible, and the infinite; the moral predominates over the speculative and scientific, and the man is awed before the divine law, crushed with the sense of guilt and the expectation of punishment, terrified before the inexorable Judge to whom he must give account of every secret of his life. From these impressions with which his soul trembles, he passes to believe the reality of the infinite and the unseen, as easily as from impressions on the eye and ear he passes to believe the reality of the outward world. The world unseen is real to him; he expects it to manifest itself supernaturally; he is prepared to hear voices from heaven, to see spirits and visions; miracles occasion no difficulty of belief; he regards them as the legitimate evidences of communications from the world unseen, and demands more. Nature itself he regards as a constant manifestation of the supernatural. It is God who thunders, who sends the wind and the rain.

The Jewish literature in the Old Testament contains little argument or speculative philosophy. It is mainly historical and prophetical pictures of God's action in history, with the legislation for a theocracy, with moral law, an order of worship, and devotional poetry.

In the Greek type of mind, on the contrary, the senses, the faculties of observation, and the logical powers predominate. Nature was so near to the Greek as to exclude the supernatural. His gods were the powers of nature personified. To the Jewish mind man is divine, and nature is for his use. The Hebrew literature opens with the sublime proclamation that man is above nature, appointed to possess and use its resources and powers. The thinking of the Greek scarcely rises to this grand conception. To him nature is divine, and man is its servant and worshipper. His thinking is a philosophy, elaborating by logical processes a system of the universe — starting, sometimes, with fire or water or some material principle. In this type of mind the aesthetic element predominates over the moral; the sense of beauty displaces the sense of obligation; and joy in the present displaces the sense of what ought to be, the consciousness of sin, and the foreboding of judgment. To this type of mind nature is all-sufficient. Miracles, instead of being helps to faith, are themselves its greatest difficulties. Accordingly, in the education of the race, the Greek has contributed philosophical inquiry and scepticism, logic, art, and, if not physical science, the type of thought from which science comes.

2. Christianity is to meet both of these types of thought, and to develop a higher type, in which both co-exist in completeness and harmony.

The characteristics of each type are found in all minds. The type is characterized not by the exclusion of either, but by the predominance of one. Complete culture must take up and develop both in the same age and the same mind.

It is not true that the Jewish type belongs to the earlier stages of progress, and the Greek type to the later. The Jewish type is as high an order of mental culture as the Greek. Comte's hypothesis, that it is an infantile condition which the race necessarily outgrows, is contrary both to philosophy and to fact. The characteristics of the Jewish type are in all ages necessary to the highest development of mind, and to the completeness and harmony of human thought. They rest intellectually on those faculties of intuition and faith which are involved in and underlie all intellectual action, without which thought withers into words and reality fades into phenomenality; without which nothing can be explained in its rational ground, law, and end; the questions which reason necessarily asks it is unscientific to propound; the deepest wants of the human soul remain forever unsatisfied, and their existence without significance or explanation. Christianity offers a culture which takes up and develops both of these types. This is the explicit assertion of Paul — not that Christianity sets aside the demand of the Jew for signs, nor the quest of the Greek for wisdom, but that it meets and satisfies both. We preach Christ crucified, to the Jew a stumbling-block and to the Greek foolishness, so long as they reject him; but to all who receive him, whether Jew or Greek, Christ, the power of God satisfying the Jewish type of thought, and the wisdom of God satisfying the Greek.

3. In this age, which is commonly characterized as rationalistic and scientific, and supposed to belong exclusively to the Greek type of thought, the Jewish type survives, and the power of the world to come is felt. We multiply the evidences of Christianity, as if its continuance depended on logical proof. But it is a significant fact that the other religions of the world have been originated and sustained

without any discussion of their evidences. They address the spiritual capacity and wants of the soul, and they are received, and are believed, till they degenerate, and are superseded by some other religion more completely satisfying the spiritual intuitions and sentiments. As the strings of a viol respond with music to the touch of the bow, the spiritual in man responds to the presentation of spiritual realities. The basis of religious faith is in the constitution of man. When atheism sweeps away religious belief, as in the French Revolution, presently it re-appears, as verdure springs up spontaneously on burnt land.

This susceptibility exists in the nineteenth century, as really as in the first; for it is inseparable from the human soul. To this, in preaching, we safely address ourselves. Mere argument cannot bring men to Christ. By its very processes, dissecting the living body of spiritual truth, it deprives it of its power. It is the presentation of spiritual reality to the soul which moves it. The law of God burning on the conscience, God's redeeming love in Christ, the beauty of Christ's character — these and the like realities constitute the power of the world unseen, which every human soul must feel, if clearly before the mental vision.

In this so-called rationalistic and sceptical age, we find even the very error of the Jewish type of thought, the insatiable demand for sensible manifestations of the spiritual world. The belief in spiritual rappings is proof; meriting the indignant words of Professor Ferrier: "Oh ye miserable mystics, when will ye know that all God's truths and all man's blessings lie in the broad health, in the trodden ways, and in the laughing sunshine of the universe; and that all intellect, all genius is merely the power of seeing wonders in common things."[1]

Thus, even in this age, there is occasion for our Saviour's rebuke of those who sought of him a sign: There shall no sign be given them, but the great facts which Jonah typified — the death, the resurrection, and ascension of our Lord.

[1] Institutes of Metaphysics, p. 225.

If this age be compared with the first centuries of the Christian era, — with their Epicureanism, Gnosticism, and New Platonism, — it will be apparent that its rationalism and scepticism are at least not more formidable hinderances to faith than the rationalism of those centuries of Christian triumph.

II. This Age is characterized by the Spirit of Free Inquiry, and by Love of the Truth, as distinguished from Religious Faith.

1. In the outset, I must point out the inadequacy of this spirit of free inquiry to realize the highest results. Freedom of inquiry and love of the truth are conditions of thought, not principles of action. The attitude of inquiry is an attitude of weakness. It implies uncertainty, doubt, therefore irresolution, inaction, inefficiency. The action of the soul must be internal to resolve its own doubts and answer its own questions. It wears itself out in inward friction. Such were Sterling and James Blanco White, passing from one belief to another, unable to rest in any; the whole action of life like that of a man lost in a dismal swamp, leaping from one shaking tussock to another, unable to stay his foot on any, and sinking at last in the smothering quagmire. So Paul describes the Greek as seeking wisdom, rather than finding it — "ever learning, and never able to come to the knowledge of the truth." On the contrary, action, energy, power come from faith. Men do not go into all the world and preach the gospel to every creature, they do not rebuke wickedness nor demand the reform of abuses and the removal of oppression, merely as inquirers after truth. A missionary does not go to the heathen as an inquirer, as ready to receive Brahma as Jesus, and the Vedas as the Bible. The very idea of prophet and apostle, of missionary and reformer, implies intense, overmastering faith. When Lecky and writers of his school exalt the spirit of inquiry above faith, they take a position which would make scepticism universal, as the highest condition of human thought, would make missionaries, reformers,

martyrs, and prophets impossible, and condemn mankind always to inquire and never to believe.

But it is not possible for man to remain a mere inquirer. Scepticism in its primitive and philosophical sense, as the spirit of inquiry and investigation, must either lead to established belief, or else pass over into scepticism in its bad sense, as the spirit of denial. It begins to dogmatize. And when it begins to dogmatize, it ceases to be scepticism in the philosophical sense; it becomes dogmatic and arrogant; it demands that its negations be received as knowledge; it transforms its questions into negations, and then its negations into affirmations, and propounds as positive knowledge the proposition that knowledge is impossible. One of the French Encyclopaedists said: "I am as sure that there is no God in heaven as I am that Homer is a fool." Of such Jacobi said: "They believe that their opinion is reason, and that reason is their opinion."

In its further development, the spirit of inquiry becomes irreverent, revolutionary, and destructive. The anatomist cannot reverence the body which he dissects. The inquirer gradually comes to regard everything as only an object of inquiry, therefore to be questioned, analyzed, dissected. Hence the spirit of inquiry becomes revolutionary and destructive. It accepts nothing as established. It doubts if the old can be true. It becomes arrogant, coarse, and terrible; saying, as did the French Revolutionists: "With the guts of the last priest we will strangle the last king."

2. Free inquiry and the love of the truth presuppose the reality of truth and the possibility of knowing it. They are, therefore, consistent with faith, not destructive of it. It is only when inquiry, which is a condition of the enlargement of knowledge, is exalted into the essence of knowledge, and scepticism becomes dogmatic, that it is in antagonism to faith. After the investigations of ages, it may be assumed that some truths are established, and are no longer open to doubt. The human mind, being in its nature knowing, may be assumed to know something beyond the possibility of

question. It is a total misconception of free inquiry to suppose that it implies an abiding indifference to opinion and an equal readiness to believe every proposition. On the contrary, free inquiry presupposes the possibility of knowledge, and is compatible with belief of a truth so strong as to make the believer willing to die for it.

3. Christianity does not acknowledge the love of the truth as the ruling principle of action. Life does not culminate in thought, but in action. Man's business is not to seek after wisdom, but to do the work of love. The love of truth is a ruling principle of investigation, not the supreme law of action. Christianity presents as the supreme law, love to persons, — to God and man, — not love to truth.

Bacon consecrated scientific investigation to the uses of man. From this consecration naturally followed the adoption of the right methods of investigation and the largest scientific discoveries. This is in accordance with Christianity. The love of truth is subordinate to the love of God and man; and this subordination is essential to insure the right methods of investigation, the largest knowledge of truth, and its most effective application.

Rationalism presents the love of the truth as the pre-eminent and ruling principle of all action. The evils resulting have been indicated. Candor, exalted to independence and supremacy, becomes an equal indifference to all doctrines, degenerates into *persiflage*, and at last into dogmatic denial. If a Christian exalts the love of truth to supremacy, the results, though analogous, are different. By his exaltation of the love of the truth, he accepts the principle of the rationalist; but, since he is a confirmed believer of the truth, his zeal for the truth is exalted above his love to God and man; and his danger is of bigotry and intolerance — of becoming even an inquisitor and a persecutor — of sacrificing the man needing salvation in zeal for the truth, instead of using the truth in the supremacy of love to save the man. There is danger, also, that he gradually substitute zeal for opinion instead of zeal for truth; and thus, while the exaltation of the love of the truth degenerates in the rationalist into destructive denial, it degenerates in the Christian into persecuting and destructive intolerance. The subordination of the love of truth to the love of Christ and of all for whom Christ died is the security at once against the belief of error and intolerance in zeal for truth. He who most loves like Christ will most think like him.

4. Free inquiry and love of the truth, when acknowledged as conditions of investigation which imply the reality of knowledge and faith, and which are subordinate to love, are accepted by Christianity, and are auxiliary to its progress. The mind is delivered from the enforcement of opinion and the oppression of authority, and aroused to its most vigorous action. Opportunity is given for the detection and removal of errors and abuses, and the ground is prepared to receive new seed and to bear new harvests of Christian truth. Candor and docility prepare for a consideration and acceptance of the claims of the gospel. The critical scrutiny of all arguments demonstrates anew all Christian truth that abides it. The Christian believer himself receives truth not blindly and traditionally, but on conviction; he is better able to defend it; he is more in sympathy with others who find difficulty in believing; he does not denounce doubt as a sin, nor quench the smoking flax. The very process of argument and rationalistic speculation brings the church back to the simplicity that is in Christ, brings anew into prominence the spiritual part of our nature on which Christian faith rests, and enables us to appreciate the meaning of the Saviour's blessing on those who have not seen, and yet have believed.

5. The quest after wisdom which characterizes this age will ultimate in the recognition of the true rationalism which Christianity carries in it. In other words, this type of mind will find its complete satisfaction and rest in Christianity itself.

Christianity teaches that, whatever may be known by reason, that is not sufficient to save man from sin, but that he also needs the redemption wrought by God through Christ and the Holy Spirit. It finds this fact of redemption to be accordant with reason. It finds in it the rational solution of man's condition and destiny, which without this fact is impossible. It finds in it the only complete and satisfactory philosophy of history. The unbelieving rationalism is irrational in assuming the sufficiency of human reason to save man from sin. It therefore necessarily ceases to be a religion, and degenerates into an unbelieving philosophy. But I affirm that the facts of Christianity are the data for interpreting and vindicating to the reason the phenomena of man's moral and spiritual life. Ultimately this interpretation and vindication will be complete. Ultimately, it may be after long struggles, Christ will become the Saviour from intellectual perplexity and doubt, not less than from sin. He is the rest for the intellect, not less than for the heart.

Christianity, therefore, is to meet the quest for wisdom by satisfying it. Because man is rational, he must interpret and vindicate to his reason the facts of his moral and spiritual being. Rationalism cannot be put out of the way by being suppressed. To suppress inquiries of this sort would be to suppress reason itself. We can meet the rationalistic spirit of the day only as we show that "in Christ are hid all the treasures of wisdom and knowledge" — that "he is made unto us wisdom," as well as righteousness, sanctification, and redemption.

This process is far from complete; but it has advanced far enough to exemplify its nature. Science, by its speculations on force, admits what necessitates the admission of a First Cause of force; and thus the last word of science is the first word of theology. Christianity, in the doctrine of a personal God whose will is the source of all power, gives the complete reality which science obscurely intimates. Science insists on law, and tends to establish a uniformity of necessity. But Christianity recognizes a moral order, a uniformity of perfect reason and perfect love, as complete as the uniformity and order of necessity. The action of nature is the power of will expressing evermore the thoughts of reason and the purposes of love. And this alone meets the true scientific idea of order and law; for blind necessity is but another name for chance, and gives no rational principle of order nor basis for either its universality or perpetuity.

The doctrine of the Trinity is acknowledged by some who do not accept it as an article of religious faith, as satisfying as no other doctrine does the necessities of the most profound philosophical thought respecting the being and personality of God.

In the atonement we find the fact which alone can harmonize immutable morality with divine mercy, and set forth as elements of one all-embracing love the mercy that pardons and the justice that condemns.

In the incarnation we have an entrance of God into human history and relations — a union of God and man which all religious thought of the East and of the West has known as necessary to the realization of religion, and in different directions has groped to find.[1]

In the fact of Christ's kingdom on the earth, we have the principles which underlie all human progress and the realization of the social well-being and complete civilization of man. Christianity, lovingly studied, reveals within itself the true philosophy on which modern thought must rest, and by which modern civilization must advance.

Thus philosophy itself, rightly understood, becomes the ally of Christianity. In the words of Lord Bacon: "Philosophia obiter libata abducit a Deo, penitus hausta reducit ad eundem." Thus Christianity is at last received as satisfying the reason, as well as renewing the heart, both by philosophy and by faith, as Augustine enthusiastically exclaims: "Certissima scientia et clamante conscientia."

III. This Age is characterized by Positiveness and Vastness of Scientific Knowledge.

There is no antagonism of science to religion, so long as

[1] See Dorner's Doctrine of the Person of Christ; the Introduction.

science defines its sphere to be the observation of phenomena, their classification by common characteristics, and the determination of their uniform sequences, and does not dogmatically deny the reality of other knowledge. Philosophy is then distinguished from science, as the interpretation and justification of phenomena to the reason by showing their rational grounds, principles, laws, and ends; and philosophy and theology are both acknowledged as legitimate spheres of thought. But when science denies that any knowledge is possible, except of phenomena of nature and their common characteristics and uniform sequences, it becomes dogmatic unbelief, and stands in direct antagonism to Christianity. It must then be opposed as error, and exposed as, in the name of science, denying and repudiating reason itself. In this attitude science is opposed to the Greek quest for wisdom, not less than to the Jewish demand for signs.

It is thought that the vastness of human knowledge overpowers faith. But, in reality, the greatness of the universe is not so much its bigness as its varied manifestations of mind. The three-storied or seven-storied heaven of the Jew, with the throne of God above it and the love of God filling it, and redemption wrought in it, and earth beneath it opening out into the grandeurs of immortality, is a grander universe than the immeasurable masses and spaces of Astronomy, in which no God is, no love reigns, and only unconscious force acts under blind necessity evermore.

And, so long as science remains within its distinct sphere, the enlargement of scientific knowledge does not hinder faith. It was a great enlargement of knowledge when the Copernican system of Astronomy was received; yet it neither magnified nor lessened the creations of mind. The works of Homer and Virgil remained the same. The ideas of God, of sin, of redemption, remained unchanged. The increase of scientific knowledge may even be a help to faith. Faith feeds itself on all knowledge, manifesting in new aspects the wisdom and love of God. It expatiates through the vast distances of the universe in wonder and adoration. At the same time, innumerable puerilities, which once crept into the place of the true objects of faith, and degraded the soul, instead of elevating it, are swept away. The wonder of knowledge is greater than the wonder of ignorance, and a greater help to faith.

IV. The Age is Realistic and practical, as opposed both to Philosophical Inquiry and to Sentiment and Enthusiasm.

Even this presents advantages to Christianity. Thought for the sole end of seeking truth, with no reference to its uses, is liable to degenerate into verbiage or frivolousness or intolerance. Zeal for truth is never safe, except when vitalized and controlled by love to God and man.

The great objection to the practical character of modern thought is that it concerns itself mainly with material interests. But, even so, it is better than merely speculative inquiry, with no reference to the welfare of man.

It is not true, however, that the age is occupied exclusively with material interests. The great questions which agitate modern society are largely moral and religious. And, however realistic the age may be, it is certain that this century has witnessed as marked instances of the uprising of whole peoples in enthusiasm for ideas as were ever witnessed in the "ages of faith."

We differ, to our advantage, from the primitive churches in this, that they had Christian ideas to create in the midst of heathenish corruption, in which the very ideas of Christian purity, of philanthropy, of human rights and brotherhood were wanting. But now many of the great principles of Christianity are generally accepted and practically applied; they are axioms of reform and of social progress, and powers in civilization. Especially, all thinking and all great movements which lay hold of the heart of the people, take on a philanthropic character.

In such an age Christianity has an eminent advantage in its beneficent character, as the redemption of the world from sin. And so far as the age is realistic and practical, it meets its thinking and its wants by the manifestation of its quickening and saving power. And if each successive age of the Christian era has had some specific doctrine of Christianity to develop, that which is given to this generation to study and unfold is the Christian doctrine of Christ's kingdom as the reign of righteousness and love over all the earth in the life and civilization of men.

V. It remains to consider the Industrial and Social Condition of Christendom in its Relations to the Progress of Christ's Kingdom.

Time permits, however, but a glance at this great subject.

Through the art of printing each age has all the ages past in its presence, and is instructed both by their failures and their successes. The progress of Christ's kingdom, therefore, need no longer be lineal, partial, and one-sided, but rounded and complete. Christianity, instructed by the life of the past, may be expected to become broader and more complete in doctrine, character, and life.

Through commerce and the facilities of intercommunication the existing nations live in the presence of each other, and by travel and emigration the peoples are interfused. The time is past when the nations were in ignorance of each other; when their natural relations were those of enmity; when the thought and life of one nation had no influence on another; and progress in one locality was without effect elsewhere. The earth is practically smaller, its countries nearer together, its nations in constant communication, serving each other by their industry. Whatever effects a change at one point extends its influence to all. For these reasons and by the necessities of industry and commerce, the nations are coming to recognize that they are members of one family. The idea of nations confederated to preserve universal peace and to secure the common welfare has ceased to be chimerical; has become already a possibility, the realization of which, not the enthusiasm of Christian love only, but the wisdom of sound statesmanship predicts. And the settlement of the great questions which divide the nations is more and more sought and attained by peaceful methods, and made in the interest of the peoples and not of the dynasties.

The Christian nations are characterized by energy, progressiveness, and expansiveness. The close connection of the nations brings this superiority home to the heathen and Mohammedan nations and makes it a constant influence upon them. Idolatry cannot live by the side of steam-engines and telegraphs.

These characteristics also distinguish Protestant nations from Catholic. They seem always to be most marked where Christianity is purest and most effective. The most christianized nations are those which are gaining the preponderating influence in Christendom. Particularly noticeable is the spread of the English speaking race, and the immense extent of the world's surface in which that language is spoken. De Tocqueville, speaking of the spread of the English-speaking people in America, says: "This gradual and continued progress of the race towards the Rocky Mountains has the solemnity of a providential event; it is like a deluge of men rising unabatedly and driven by the hand of God. ..... This is a fact new to the world, a fact fraught with such portentous consequences as to baffle the efforts even of the imagination." To this must now be added other immense regions in which the English language is spoken. A wonderful contrast this to the anticipations cherished not very long ago. Lord Bacon published his great works in Latin, saying that "English would bankrupt all our books." And Alexander Pope in his preface to an edition of his poems, contrasts the limited use of English with the universal use of Greek and Latin: "They writ in languages that became universal and everlasting, while ours are exceedingly limited both in extent and duration. A mighty foundation for our pride! when the utmost we can hope is to be read in one island, and to be thrown aside at the end of one age."

God has always acted by chosen peoples. To the English-speaking people more than to any other the world is now indebted for the propagation of Christian ideas and Christian civilization. It is a remarkable fact in this day that the thinking of the world is done by the Christian nations; that the enterprise and energy of the world are mainly theirs. They alone are colonizing, and by their commerce and enterprise pushing their influence throughout the world. So also the political condition of the Protestant nations is that of constitutional government, popular education, and a growing regard for the rights and welfare of the people.

These are conditions more favorable to the advancement of Christ's kingdom than have ever before existed. And in view of both the thinking and the practical life and character of the age, I believe that no preceding age has presented conditions so favorable to the advancement of Christ's kingdom and so encouraging to faithful Christian effort.

# COMMENTARIES

PUBLISHED BY

# WARREN F. DRAPER,

## ANDOVER, MASS.

**These Books will be sent, post-paid, on receipt of the price affixed.**

## MURPHY.

***Critical and Exegetical Commentaries, by Prof. James G. Murphy, LL.D., T.C.D., viz. on***

GENESIS. With a Preface by J. P. THOMPSON, D.D., New York. 8vo. pp. 535. Cloth, rounded edges. **$3.50**

EXODUS. (Uniform with Genesis). 8vo. pp. 385. **3.0C**

LEVITICUS. (Uniform with Genesis and Exodus). pp. 318. **2.50**

"Dr. Murphy in his commentaries has a definite plan, which he carries out. The text is explained, translated anew, and comments are added on the difficult and mooted points. He is a fair, clear, and candid interpreter. His aim is to reconcile the Scriptures with science by an impartial examination of the text."—*Amer. Presbyterian and Theological Review.*

"Thus far nothing has appeared in this country for half a century on the first two books of the Pentateuch so valuable as the present two volumes. His style is lucid, animated, and often eloquent. His pages afford golden suggestions and key-thoughts. . . . . Some of the laws of interpretation are stated with so fresh and natural a clearness and force that they will permanently stand." —*Methodist Quarterly.*

"The most valuable contribution that has for a long time been made to the many aids for the critical study of the Old Testament is Mr. Draper's republication of Dr. Murphy on Genesis, in one octavo volume. It is a good deal to say of a commentary, but we say it in all sincerity, that this volume furnishes about as fascinating work for one's hours for reading as any volume of the day, in any department of literature; while its general influence will be salutary and effective for the truth. . . . . The English reader will find nothing accessible to him which will compare favorably with this as a help in the study of this portion of the divine word; while he will, of course, read always with his own judgment upon the views which find expression." —*Congregationalist.*

## STUART.

***Critical and Exegetical Commentaries, by Moses Stuart, late Professor in Andover Theological Seminary, viz. on***

ROMANS. Third Edition. Edited and revised by PROF. R. D. C. ROBBINS. 12mo. pp. 544. **$2.25**

HEBREWS. Third Edition. Edited and revised by PROF. R. D. C. ROBBINS. 12mo. pp. 575. **$2.25**

ECCLESIASTES. Second Edition. Edited and revised by PROF. R. D. C. ROBBINS. 12mo. pp. 346. **$1.50**

BOOK OF PROVERBS. 12mo. pp. 432. 1.75

"The first characteristic of Professor Stuart as a commentator is the exhaustive thoroughness of his labors. His exegesis is in general skilful and felicitous, especially in bringing out the meaning of the obscure passages, and adding new and delicate shades of thought to the more obvious and superficial sense." —*North American Review.*

"The exegetical works of Prof. Stuart have many excellences, and it will be a long time before the student of the Bible in the original will be willing to dispense with them as a part of his critical apparatus."—*Boston Recorder.*

"The spirit of the man is so intertwined with them as to be a perpetual stimulant and benediction to the reader." —*Congregationalist.*

"In turning over its pages we recall the learning, the zeal, the acumen, and the idiosyncrasies of one of the most remarkable of the great and good men which our theological world has produced. . . . . This contribution by Prof. Stuart has justly taken a high place among the Commentaries on the Epistle to the Romans, and, with his other works, will always be held in high estimation by students of the Sacred Scriptures."—*N. Y. Observer*

## ELLICOTT.

### *Commentaries, Critical and Grammatical, by C. J. Ellicott, Bishop of Gloucester and Bristol, viz. on*

GALATIANS. With an Introductory Notice by C. E. STOWE, lately Professor in Andover Theological Seminary. 8vo. pp. 183. $1.50

EPHESIANS. 8vo. pp. 190. 1.50

THESSALONIANS. 8vo. pp. 171. 1.50

THE PASTORAL EPISTLES. 8vo. pp. 265. 2.00

PHILIPPIANS, COLOSSIANS, AND PHILEMON. 8vo. pp. 265. 2.00

THE SET in five volumes, tinted paper, bevelled edges, gilt tops, 10.00

THE SET in two volumes,

THE SET in two volumes, black cloth, rounded edges, 8.00

"We would recommend all scholars of the original Scriptures who seek directness, luminous brevity, the absence of everything irrelevant to strict grammatical inquiry, with a concise and yet very complete view of the opinions of others, to possess themselves of Ellicott's Commentaries." — *American Presbyterian.*

"His Commentaries are among the best, if not the very best, helps a student can have." — *American Presbyterian and Theological Review.*

"Ellicott is one of the best commentators of this class." — *Princeton Review.*

"I do not know of anything superior to them in their own particular line."—*Dean Alford.*

"We have never met with a learned commentary on any book of the New Testament so nearly perfect in every respect as the Commentary on the Epistle to the Galatians, by Prof. Ellicott, of King's College, London — learned, devout, and orthodox." — *Independent.*

"They fill the scholar with genuine admiration." — *Watchman and Reflector.*

"The Commentaries of Prof. Ellicott belong to the first class of critical writings of the New Testament." — *Boston Recorder.*

"To Bishop Ellicott must be assigned the first rank, if not the first place in the first rank, of English biblical scholarship. The series of Commentaries on the Pauline Epistles are in the highest style of critical exegesis." — *Methodist Quarterly.*

"The best English work of this character."— *New Englander.*

"Strictly grammatical and critical, thorough and fearless, concise yet complete, worthy of all confidence." — *Evangelical Review.*

## HENDERSON.

### *Commentaries, Critical, Philological, and Exegetical, by E. Henderson, D.D., viz. on*

THE BOOK OF THE TWELVE MINOR PROPHETS. Translated from the Original Hebrew. With a Biographical Sketch of the Author, by E. P. BARROWS, Hitchcock Professor in Andover Theological Seminary. 8vo. pp. 490. $3.50

JEREMIAH AND LAMENTATIONS. Translated from the Original Hebrew. 8vo. pp. 315. $2.50

EZEKIEL. Translated from the Original Hebrew. 8vo. pp. 228. 2.00

"Dr. Henderson's Commentaries are rich in wholesome and true exposition." — *Presbyterian Magazine.*

"The work is invaluable for its philological research and critical acumen. . . . . The notes are replete with the fruits of varied learning." — *The Presbyterian.*

"Dr. Henderson is one of the most eminent of modern biblical critics. One of the leading features of his mode of treating Scripture is his happy blending of textual with exegetical comment. His treatise on Jeremiah is well worthy, by its elevated scholarship, to take a place side by side with the commentaries of Bishop Ellicott and of Professor Murphy, also issued by Mr. Draper." — *Publishers' Circular.*

"He excelled in weighing evidence, and impressing upon it its relative value. His discrimination was clear and his judgment was sound. He dealt with fact, not with fiction. He searched for data, not for opinions. Dr. Henderson was not only well versed in the Hebrew language, but also in its cognates. Few men, either in England or America, have been his equals in Oriental literature. His Commentary on Jeremiah has the same general characteristics which appear in his Commentary on the Minor Prophets." — *Bib. Sacra.*

"The only satisfactory commentary on the Minor Prophets we know of in the English language." — *Episcopal Recorder.*

"The volume before us gives abundant evidence of patient scholarship and clear conceptions of evangelical truth." — *Evangelical Quarterly.*

"**We have met with no so satisfactory a commentary on this part of the prophetic scriptures.**"— ***Watchman and Reflector.***

**Commentary on the Epistle to the Hebrews.** By PROF. MOSES STUART. Third Edition. Edited and revised by PROF. R. D. C. ROBBINS. 12mo. pp. 575. $2.25

"The Commentaries of Prof. Stuart abide the test of time. Though somewhat diffusive in style, they contain so much thorough discussion of doctrinal points, so much valuable criticism on pregnant words, and such an earnest religious spirit, that they must live for generations as a part of the apparatus for the biblical student." —*Independent.*

"It is from the mind and heart of an eminent biblical scholar, whose labors in the cause of sacred learning will not soon be forgotten." —*Christian Observer.*

"It is a rich treasure for the student of the original. As a commentator, Prof. Stuart was especially arduous and faithful in following up the thought, and displaying the connection of a passage, and his work as a scholar will bear comparison with any that have since appeared on either side of the Atlantic." —*American Presbyterian.*

"This Commentary is classical, both as to its literary and its theological merits. The edition before us is very skilfully edited by Prof. Robbins, and gives in full Dr. Stuart's text, with additions bringing it down to the present day." —*Episcopal Recorder.*

"We have always regarded this excellent Commentary as the happiest effort of the late Andover Professor. It seems to us well-nigh to exhaust the subjects which the author comprehended in his plan." —*Boston Recorder.*

"Professor Stuart has held a large place in the eye of the church, as a man well furnished with all the learning required in a scriptural commentator; and we recognize his merit, while we do not always rely on the theology of his comments." —*Presbyterian.*

**Commentary on Ecclesiastes.** By PROF. MOSES STUART. Second Edition. Edited and Revised by R. D. C. ROBBINS, Professor in Middlebury College. 12mo. pp. 346. $1.50

"A most thorough, plain, careful, faithful Commentary. It consists of a preliminary dissertation on the nature, design, method, and history of the book; a translation having the commentary after each verse, and a brief final summary of most of the chapters. The commentary is worked out in a most thorough manner, both its philosophy and exegesis." —*Independent.*

"The first characteristic of Professor Stuart as a commentator is the exhaustive thoroughness of his labors. His exegesis is in general skilful and felicitous, especially in bringing out the meaning of the obscure passages, and adding new and delicate shades of thought to the more obvious and superficial sense." —*North American Review.*

"This Commentary casts much light on this difficult portion of God's word." —*Boston Review.*

"The Commentary on Ecclesiastes was among the latest and ripest of its author's works." —*Christian Review.*

"It bears the marks of his vigorous and intuitive mind on every page." —*Boston Transcript.*

"One of the ripest and most interesting of Dr. Stuart's works." —*The Lutheran.*

**Commentary on the Book of Proverbs.** By PROF. MOSES STUART. 12mo. pp. 432. $1.75

"This is the last work from the pen of Prof. Stuart. Both this Commentary and the one preceding it on Ecclesiastes, exhibit a mellowness of spirit which savors of the good man ripening for heaven; and the style is more condensed, and, in that respect more agreeable, than in some of the works which were written in the unabated freshness and exuberant vigor of his mind. In learning and critical acumen they are equal to his former works. No English reader, we venture to say, can elsewhere find so complete a philological exposition of these two important books of the Old Testament." —*Bibliotheca Sacra.*

**An Examination of the Alleged Discrepancies of the Bible.** By JOHN W. HALEY, M.A. With an Introduction by ALVAH HOVEY, D.D., Professor in the Newton Theological Institution. 12mo. pp. xii. and 473. Price, $2.25.

"I have examined a part of the manuscript copy of the Rev. J. W. Haley's work on the Apparent Contradictions of the Bible and the reconciliation of them. The work is the fruit of lengthened and laborious research. It will be of great use to every minister who will study it. Every minister ought to be familiar with the principles stated in the work. I do not know any volume which gives to the English reader such a compressed amount of suggestion and instruction on this theme as is given in this volume, so far as I have examined it. I discover no trace of a sectarian spirit in the manuscript. I hope that, for the benefit of all Christians who are called to defend the Bible against infidels, the manuscript will be published in good type and on good paper very soon." —*Prof. Edwards A. Park.*

"In the first part, which is in the nature of an introduction, Mr. Haley outlines the field of investigation, acquainting the reader with the character of the difficulties to be met with and the nature of the process by which they are to be removed.

"Having briefly unfolded the principles which underlie the investigation, Mr. Haley enters, with Part II., upon the body of his work, taking up in order every discrepancy of which he has been able anywhere to find mention, and attempting its explanation. There are nearly six hundred passages which receive this separate treatment; in the course of which fully three thousand distinct texts are cited.

"The hints we have given above convey only a very general idea of a work which it is hard to describe as it deserves. As a whole, it is an honor to American scholarship, and a contribution of the highest value to our existing apparatus for the study and use of the Bible. Mr. Haley has performed a difficult and laborious task in a most admirable manner. The amount of toil which has been involved in it can only be justly appreciated by the professional few. Not its least valuable element consists in its copious citations from biblical scholars of all schools and ages, whom the author has here gathered about him as a great class of witnesses, soliciting their testimony upon every point, and giving it mainly in their own words; so adding to the general discussion the feature of a digest of interpretations. If we cannot always assent to Mr. Haley's own expressed preferences, we certainly can never deny their temperateness and candor. The arrangement of materials is strikingly methodical and convenient, and the style might well be a model to us all, being uniformly compact, clear, and exact.

"A book so costly in great qualities, yet so cheap and accessible to all; one so scholarly and yet so simple and usable; one so creditable to its author, and yet so modestly sent forth, does not every day appear. As an example of thorough and painstaking scholarship, as a serviceable handbook for all Bible students, and as a popular defence of revealed truth, it will take high rank, and fill an important place which up to this time has been conspicuously vacant."—*Congregationalist.*

"In many of the instances of alleged discrepancy the explanation or interpretation of our author will be satisfactory to all lovers of the Bible; and some of them will satisfy even those who discredit divine revelation — candid men, who will remand the question of its acceptance to some other tribunal, or upon some other ground of faith or of discredit. It is not likely that the very best interpretation has everywhere been given to an apparent discrepancy in this work; nor is such to be found in any commentary; but there is an evident fairness in the writer's method, a brevity of expression, and good scholarship, all which commend themselves and the work to popular favor."—*The Commonwealth.*

"He has gathered these alleged discrepancies out of a large number of authors, consisting mainly of English, French, and German rationalists and infidels. He has classified these as far as he could, and then proposed solutions for them — solutions not always original, but gathered from all the critics and commentators of note. His citations are very copious, and add very much to the value of the book. ... The texts which are supposed to be contradictory are quoted, and set over against each other in parallel columns, that their full force may be seen. ... The book is fitted to be very useful, and fills a niche which has not yet been occupied."—*The Presbyterian.*

**A GUIDE TO READING THE HEBREW TEXT**; for the Use of Beginners. By Rev. W. H. Vibbert, M.A., Professor of Hebrew in the Berkeley Divinity School. 12mo. pp. 67. $1.25.

"The aim of this work is to give the student all that is needful to enable him to read the text of the Old Testament, keeping rigorously to the plan of stating clearly and precisely everything that is essential to the purpose. This work is not a Hebrew Grammar, but it is a guide and a help to the reading of the text of the Hebrew Bible. One thing is given at a time, with exercises for practice, so that each point may be perfectly comprehended. It is hoped that the book is so constructed as to enable the learner to read the Hebrew text without the services of the living teacher. Nothing has been taken for granted on the part of the student. By a systematic and progressive plan of arrangement, which he must follow closely and steadily, he is lead on from section to section, until perfect familiarity with the forms and sounds of characters and signs is acquired." — *Author's Preface.*

"Mr. Vibbert's manual is what it claims to be. It really gives, in a perspicuous and exact manner, an initiation into the mysteries of the Hebrew tongue, and the rudiments of Hebrew study are all contained in these simple rules and illustrated in these practical exercises. The method is the excellent method of Kalisch which insists upon orthography as the needful preliminary to grammar and syntax. One who faithfully follows Mr. Vibbert's directions will be able to use with profit the lexicon and the chrestomathy, and in a little time to read the Word of the Lord in the character which it had when the Scribes expounded it." — *Christian Register.*

**HEBREW GRAMMAR.** The Elements of the Hebrew Language. By Rev. A. D. Jones, A.M. 8vo. pp. 168. $1.75.

"By a simple and progressive series of exercise, and by a perfectly plain exposition of the syntax, the student is enabled to take up Hebrew just as he would the *Initia Latina*, and just as easily." — *Publisher's Circular*, Apr. 15, 1870.

"The plan of the work is admirable, and happily executed." — *Reformed Church Messenger.*

**HEBREW ENGLISH PSALTER.** The Book of Psalms, in Hebrew and English, arranged in Parallelism. 16mo. pp. 194. $1.25.

"The preacher in expounding to his congregation one of the Psalms of David, will find it very convenient to have the original by the side of the English version. For private reading and meditation, also such an arrangement will be found very pleasant and profitable. We feel confident that this little volume will be a favorite with Hebrew scholars; and that, when they have once become habituated to it, it will be, to many of them, a *vade mecum*." — *Bibliotheca Sacra.*

"A handsome edition of the Book of Psalms, which will be quite a favorite with clergymen and theological students." — *New Englander.*

"A very convenient and admirable manual, and we beg leave to thank our Andover friend for it." — *Presbyterian Quarterly.*

"The volume is beautifully printed, of convenient size for use, and of admirable adaptation to the service of those whose Hebrew has become a dim reminiscence." — *North American.*

**RIGGS'S O.T. EMENDATIONS.** Suggested Emendations of the Authorized English Version of the Old Testament. By Elias Riggs, Missionary of the A. B. C. F. M., at Constantinople. 12mo. pp. 130. $1.00.

"The amendments here suggested are the result, not of a systematic revision of the English Version, which I have never attempted, but of comparisons made in the course of translating the Scriptures into the Armenian and Bulgarian languages. They are offered to the candid consideration of all who feel especial interest in the correction of the English Version, and specially of those providentially called to the work of translating the word of God into other tongues." — *Author's Preface.*

"W. F. Draper, publisher of the Bibliotheca Sacra, has issued an interesting and suggestive little treatise, written by Rev. Elias Riggs, Missionary of the A. B. C. F. M., at Constantinople, which is introduced by an Introductory Note of Prof. Thayer of Andover. It is intended to suggest some of the philological changes in the version of the Old Testament, rendered advisable by the advanced scholarship in Oriental tongues, attained especially by our missionaries of the East. The criticism upon the New Testament has been very full. The present is a work of the same description upon the Old, but is one upon which fewer eminent scholars have entered. Obscure passages are found to yield their long-hidden meaning through an acquaintance with the idioms of Oriental languages, and a personal familiarity with the unchanging customs of that stereotyped land. The volume is a valuable reflex contribution to the churches at the West, from the mission fields supported by their gifts in the East. It comes at an hour when its modest and well-defended suggestions will secure a careful examination on the part of the Biblical scholars now engaged in Great Britain and in this country upon a new version of the English Bible." — *Zion's Herald.*

www.ingramcontent.com/pod-product-compliance
Lightning Source LLC
LaVergne TN
LVHW010236110826
845151LV00004B/1309

* 9 7 8 1 4 2 5 5 2 5 2 1 7 *